CREATING INSTRUCTIONAL MATERIALS

Second Edition

CREATING INSTRUCTIONAL MATERIALS

Second Edition

ROBERT V. BULLOUGH, SR.
University of Utah

Charles E. Merrill Publishing Company
A Bell & Howell Company
Columbus   Toronto   London   Sydney

Published by
CHARLES E. MERRILL PUBLISHING COMPANY
A Bell and Howell Company
Columbus, Ohio 43216

This book was set in Optima.
The production editor was Elizabeth A. Martin.
The cover was prepared by Will Chenoweth.

Library of Congress Catalog Card Number: 77-15677

International Standard Book Number: 0-675-08361-3

1 2 3 4 5 6 7 8 9 10/ 85 84 83 82 80 79 78

Printed in the United States of America

1|8|79 Baker & Taylor 8.95

PREFACE

The importance of visual teaching materials has been recognized for centuries, but only in recent years have the vast implications for the use of such materials been fully appreciated. Still pictures were formerly the most common kind of media used in the classroom. These were generally employed in a rather passive manner under the label of "visual aids" as adjuncts to the traditional lecture and textbook assignment. Today, media are finally being utilized as something other than mere embellishments. As a matter of fact, it now appears obvious that properly designed media "packages" can assume at least part of the teacher's traditional role and can, in fact, "teach" the student many of the things that formerly were considered within the domain of the teacher exclusively. The new role for media is, in turn, creating a new role for the teacher. Instead of functioning as an imparter of facts and knowledge, the modern teacher can leave that aspect of teaching to the mediated "package" and can concentrate on the more personal and human dimensions of education.

Frequently, the teacher finds it necessary to create materials that, for one reason or another, are not available in a ready-made format. The principal objective of this book is to furnish the teacher, or anyone else who is concerned with the communication of information, with a basic knowledge of the fundamental design and production techniques that are useful in the creation of instructional materials. The second objective is to acquaint the individual with at least one rationale for the utilization of media in the teaching-learning process.

In the second edition of *Creating Instructional Materials*, an attempt has been made to update the contents so that they will be in keeping with the current state-of-the-art. Many new products have reached the marketplace since the first edition was published in 1974. Information on the characteristics of such materials along with methods for using them has been included where this was deemed appropriate. Additionally, three years of use in the classroom and other environments has led to considerable input relative to various organizational and content aspects of the book. A number of changes have evolved from such input, including the addition of a chapter on audio recording techniques.

This text can be used as the basis for a course, or as a source book that offers self-contained chapters which are based on individual production processes. A bibliography has been provided that includes books and articles that will serve as a source of additional information in the many fields that are encompassed by instructional media. Finally, a "sources" section is included that contains information on both materials and equipment.

Many individuals have contributed to the creation of this text. The greatest input, however, has come from the teachers in the field and the education majors on the University of Utah campus who have been more than generous with their suggestions and practical help.

It is hoped that this information will be of value to anyone who finds it necessary or desirable to create his or her own instructional materials.

R. V. B.

CONTENTS

1   A Basis for the Design and Selection of Media   1

2   Picture Preservation   19

3   Illustration   43

4   Lettering Techniques   63

5   Visual Design   87

6   Posters, Charts, and Graphs   113

7   Copying and Duplicating Processes   125

8   Overhead Transparencies   137

9   Display and Demonstration Boards   165

10   Three-Dimensional Teaching Devices   181

11   Photography   201

12   Audio Techniques   235

13   Television   249

Materials and Equipment Sources   269

Index   273

A BASIS FOR THE DESIGN AND SELECTION OF MEDIA

A RATIONALE FOR THE USE OF MEDIA

When the question "Why use media?" is asked, teachers will respond with almost as many different answers as there are respondents. "Because students learn more," "Because the class gets tired of lectures only," "Because pictures are better than words," and so forth, are typical answers to this question. There probably is some validity to most of these statements, but none of them adequately satisfies the need for a functional rationale for the use of media in the classroom. Actually, the statements above must be qualified by prefixing the word "sometimes" to each of them. It does not follow that "Pictures are better than words alone," however, they **sometimes** are.

The acquisition of a wide range of concepts is an essential prerequisite to such higher order processes as problem solving and principle formulation. The extent to which an individual is able to function abstractly dedends in large part upon the extent to which he has been able to learn concepts through both direct and contrived experiences. Perception occurs when an individual receives sensory inputs from the immediate environment; percepts are the raw material from which concepts are formed. Because of the concrete nature of most media, they can play an important role in concept learning; indeed, this might well be the most congent reason for using them in instructional situations.

Concept development is dependent upon the "internalization" of the environment. The sensory inputs from the environment are basically nonverbal in nature and consist of the essential properties of the world "out there," that is, color, form, position, size, texture, and so on. These critical qualities are manipulated internally in various ways to form patterns in an attempt to come up with a meaningful match for subsequent perceptual inputs. As the individual's store of percepts increases, so too does the potential for increased concept development and, as a consequence, also the potential for dealing adequately with his or her world. Nonverbal media, being highly sensory in nature, can serve an important function in the perceptual portion of the process of concept development. Words, on the other hand, have little to do with perception, but much to do with conception.

Verbal labels (names) are assigned to objects and become so intimately associated with them that they are capable of calling up the concept of the object even in its absence. But a label is meaningless unless an equivalent concept is already in storage in the brain. If a prior knowlede of elephants has not been attained by an individual, the term "elephant" is nothing better than a nonsense word.

At times, teachers unwittingly attempt to teach concepts to students through verbal means, but words are frequently inadequate for the task, particularly where young children are involved. In order for basic concepts to be learned, it is necessary that the individual have direct encounters with the elements that make up the concept somewhere in his or her experience. Media—including real objects of course—provide the individual with an input of perceptual bits from which logical patterns can be constructed. These patterns are categorized and stored for future use in a way somewhat like a computer data bank might store information. The analogy between the brain and the computer can be carried one step further: if the data bank does not contain the specific information required, then this information cannot be elicited on signal—the computer must be programmed properly in order that the desired responses will be forthcoming.

Words can put the "computer" to work. They can serve as the signal that triggers the search for the appropriate stored data. If a teacher wishes to communicate verbally, there must be no doubt that the "computers" at their desks are programmed to respond to specific verbal signals. If the subject is crustacea, the teacher must be certain that the concept "crustacea" is in the data bank of each individual. If such is the case, then the word "crustacean" will trigger the recall of the critical properties of this group of creatures and understanding and communication will result (See Figure 1-1). This is why it is so essential that somewhere in the process of growing up, children have enough actual and contrived experiences that they can survive in the verbal world.

Concepts can be divided into two large classes, namely, those that are concrete, and those that are abstract. As you might expect, concrete concepts are more readily learned than are abstract ones. Experiments indicate that it takes considerably more practice—and thus more time—to learn a concept such as "democracy" than it does to learn one such as "insect." Such findings should furnish educators with an added incentive to create and utilize appropriate and imaginative kinds of media that will bring to the learning of abstract concepts a degree of concreteness.

The cuisenaire rods and squares described by Bruner are examples of this kind of approach. These simple media represent a successful effort at encoding

FIGURE 1-1

a nontangible concept (equations) into a tangible form. Through the manipulation of such objects, children ultimately learn basic mathematical principles that will enable them at a later stage to successfully solve problems at a higher level of abstraction. The squares are highly sensory in nature and permit children to learn in the manner that suits them best—through interactions with concrete things. It is interesting to note that adults can also profit from this approach. When new concepts are being introduced, adults can be much like children in their need for concrete experiences.

In addition to such contrivances as the rods discussed above, a wide variety of media, including models and graphic representations, can be quite effective in translating abstract concepts into concrete form if they are thoughtfully and carefully designed. Some concepts, however, present a unique challenge to the instructor. Although it is a rather simple task to display the grasshopper in various concrete forms, it is another matter to try to accomplish this with concepts such as diligence or hopefulness for example. Consider also such attributes as honesty, valor, bravery, loyalty. A picture of a person displaying loyalty might be construed to mean many different things.

Although it is difficult, if not impossible to determine precisely how such complex concepts are learned, it seems reasonable to assume that we learn about these kinds of affective things through encounters that very closely resemble our encounters with more tangible types of phenomena. When children are developing the concept of "ball," they manipulate the ball in different ways and then assess the results. In this way, they determine which of their conceptions are accurate and which are not. A similar thing occurs when they learn the concept of "truth," a much more complex concept than "ball," of course. Children attempt to satisfy a felt need through manipulating the variables in a given situation. They find that certain actions are acceptable, while certain others are not. If, for example, a child breaks a jar while attempting to discover what it contains and then blames the accident on the cat, his or her mother will admonish the child to "tell the truth." Through encounters with reality such as this, children develop concepts not only of concrete referents, but also of highly abstract things as well.

Mediated strategies such as simulation, role playing, and certain types of gaming incorporate encounters with things that do not exist in nature as concrete objects. Pictorial (iconic) types of media are often employed to establish an environment in which these activities can take place.

The model or paradigm is another example of a medium that lacks a tangible referent. The model of communication, to use one of the more common ones, has no physical referent in nature—it represents a process rather than a thing. Yet the process it represents in a contrived graphic format seems to make logically visible that which is not visible.

Models (like the communication model, not three-dimensional iconic models), graphs, certain charts and much other material of this nature are often too esoteric for use with children. Children must build a store of concepts before they can comprehend the symbolism which is inherent in such media. For this reason, the use of graphs, maps, etc., is generally delayed until such a time as the child demonstrates the ability to handle the symbology involved.

At this point, it seems advisable to attempt to better define the term "concept development" and to place it in proper perspective with other kinds of learning. Concept development has to do with abstracting the critical properties that cause elements to be logically related and then generalizing to other like cases while limiting this by accurate discrimination. At a basic level, the critical properties of triangles include three sides and three angles. The concept has been learned when similar figures, say the gable of a house, a paper hat, and an artist's plastic triangle, are singled out from an array of nontriangular figures and correctly identified.

To a large extent, the concepts which an individual is able to develop depend on his age and previous experience. Learning can be facilitated greatly through the use of strategies that tend to make experiences more concrete as age decreases. First grade children use such things as cuisenaire rods when learning math; older children learn about chemical compounds by constructing models and charts. By the time adulthood is reached, a sufficient store of concepts has been developed that the adult often uses a different kind of strategy to acquire new ones. This is done by linking the word that identifies the new concept with concepts that are already formed. This is certainly a far cry from the sometimes laborious efforts that children engage in as they learn a new (for them) concept. Once a concept has been learned, it can be verbalized and expanded. Additionally, principles can be developed once concepts are mastered. The learning of principles—a high level type of learning—is accomplished in large measure through the use of verbal stimuli. Words are used to set the stage for the learning; they can be used for assessment; they are useful as directive devices; they can also be used for reinforcement. It must be stressed, however, that none of these verbal strategies will be effective in the teaching of a principle unless the student first has mastered the concepts basic to the principle.

An example of a principle might be "crustacea shed their skins as they grow." Involved here are the concepts of crustacean, shedding, skin, and growth. In order for students to fully understand this seemingly simple statement, they must have first mastered these four concepts through actual or contrived experiences with crustacea, skin, and so forth; otherwise, this principle, like many others that children "learn" will be little more than a hazy, memorized statement of questionable value.

Problem-solving experiences that include such techniques as the "discovery method" are among the highest order kinds of activities that occur in the classroom. Problems are solved through the application of sets of logically combined principles; problem solving is therefore highly verbal in nature. Pictorial types of materials are frequently used to establish the problem situation, however. For example, in learning how to mix colors, such actual and contrived materials as paints, brushes, worksheets, charts, etc., are necessary for the experience to be a meaningful one.

In this kind of activity students would need to possess the concepts of "color" and "mixing" among others. They should also understand the principles that apply when pigments are combined in various ways. An example of a principle related to color mixing might be the following: "When complements are combined, a neutralizing effect is achieved and the nearer the combined hues come to being equal, the nearer to a true neutral will be the visual effect of the mixture."

Perhaps the problem to be solved might involve the creation of a scene or still life with emphasis on naturalness of color. Given the basic primary and secondary colors, and the prerequisite concepts and principles, students would be expected to put these to use in an effort to solve the problem.

To sum up what has been covered, then, we can say that basic concepts are formed through encounters with "reality." When new concepts are being introduced, an effort should be made to provide an environment in which the student can experience direct encounters with the phenomena involved—this is where media come into the picture.

SELECTING MEDIA AND CHARACTERISTICS OF DIFFERENT MEDIA

Selection

In selecting media for instruction, the teacher must decide exactly what the students are to learn and then select the most appropriate types of media for the task. For example, if the teacher wishes the students to be able to identify several species of native birds in their natural habitats, media should be selected that will enable them to perform this task. Obviously, color is an important aspect of field identification and should be included in the media. The habitat that would be favored by one species might not be favored by another; therefore, habitat might be stressed. Size and shape also are considerations in the identification of birds, as are distinctive flight peculiarities. The teacher probably should select colored pictures that display the proportions and relative sizes of the birds.

Additionally, habitats should be displayed in the pictures and on charts; they may also be described verbally. Flight patterns can best be shown through the use of motion pictures and trips to the field and can be described in part through the use of verbal descriptions where the students are sophisticated enough to understand the meanings of the terms used.

When affective (emotional) behaviors are to be emphasized, thoughtfully designed photographs and photographic essays along with carefully selected motion pictures can be useful. Simulated situations, role-playing, recording and play-back techniques using television equipment, visits to institutions such as hospitals and prisons, are all useful ways in which attitudes and feelings can be modified. Media can effectively help to "set the stage" in simulated and role-playing situations.

If the objective is to have the students learn certain factual information, then a textbook or oral presentation may be satisfactory. Pictures can also contain certain specific factual material and can be used, together with verbal directions, to impart information.

Demonstrations and self-instructional "packages" lend themselves nicely to the teaching of procedures. Programmed texts are also suitable for this purpose. If the objective of the lesson is to teach the students to perform certain skilled psychomotor acts then media that incorporate motion might be desirable. Motion pictures, single concept film loops, television presentations, demonstrations and similar materials will be useful for this purpose.

Perhaps a point should be made of the fact that most mediated experiences involve many kinds of media and that no single type will invariably give the "best fit" for a specific teaching situation. Additionally, it would be a unique teaching situation if it did not include some kind of verbal accompaniment. In other words, it is difficult, if not impossible, to establish definite, discrete categories into which each type of media will fit without overlapping other media categories. Therefore, it might not be entirely satisfactory to base the selection of teaching materials on objectives alone. So, in addition to particular kinds of media and specific objectives, the teacher may find it necessary to consider other kinds of criteria when creating learning experiences.

For example, a videotape that is checked out from the district media center might not be compatible with the equipment that is available in the school. The alternatives are to find some other kinds of media that will achieve the desired effect, or to acquire equipment that will handle the tape—a task that may not be practical.

Knowing the level of sophistication of the students will further enable the teacher to select the proper types of media. The vocabulary level should be considered as well as the nature of the pictorial content. The type of pictorial rendering may determine in part the level of sophistication of a visual: a conventionalized drawing may appeal to older students but not to younger ones; a simple picture might be fine for preschoolers, but would be totally inadequate for sixth graders.

It is well to be idealistic when it comes to teaching; however, when it comes right down to the selection and implementation level, teachers often are forced to forego certain superior types of materials simply because they are too expensive. So, cost is an important factor in the selection of materials. The rule here is: if it is too expensive, use something else. Often, homemade materials will solve the problem and fill the gap, but these, too, can be expensive, if not in money, in the expenditure of time and effort.

At times, homemade or locally produced materials may not be of the same quality as the commercially produced variety. However, simply because a particular item is produced by a large, well-known firm does not automatically mean that it will be of superior quality. An item often is created to serve as large a segment of the potential market as possible. It is common to find that the literature accompanying a commerical film lists it as being satisfactory for a range of students all the way from elementary to high school grades. This is not to say that some films do not accomplish this, but in many cases, producers simply attempt to get as much mileage as possible out of a film.

Many commercially produced materials are too overburdened with information and detail to be effective. Often they go to the other extreme and are too simple. Some materials, both commercially produced and locally produced, exhibit poor color qualities, ineffective contrast, illegible lettering, etc. A common fault of the hand-drawn transparency is that it is smeared, spotted, and streaked to the point of distraction; it may also exhibit poor lettering and even misspelled words.

Sound tapes sometimes have poor fidelity, volume that oscillates, too much background noise, or inappropriate musical accompaniments. These faults are most common in locally produced tapes, but the problem of inappropriate or overwhelming background music is also common to the commercial tape as well as to motion picture and slide sound tracks.

Through frequent encounters with media, teachers develop an eye for quality. They come to know what is good, mediocre, and poor, and can act accordingly. It would be advisable to forego the use of certain media if they are of such poor quality that they are going to detract from, rather than add to, the lesson. A particular case in point is the frequent use of transparencies that are simply lifted from the printed page and then projected. Generally, the students in the back of the room cannot see what is on the screen, and those in the front of the room who might read the information find that there is too much of it for them to handle in the time provided.

Finally, when selecting media, whether or not they can be obtained when they are needed is a very real problem. Often excellent pictures are available in magazines and on calendars; they may be trimmed and mounted with little or no cost to the school. On the other hand, beautiful films that would dovetail nicely with a unit being taught on a particular subject may be completely out of reach because of rental or purchase fees. Often a film is not available when needed simply because someone else has it checked out. When selecting the media for a learning unit, it is well to determine ahead of time if they will be available.

The considerations that relate to selection can be used also as the basis for making the decision as to whether or not you want to create your own instructional materials. For example, if a good set of transparencies is available from the media center that will fit your needs, you wouldn't want to go through the process of reinventing the wheel so to speak. So, before getting involved in local production, make it a habit to consider these points:

Are the needed media AVAILABLE? If so,

Are the media free, or must they be purchased? If they must be purchased

What is the COST? If you can afford them, how about

TECHNICAL QUALITY? If they appear to be of good quality, are they

APPROPRIATE to the task at hand? You must also consider the

LEVEL OF SOPHISTICATION. If everything appears acceptable to this point, you are in business—no need to create your own teaching materials. However, If you were unable to make it through the checklist for one reason or another, you will probably find it necessary to move into production. If this is your decision, then the following must be considered:

Is sufficient TIME available to do the job? If so, what about

TALENT? Perhaps you have the skills, or maybe a student or media coordinator has them. If the

MATERIALS AND EQUIPMENT are available your problems are solved. Get on with the creation of your instructional materials.

Characteristics

Different types of media display different kinds of characteristics that influence their selection. The following description of media types is not meant to be all-inclusive, but rather to cover only those types that will commonly be found in a typical school; and particularly those types that can be created at the local level using this text as a guide. Therefore, certain obvious exclusions will be apparent. Programmed instruction, computer-based instruction, dial-access retrieval systems, and other sophisticated media have been intentionally excluded—the emphasis is upon less sophisticated, but still effective, media.

35 mm slides. Slides are miniature transparencies. They can be created with simple cameras and simple equipment; however, if a camera is to be acquired for this purpose it would be well to obtain the best one available for the funds allocated. A good camera will provide versatility that will permit the satisfactory and consistent production of slides under a variety of conditions. Slides are types of still pictures; however, they lend themselves to much greater enlargement (through projection) than do typical mounted pictures. They also display color in a realistic manner that replicates with considerable fidelity the actual colors of the object being photographed.

A 35 mm camera permits the production of visuals from flat pictures or from actual objects. Artwork can be produced and photographed; titles can easily be constructed and reproduced on film. Interesting candid shots can be taken of children at work or at play, of field trips and interesting natural phenomena, important visitors, etc. The slides can then be edited and placed in the proper sequence for projection. If the sequence must be lengthened, shortened, or otherwise modified, it is a simple matter of merely extracting or adding the necessary slides.

A disadvantage of the slide series is that it may become unintentionally disarranged, or some of the slides may be placed in the projector upsidedown or backwards. Numbering the slides and placing a mark in the upper righthand corner should solve at least part of this problem. Another disadvantage has to do with the cost of color film and processing. When one considers the number of transparencies that can be obtained from a single roll of film, however, the cost per frame actually is very reasonable.

Mounted still pictures. Pictures need not be mounted but they are much more functional if they are. Pictures are much like the slides described above in that they lack motion, are two-dimensional, and can be displayed for any length of time desired. They differ from the slide, however, in that they are not generally projected. If it seems advantageous to do so a picture can be projected and enlarged through the use of the opaque projector. The typical nonprojected still picture has several virtues including its very low cost (it may cost nothing), its availability, its lack of a need for special display equipment (such as a projector), and its "self-paced nature (a child can examine it at leisure because once it is displayed on a bulletin board or elsewhere it is permanently accessible until removed).

Pictures have certain disadvantages, however. Some of them are too small for the total class to see as a unit. Others contain false colors or no colors at all, which may detract from their value when certain concepts are being taught. Pictures may contain too much information, much of which might be irrelevant, or they may contain too little to do an adequate job with a particular concept. It is difficult to find exactly the one picture (or even a group of pictures) that will communicate the precise idea that needs to be learned by the student.

Overhead transparencies. Overhead transparencies are like large slides in the sense that they are enlarged onto a screen through projection. Certain advantages are realized through the use of the overhead system that are not inherent to the 35 mm slide system. For one thing, overhead transparencies can be produced in the classroom or workroom through a multitude of processes that range from a simple tracing approach to a rather sophisticated machine-made approach. Transparencies lend themselves to special projection techniques that add interest to a presentation. The teacher might write on the surface of the film, might point with a pointer, reveal one segment of the image at a time, utilize overlays to build concepts, or color over the important cues with a marker. The projector itself is used in the front of a lighted room, thus enabling the teacher to maintain eye contact with the students.

Unlike the 35 mm slide, however, it is very costly to photograph a full color image onto the large 8 x 10 overhead format. Usually color must be obtained through use of markers, or by the "lift" process (see section on transparencies). Diazo gives beautiful colors, but these are flat and do not replicate the actual blended colors to be found in the real objects. Another disadvantage of the overhead system results from the ease with which transparencies can be produced on certain machines such as the thermal transfer machine. This disadvantage has to do with the inferior transparency that often results through the misuse of the process. Many teachers feel that anything that can be transferred to a sheet of film is satisfactory for projection; this simply is not true. A typed or printed page seldom is good original copy for a transparency. There generally is too much information concentrated on the page and the letters are too small to be adequately seen and read by the students. The use of common sense in the selection and preparation of transparency masters will preclude the problem of inadequate transparencies to a large extent.

Motion pictures. Motion pictures of considerable quality can be produced by teachers and students with the modern super 8 equipment now available. The 16 mm format is still the most popular for commercially produced films and gives a larger, sharper image than does the super or standard 8 mm system.

Where motion is desirable (as in the area of psychomotor skills teaching), this medium is excellent. It is next to impossible to learn to execute proper turns in skiing through the use of still pictures. Motion pictures that take advantage of such techniques as close-ups and slow motion can be excellent for teaching this type of skill. Of course, much depends on how diligently the student practices his lesson—a good instructor helps a lot, too!

Many materials do not gain by being encoded into the motion picture format. For example, a trip through an art museum where the camera merely records one still picture after another for a period of time may be as effectively conducted with a set of slides. However, the motion picture can be used in many creative ways—the trip through the art museum might gain additional impact and interest through the use of intimate detailed close-ups of parts of certain pictures, or zooms and pans that add movement to an otherwise still visual.

Time lapse and slow motion techniques permit observations to take place that could not possibly be realized in any other way. The motion picture camera can also faithfully record sequential events as they occur and preserve them for study at some later time. A dimension of realism is inherent within the motion picture format that is impossible to obtain with any other medium (including television, due to its lack of color fidelity and sharpness of image).

There are certain disadvantages that accompany the advantages that are presented by the motion picture. One definite disadvantage of the 16 mm commercial film is its high acquisition cost. Even a short film probably would be out of reach for the average school and would have to be purchased by the central film library for distribution to the school on request. This leads to another problem: the desired film frequently is not available when it is needed, and unless teachers can anticipate their needs far in advance, they may have to do without a particular film. After a few discouraging experiences of this nature, teachers learn either to order popular films weeks and months in advance, or simply forget about them and utilize some other approach in their teaching. Super 8 films are not nearly so expensive as the 16 mm, and as these become increasingly more available in a wider range of subjects they will help to alleviate the problems of cost and availability.

Many teachers are frightened by projectors, which they consider to be highly technical and difficult to operate. Often, a single negative experience, such as having a film break in the middle of a presentation, will tend to discourage teachers from using projection equipment. When available, "self-loading" projectors help to make the operation more simple; also, presenting in-service training sessions in the use of equipment is an excellent way in which to encourage the use of films and other types of equipment-dependent media.

Projected types of media such as slides, motion pictures, filmstrips, and transparencies have the additional disadvantage of being fixed-paced unless they are housed in some type of self-instructional unit such as a carrel. Once the projector is turned off, the image is gone and it is pretty final. This can be frustrating for the child who has not finished interacting with the media. Still pictures, handouts, and other types of nonprojected visual media do not suffer from this disadvantage if properly used. Whenever it is practical to do so, projected kinds of media should be made available to those students who desire additional interactions with them.

Duplicated handouts. Machines are available in every school for the production of duplicated handouts. These simple media are among the most effective learning devices available, and for the teaching of certain kinds of concepts are unsurpassed. Printed handouts can teach such things as vocabulary, word identification, sentence structure, and so on. Illustrations of a simple nature can be encoded in this form and can permit every child to have an equivalent experience. Handouts can be used in conjunction with a transparency in such a way that the students can actively work along with the teacher and can match the responses that they are making with those that the teacher is making. Handouts cost very little; they can be produced rapidly through the use of either handmade or machine-made masters. Enough copies can be pulled from one master to satisfy the needs of a total class. Additionally, transparencies can be made directly from the master that will exactly conform to the pattern of the handouts and therefore be an exact replica of them.

If it is desirable that the students have access to a printed or typed page, then the handout is the answer. As has been mentioned, a slide or transparency of a typed or printed page is not a satisfactory teaching device due to the abundance of information contained on the page and the small size of the print. Handouts also give the students the opportunity to pace themselves, they may interact with the handout at their own speed, and may take the handout home with them for additional perusal at their leisure.

Many varieties of duplicated handouts are very simple to create. Because of this, there are times when insufficient care is taken in their preparation, and they suffer from poor quality. Occasionally, the master will wrinkle and portions of a word will be obliterated. This is true mainly of the mimeograph and spirit processes, particularly when thin gauge thermal masters are involved.

The carbon coating on spirit masters becomes increasingly depleted during the course of a duplicating run so that copies appear less intense as the run nears its conclusion. This problem is easily solved by creating another master. However, in an effort to squeeze out every possible copy, teachers sometimes find themselves with a number of handouts that are faint and difficult to read.

Care should be taken when creating drawings on spirit masters. Lines should be precise, large areas of solid color should be avoided, drawings should be simplified. Creating drawings by hand on the mimeograph master can be quite a chore because they must be done with crude stylus-like tools that severely limit technique. Offset processes are best for high quality long runs, but the average teachers do not possess the knowledge and skill to run a modern office offset press and must rely on the expert to do this for them.

Television. The applications of this potent medium are extremely varied and numerous. They range all the way from home viewing for entertainment purposes to highly structured educational sessions during which prescribed objectives are addressed. Television can be used by students as a substitute for or adjunct to the traditional modes of reporting or responding. In many schools, television"reports" are as common as the written theme or verbal presentation.

Teachers use television to present in-class information of various kinds. Much of this information is derived from sources outside of the school, however, varying amounts might be made up of locally produced segments. Creative teaching involves much more than merely playing a tape which the students passively view. Preliminary activities can include not only discussion, but also the creation of a multitude of different kinds of visual and verbal products such as illustrations, television programs, short stories, analytical essays, and photographic materials.

The videocassette format has led to the development of a number of strategies that were less common in the days of open-reel recorders. For example, many schools have libraries of cassettes which reside in the media center. This arrangement leads to a more extensive usage of the materials due to the increased availability that this system provides. Some districts have contractual agreements with film producers that enable them to tape selected motion pictures. The problem of scheduling that is common to motion pictures (as well as to broadcast television) is thereby alleviated to a large extent.

As with the motion picture, the characteristic of movement is an important aspect of television. Additionally, however, the immediacy of the television medium gives it at least a degree of superiority if this factor is essential to a particular undertaking. For example, a videotape can be made, and can be played back immediately without the need for an interim processing step.

There exist certain problems in the production and utilization of television programs. Once again, some teachers have a fear of equipment and may shun the medium if it involves anything more than turning on the receiver. In some situations, scheduling can be frustrating; however, a cassette library can help to solve this shortcoming.

Tape Recordings. Tape recordings may be used in conjunction with visual presentations or alone depending on the concepts to be taught and the objectives that have been established. Most generally, teachers lecture, describe, interact with the students, question, cajole, and use other verbal approaches as they proceed with a lesson. At times, however, some things verbal are worth encoding on a tape for replay at some future time. Such events as a forensic meet, a band recital, or a visit from a famous personality might be recorded on tape for preservation. Lectures and lessons often are placed on cassettes which are made available to students for study. Often these may be checked out from the school and taken home overnight. Some cassette tape units are playback instruments only and do not record. This tape of machine is less expensive than the recording variety and is useful when the primary activity is that of listening. When learning to speak a language, students will find the recorder player unit to be more satisfactory than the playback unit because it enables them to record their own voices and then listen to it as playback.

Simple tape recorders are very inexpensive and readily obtainable. They are small, and the cassette variety is pretty much self-contained. Although reel-to-reel recorders may be large and heavy, many of them are small and compact and easily transported to the recording area.

Some people find the tape recorder to be as mysterious a piece of hardware as the 16 mm projector. They have a fear of erasing something that is important and they have difficulty finding and pushing all of the proper buttons in the proper sequence to make the machine function. Once again, the answer to this is training and practice. An in-service workshop on tape recorders will take most of the uncertainty out of using this very functional device.

There is also the problem of compatibility between machines. When attempting to dub one tape from another, incompatibility can be very frustrating: patch cords do not fit, the machines may have different track arrangements, and so on. But, as with the other types of media mentioned above, the advantages almost always outweigh the disadvantages and the final results make whatever trouble was encountered in the production of the media seem unimportant and insignificant.

THE COMMUNICATION MODEL

A number of models have been developed in an effort to visually portray the process of communication. Although these might differ from one another in detail, they are all basically the same as far as content is concerned.

The model shown in Figure 1-2 includes the basic mechanical components of communication, but it does not take into consideration such psychological prerequisites as readiness and attitude. Nevertheless, the model is useful to the extent that it enables us to better understand the complex phenomenon of communication.

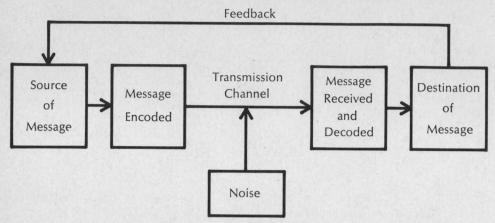

FIGURE 1-2   A Communication Model

The source of the message is an individual who has some data to transmit. The data are generally in the form of an idea, some facts, a concept, and so on. The source might be the teacher, a student, or anyone who has something in mind that he wishes to share with others.

Encoding is the process of changing the data into some form that can be transmitted. Obviously, a thought in one's mind does not lend itself to transmission without some kind of encoding—unless one accepts the theory of ESP. Encoding involves transferring the intangible thought into something more or less tangible—this is where media come into play. Examples of encoding might be making a transparency, creating a poster, making a filmstrip, lettering a caption, giving a lecture, and so forth.

After the information is coded for transmission, it must be sent to its destination via some kind of channel. The channel may consist of certain wave lengths along which radio signals are broadcast. It may consist of reflected rays of light emitting from the illuminated projection screen. It may be the air between speaker and audience which carries the audio signals.

Often the transmission channel functions in a less than perfect fashion due to the factor of "noise." Noise can be almost anything—it doesn't necessarily have to be a sound. For example, a room that is too warm or too cold introduces the noise factor which is nothing more or less than a deterrent to effective message transmission. Redundancy built into the message helps to overcome the problem of noise.

Ultimately, the message reaches the receiver who decodes it. This act of decoding has to do with putting the message back into its original form. It is important to recognize that although the message may have been decoded, it may not have been decoded accurately. That is, it may not at this end resemble what it was originally at the other end. This may be the fault of the encoder, the decoder, the transmission channel or a combination of these elements. Often the encoder encodes the message in a language that the decoder cannot entirely comprehend. This can happen when words are used in an attempt to develop concepts.

At any rate, if the message is finally internalized and becomes an accurate mental image in the mind of the receiver, then the message has reached its destination. It is entirely possible for the recipient of the message to comprehend every visual and verbal element in the message and yet not be able to form an accurate mental image of the referent (that which was referred to). This is very often the fault of inadequate message design. Even photographs and motion pictures can convey faulty impressions, although we consider these types of media to be high in fidelity. An example might have to do with the size of an object. One small child was terrified by a motion picture which displayed close-up shots of groundhogs because she considered groundhogs to be as huge as they were displayed on the screen. No adequate known reference object was employed in order that an accurate idea of the size of a groundhog might be formed.

The manner in which the degree of success of the communication is assessed is through the process called "feedback." Feedback has to do with the response of the recipient to the message. This response is communicated back to the sender and completes the communication loop. The communication loop is a constantly moving, active cycle and it enables the sender of the message to continually modify the message in order that communication becomes more and more effective and accurate.

Tests frequently are used as feedback devices. Another feedback strategy involves verbal interaction. Receiver performance after communication enables the sender to assess the degree of success. In order that the effect of the communication might be accurately measured, it is essential that some knowledge of the prior capability of the subject be known. This knowledge often is gained through the use of a pretest.

A practical illustration of the model in action might be as follows: a zoology teacher wants his students to be able to identify the major groups of living fishes (message source). The teacher knows that this concept is highly visual in nature so he decides to use a visual technique for encoding his message. Motion is not an important factor in this concept, so a still picture is selected. The class is a large one and therefore magnification or multiplication is needed. The overhead transparency along with duplicated handouts are selected (redundancy). Color in fish classification at this level is not needed—as a matter of fact, color could introduce an ambiguous element into the visuals since to color a fish red, for example, might lead some students to conclude that all fish of this particular group are red. The final version of the transparency becomes a black and white photocopy or thermal copy visual (the message is encoded). After appropriate preparation, the transparency is placed on the projector stage and projected onto the screen. The image is carried through reflected light rays to the audience (transmission channel). Several students who are on the student council enter the room late (noise) and the teacher must repeat part of his presentation.The reflected image of the fishes impinges upon the sensory modalities (eyes) of the students and the teacher's verbal message enters a second modality (ears). The duplicated sheets also are distributed and become a part of the communication.

The students begin to interpret, make associations, and selections from the incoming information. They begin to structure the information into a meaningful message (message received and decoded). The students now have in their minds the same message as their teacher (destination of message). The only way that the teacher can assess the degree of correspondence of the concept that the pupil has with the concept that he wishes them to have is to elicit feedback from his students. He may do this simply by asking questions, or he may administer an examination which might be written or drawn. He may also ask the students to put appropriate labels on the duplicated materials which he gave to them (all of this is feedback). If a teacher finds that the students are not able to respond satisfactorily to his test, he may revamp his message by adding printed labels to the visuals, or he may wish to modify the visuals in some way, or allocate more time and/or resources to the task. He would then repeat the process and continue to modify until the students were able to achieve their objectives. This is the communication model in action.

A SYSTEMATIC APPROACH FOR THE DESIGN OF LEARNING EXPERIENCES

Just as media are an integral part of the communication process, they are also a very essential part of most learning experiences. It is difficult if not impossible to select the appropriate types of media without first knowing precisely what it is that the students are expected to learn. Stating objectives is a first step in the systematic approach to instruction and should precede anything else that might be undertaken in the teaching unit.

In order to more adequately address the problem of writing objectives, it might be useful at this point to define what has come to be known as the three domains of learning, i.e., the cognitive, the affective, and the psychomotor domains.

Cognitive. This domain includes those kinds of functions that relate to remembering or recalling something previously learned. It also has to do with high level problem-solving activities as well as with various kinds of synthesizing activities. It has to do with the manipulation of knowledge.

Affective. This domain includes the emotional, attitudinal, value-related kinds of things. It is a difficult domain with which to deal because conclusive methods of accurately measuring such functions have not been fully validated.

Psychomotor. Has to do with muscular or motor skills. It involves the physical manipulation of things or the performance of some kind of coordinated movement.

It should be obvious that it is much simpler to write objectives for the cognitive than for the affective domain because of the nature of the content. Indeed, most of what is measured in the schools is of cognitive nature— paper-and-pencil tests represent the traditional way of assessing the student's knowledge.

When you are writing objectives, you might describe the kind of behavior in which the students are to engage, or you might describe the type of product that they are required to produce. Under behaviors, you could include such things as dance performances, athletic activities, speech presentations, and so forth. Products would include drawings and paintings, objective tests, essays, and so forth. Your objectives should be written in such a manner that either the product or the activity (or both, if applicable) is clearly defined and identifiable. Use specific terms such as "list," "describe," "identify," rather than illusive ones such as "understand," "know," "appreciate." Specify the level of performance that is desired. This can be done by establishing a minimal level in terms of a percentage of the total possible score or by indicating the minimal number of responses required. Finally, you might also wish to state the conditions under which the students are to demonstrate their competence.

Here is an example of a behavioral objective: "Given a sheet of lettering samples, the student will correctly classify at least eighty percent of the samples as to style."

Don't feel that you must slavishly follow one prescribed pattern for educational objectives. Alter the pattern, or devise your own. But, in any case, get used to writing down some kind of objectives before you begin developing your learning materials. It will be well worth the trouble.

After the objectives have been clearly specified, it is a good policy to determine what it is that the students already know about the concepts to be presented. This pretest may be compared to the test that is given after the students have been through the learning experience to determine whether or not the experience accomplished what it was supposed to. The pretest also is useful as a basis for the restructuring of the original set of objectives. If the group already possesses certain skills or information that was included in the initial objectives, the objectives should be altered to include other kinds of requirements or should be excluded.

Now decide on what types of experiences should be built into the instructional portion of the system. This is a demanding kind of decision which can only be made after an assessment of the objectives and purposes of the lesson. Additionally, available resources should be inventoried so that experiences can be realistically designed. Then acquire or create the media that are needed for the unit of instruction. Think in terms of the differentiated grouping of students if this seems appropriate; or consider an individualized approach if the necessary requisites are available. After everything is in order, teach the lesson.

After the learning sequence, it is necessary to administer a post-test in order to evaluate the efficacy of the teaching process. It is probably desirable to test in the manner in which teaching was conducted if possible. In other words, if the students were trained with an actual camera, they should probably be given a performance test using an actual camera; but this relates back to the objectives as stated at the beginning of the sequence—they should determine precisely what the students' competencies should be.

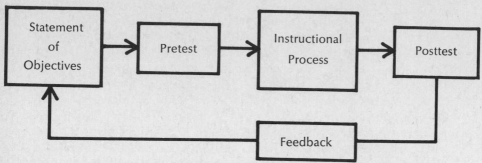

FIGURE 1-3   A Model of an Instructional System

The post-test gives information (called feedback) to the teacher who may then wish to alter methods, media, or objectives in order that a more appropriate terminal performance might be obtained.

BIBLIOGRAPHY

Arnheim, Rudolf. **Visual Thinking.** London: Faber & Faber Ltd., 1969.

Bloom, Benjamin S., ed. **Taxonomy of Educational Objectives, Handbook I: Cognitive Domain.** New York: David McKay Co., Inc., 1956.

Bruner, Jerome S. **Toward a Theory of Instruction.** Cambridge, Mass.: Harvard University Press, 1967.

Dondis, Donis A. **A Primer of Visual Literacy.** Cambridge, Mass.: The MIT Press, 1973.

Eliot, John, ed. **Human Development and Cognitive Processes.** New York: Holt, Rinehart and Winston, Inc., 1971.

Forgus, Ronald H. **Perception.** New York: McGraw-Hil' Book Co., 1966.

Gagne, Robert M. **The Conditions of Learning.** New York: Holt, Rinehart and Winston, Inc., 1965.

Gerlach, Vernon S. and Ely, Donald P. **Teaching and Media.** Englewood Cliffs, N.J.: Prentice-Hall, Inc., 1971.

Gregory, R. L. **The Intelligent Eye.** New York: McGraw-Hill Book Co., 1970.

Knowlton, James Q. "On the Definition of 'Picture,' " **AV Communication Review** 14, no. 2 (1966): 157-83.

Mager, Robert F. **Preparing Instructional Objectives.** Palo Alto, Calif.: Fearon Publishers, 1962.

National Education Association. **Research, Principles, and Practices in Visual Communication.** Washington, D.C.: 1960.

Piaget, Jean. **The Child's Conception of the World.** Totowa, N.J.: Littlefield, Adams and Co., 1965.

Popham, James W. and Baker, Eva L. **Systematic Instruction.** Englewood Cliffs, N.J.: Prentice-Hall, Inc., 1970.

Woodruff, Asahel D. "The Rationale." **Theory into Practice** 7 (December 1968): 197-202.

2

PICTURE PRESERVATION

INTRODUCTION

The still picture is widely used in the development of various kinds of concepts. As a general rule, pictures are used as components in a larger experience that almost always includes some verbal or digital material and often includes other kinds of media. When actual objects that illustrate a concept are employed, verbal cues and directions are used to call attention to the critical properties that illustrate the concept. This same strategy is employed when pictures are substituted for the objects; that is, verbal directions are used as cuing devices to point out the relevant items in the picture. This verbal cuing is accomplished with either spoken or printed symbols—in either case, similar results are obtained.

Mimetic (realistic) pictures are flat representations of three-dimensional objects. As such, they must of necessity be ambiguous where depth is concerned because it is not possible to translate three-dimensional space into two dimensions without some loss. Depth cues, such as linear and aerial perspective, overlapping planes, textures, and form are used by the artist to convey the effect of three-dimensional space. These cues are automatically encoded by the camera. However, in spite of every effort to make the picture as realistic and lifelike as possible, it will never become, in fact, the subject that is being pictured. Nevertheless, pictures serve as extremely high fidelity surrogates for the actual objects and tend to make possible visual experiences that otherwise would often be impractical.

It is not necessary for an individual to learn to "read" pictures in the same formal manner in which he or she would learn to read a verbal language. Whatever learning is involved in the understanding of pictures seems to occur in a less structured manner.

Actually, pictures are more universally comprehended than are words but only if the referent—that "thing" in the real world to which the picture refers or for which it stands—is familiar to some extent to the individual viewing and interpreting the picture. In other words, a picture of a skyscraper stands for the real thing and can be "read" by city children or by country children who may not have had a first-hand experience with skyscrapers, but who are nevertheless aware of brick and glass structures of a lesser magnitude because their town is full of them.

To Eskimo children the skyscraper is like nothing they have ever seen before. If they have no prior knowledge of the white man's structures, even simple ones, they will not be able to "read" the picture adequately, if at all. A picture of a person, however, is much more universally comprehended than is a picture of a skyscraper, for example.

We are able to identify the human figures and even most of the birds and animals which are represented in an Egyptian tomb in spite of the passage of centuries. But we find that many of the pictured artifacts seem quite esoteric simply because we do not understand what function they served in the everyday lives of the Egyptians.

Carefully composed full-color photographs possess the highest degree of fidelity of any of the two-dimensional mediums, but they still fall short of reality. What then is the function of pictures that display an even greater departure from reality (such as drawings and diagrams)? Although a perfect representational interface between the picture and its referent cannot be achieved, it is possible to obtain what amounts to a more or less perfect functional relationship. An outline drawing can show precisely how a device is constructed; a diagram can show how a muscle contracts and expands. Through the process of abstracting the essentials from a given referent, the artist can display only those elements that are essential to the functioning of the thing being portrayed.

A high-fidelity photograph, in spite of its authenticity, is seldom adequate to the task of conveying a satisfactory understanding of a complex referent to the students. Other kinds of supplementary visuals, such as diagrams, simplified drawings, cut-aways, and so on are generally needed. All of these can be preserved in ways that will enable them to sustain heavy and frequent usage in the classroom. The processes that are described in this chapter are all directed toward the preservation of valuable pictorial teaching materials.

KINDS OF STILL PICTURES

There are two basic kinds of still pictures: (1) the flat, opaque (or nonprojected) picture, and (2) the flat, transparent (or projected) picture. Category One can be illustrated by almost any of the pictures that are encountered in books and magazines. Pictures that are viewed without the aid of a projecting device and that are opaque and reflect light rather than transmit it fall into this category. Category Two can be illustrated by the film strip and slide, the overhead transparency and the lantern slide. These visuals are transparent to the extent that they permit light to pass through at least certain parts in order that an image might be projected onto a surface.

In this chapter, we shall concentrate on the first class of still pictures, the nonprojected variety. Later chapters will deal with transparencies for use on the overhead projector and 35 mm slides for use in the slide projector.

SELECTING STILL PICTURES

The selection of appropriate still pictures is dependent to a large degree on the nature of the target group and the subject matter being presented. Illustrations that are thoughtfully composed and carefully rendered, or photographs that embody powerful emotional themes can be useful when concepts that relate to the affective domain are being stressed. The more common use of the still picture, however, seems to be in the cognitive domain. It follows, therefore, that most of what a picture does relates to factual kinds of things (e.g., "What color is it?," "What shape is it?," "What does it look like?," "How does it work?," etc.).

It is important, therefore, that pictures be selected that adequately convey the information that is called for. If the concept of cows is being stressed, it is important that the physical qualities of this animal be accurately portrayed. A purple cow is cute, but if the children are to learn accurate concepts relative to what cows actually are like, they should not be misled by inaccurately colored ones.

Pictures can be used as stimulus materials rather than as strictly information imparting visuals. In a case such as this, the purple cow may stimulate the children to create all kinds of interesting creatures, but it would be well to prepare the children ahead of time for such an experience, perhaps through a simple expedient such as, "Now, children, we know that cows are not purple, but . . . etc." After children have developed some fairly accurate concepts about things, then pictures may be used that are much less real. Diagrams can be understood by older children who have some sophistication with pictures, but they may be meaningless to third graders. Cartoons are unusual because they do not replicate reality to any large extent (although some might) and yet they seem to be as readily comprehended by little children as are the real kinds of things. Cartoons can be very useful for all groups of children; however, they seem to represent a kind of "shorthand" and might pose some problems if the children are subjected to cartoon situations and then asked to perform in a real situation. A case in point might involve the child who is familiar with cartoon kinds of animals and then is asked to identify actual zoo animals. Of course, much of her success depends upon how skillfully the cartoonist has created the animals in the first place.

In essence, then, the following criteria are useful when selecting still pictures:

1. The picture should be large enough for all to see, or it should be reproduced so that each student might have a copy, or, if properly protected, it could be passed around the room.

2. If color is used and color is an important attribute of the referent that is to be learned about, then the color should be accurately portrayed.
3. Distortion, caricaturization, etc., are useful as long as they do not give the students false impressions about the referent.
4. Select visuals that are compatible with the degree of sophistication of the students. Second graders cannot comprehend a flow chart, twelfth graders might be offended by naive, childlike illustrations, and so on.
5. When using pictures as surrogates for the real thing (an example might be a picture of the Queen Mary—an object that obviously cannot be carried into the classroom), make sure that they accurately portray scale (show a person next to the ship), texture, proportion, etc.
6. Select pictures that are exciting and interesting. Use pictures that portray things going on; people looking at or interacting with things; animals in interesting poses or involved in unique activities; emotional kinds of things, and so forth.
7. Select pictures that are pertinent to the subject being taught.
8. Select pictures that are technically of high quality. The fact that a picture is reproduced does not mean that it is technically good. Sometimes colors are out of register, details are blurred, and so forth.

Some Advantages of Still Pictures

The advantages that still pictures afford are rather obvious and the list is long, but essentially the principal advantages are as follows:

- They can furnish satisfactory surrogates for referents that are not available and/or are so complex that they would not be understood, etc.
- They can faithfully replicate colors where colors are important.
- They can reduce large objects to manageable size.
- They can "freeze" motion so that the moving object can be studied more adequately.
- They can be valuable where visual identification is one of the principal objectives.
- They can serve as symbolic, graphic "maps" of the real thing (an example might be a drawing of a transistorized circuit). This type of illustration is often referred to as a diagram.
- A drawing can be modified in many ways in order that the important aspects might be emphasized or in order that a specific "feeling" might be projected; this is within the realm of the caricaturist and the cartoonist.

Some Disadvantages of Still Pictures

- It is often difficult to find appropriate pictures. Generally, teachers know exactly what is needed to communicate an idea, but are unable to find the right materials. One way to solve this problem, at least in part, is to create a file of pictures (a tear sheet file). If this file is arranged in some logical order, it will be extremely valuable when a specific picture is desired.

- Anything that involves motion as one of the most important attributes cannot be adequately visualized with the still picture. Perhaps the best way to teach a psychomotor skill is to use a demonstration, a motion picture, or television presentation.
- Still pictures may give ambiguous or false information as to the attributes of the referent. A close-up picture of a groundhog without the inclusion of a standard of measurement (such as a human figure) might cause the naive child to form concepts relative to the size of the groundhog that are totally false.
- In the absence of color (with the black and white picture) the concept of color is not projected. Of course, if color is not one of the important attributes of the object, or if the lesson does not include the identification of color, or if a knowledge of the color of the referent is not relevant, then color may not be needed.
- Sometimes, the small size of a picture can be a problem. Often the instructor will attempt to use a visual that cannot be seen by the class as a whole; this is when the technique of converting the nonprojected visual into a projected visual can be useful.

MOUNTING VISUALS

One of the basic techniques of visual communication has to do with the display of pictorial materials. Since most pictures are somewhat fragile in nature and therefore susceptible to damage and even to destruction, it is frequently desirable to preserve them by mounting them in an appropriate fashion. If expense and time are factors, rubber cement mounting or spray mounting may serve the purpose. If a permanent mount is desired, dry mounting with dry mount tissue will result in an excellent product. A picture that is frequently handled may be laminated. Rubber cement should not be used on valuable pictures for it has a tendency to leach through the surface of the paper, particularly if the paper is thin, and to discolor with age. Do not try to wet mount a picture which is printed on a clay-surfaced paper because the moisture will cause the clay to dissolve which will damage or destroy the visual. To check for clay coated paper, merely moisten your finger and rub it over the picture surface in an inconspicuous place. If a white residue comes off on your finger, the paper is clay coated.

Wet mounts may be made on sheeting, pillow cases, muslin, etc., which makes them inexpensive to produce. Chartex enables one to mount a large visual on cloth without having to resort to the use of paste and water with their resultant problems, but the cost for this material is considerably higher than the cost for equivalent wet mounting materials.

The passe partout envelope makes it possible to mount a picture permanently, but then to disassemble the mount in the event other uses for the picture are prescribed. In other words, a passe partout mount may be used in typical still, mounted picture form but the visual in the envelope may be removed and passed through a heat-transfer machine to create a transparency if desired. The basic objection to the passe partout mount has to do with cost. Also, it requires considerable time and patience to construct one of these.

The problem then becomes one of weighing the alternatives and selecting the one mounting process that will best serve the needs of the visual designer. If multiplication is a factor, perhaps a mounted picture will not meet the need; duplicated handouts may be better. If magnification is a factor, it may be advisable to use a transparency in place of the mounted picture. If action is one of the important considerations, a demonstration or motion picture might be better than the mounted, still picture. Consider all implications before proceeding with the production of the learning materials; the mere fact that a picture is "pretty" does not automatically make it a good teaching device.

Positioning a Picture

Although no "laws" exist relative to the placement of a picture on the mounting board, it is generally desirable to locate it slightly above center. This position accomplishes two things: it overcomes the tendency of the eyes to tell the observer that the visual is low (because of the apparent weight of the visual), and it leaves space for the title. Generally, the margins on either side of the mount would be equal.

To position a visual easily and attractively, follow these steps:

1. Place the visual in the upper left-hand corner of the mounting board.
2. Divide the exposed vertical space in half and draw a light pencil line (A-B). This can be done by marking a piece of scrap paper and then folding it in half as shown in Figure 2-1. Unfold the paper, place it on the card, and make a mark at the fold. The space is accurately divided in half.
3. Divide the exposed horizontal space in half and draw a light pencil line (C-D).
4. Slide the picture down so that the bottom rests on line C-D and the side rests on line A-B—this centers the picture. Now, slide the picture upward slightly so that the bottom margin is slightly larger than the top one. You may now secure the picture to the card. Or, if you are inclined to be a bit more scientific, skip step 4 and move directly from step 3 to step 5.
5. Place the ruler in a diagonal position so that a third line might be drawn that runs from the lower left corner of the picture, through line A-B, and to the point at which line C-D leaves the mounting board.
6. Where the diagonal intersects line A-B, make a mark (E).
7. Move the picture down until the right edge is tangent to line A-B and until the lower right corner touches point E.
8. Secure the picture in this position and erase pencil lines.

Rubber Cement Mounting

This is a quick, inexpensive method that is useful when permanency is not a consideration. Eventually, the cement will lose its adhesive quality and the

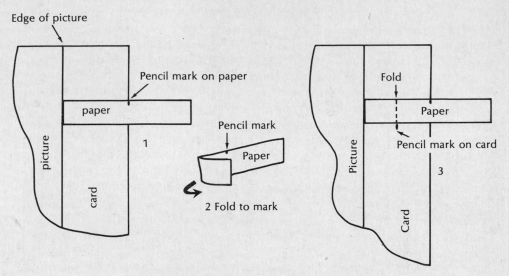

FIGURE 2-1   Dividing a Space in Half

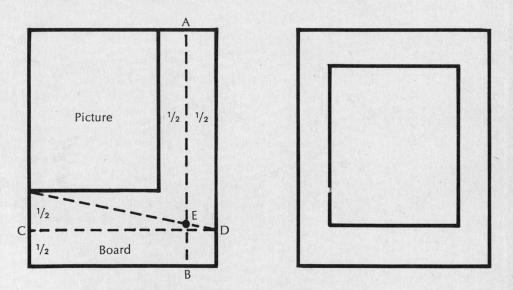

FIGURE 2-2   Positioning a Picture

picture will separate from the backing material. This may take a number of months or even years, however. In addition, thin papers become stained as the cement leaches through; this is particularly common with papers such as newsprint and thin magazine pages. Yet, even with these limitations, rubber cement mounting remains one of the most commonly used of all mounting processes.

To create a rubber cement mount, follow these steps:

1. Trim the visual so that all edges are square and even.

2. Trim the backing material (generally poster board) so that it is square and larger than the visual.
3. Mark the area on the backing material that the picture will cover.
4. Brush an even coating of rubber cement within the area indicated on the backing material. Let this dry completely.
5. Turn the visual over and coat the back with an even layer of rubber cement. Let this dry thoroughly.
6. Place two pieces of waxed paper over the mounting board so that they overlap slightly in the center.
7. Position the visual, cement side down, on the backing material. You should now have a "sandwich" consisting of the backing material on the bottom with the glued side up, the two pieces of waxed paper next, and the visual with the glued side down on top of this.
8. Position the visual so that it matches the lines drawn earlier on the backing material (you may do this merely by aiming through the transparent waxed paper).
9. Now hold the visual securely in place and slip one of the sheets of waxed paper out from under the visual. This will cause the exposed section of the visual to come into contact with the exposed section of the backing. This will result in a tight bond at this point.
10. Remove the other piece of waxed paper and rub the visual into place with your hand; you now have a rubber cement mount. You may notice, however, that some residual cement remains around the edge of the picture. You can easily remove this by using a rubber cement "mouse." A "mouse" is nothing more than a rubber cement eraser created by collecting the dry rubber cement from the sides of the container and forming it into a mass. It is possible to buy commercial rubber cement "pick-ups" or "mice" from commercial art vendors.
11. Your rubber cement mount is now completed and is ready to be displayed on bulletin boards, posters, etc.

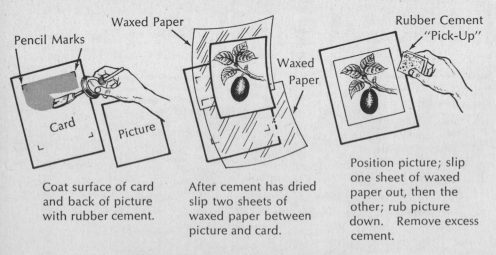

Coat surface of card and back of picture with rubber cement.

After cement has dried slip two sheets of waxed paper between picture and card.

Position picture; slip one sheet of waxed paper out, then the other; rub picture down. Remove excess cement.

FIGURE 2-3   Rubber Cement Mounting

One-Coat Rubber Cement Mounting. One-coat rubber cement is a heavy-bodied rubber adhesive that remains tacky indefinitely. It is useful for mounting materials that have irregular outlines because only one surface, rather than two, must be coated to obtain a bond. The most common variety is the *Presto* brand.

This adhesive is simple to use—merely apply a coat of cement to the back of the material to be mounted and let it dry for about two minutes. Then press the coated visual firmly into place on the backing material. Clean up any residue and that's all there is to it.

Incidentally, it is a relatively easy matter to remove a picture that has been mounted with rubber cement from its backing. Even the "permanent" double-coated mount can be disassembled in this fashion. You will need some rubber cement solvent and an eye dropper for this process; clean hands will be useful also. Carefully separate one of the corners of the picture from its backing—the merest separation is enough. Then, using the eye dropper, apply a small quantity of solvent between the picture and the backing material, gently pulling on the corner as you do this. As the dried cement is dissolved, the picture will begin to separate from the card—continue to apply the solvent while pulling on the picture, until the separation has been completed. Permit the solvent to dry and the picture will be as good as new.

Spray Adhesive Mounting

This is a popular technique that involves coating one of the surfaces to be adhered with a sticky spray. All kinds of materials can be attached to various surfaces with this substance. Spray adhesive does not soak through papers and does not age in the manner of rubber cement.

To use the adhesive, first shake the can vigorously to mix the contents uniformly. Next, hold the can about six inches away from the surface to be sprayed and apply an even coat of adhesive. For a permanent bond, coat the surface with a heavy layer of adhesive and then attach the visual to the backing material while it is still wet and tacky. For a nonpermanent bond, apply a light coat, let dry for a minute or so and then attach the visual to the backing.

Positionable Mounting Adhesive Process

Manufactured by 3M, this relatively new product consists of a layer of special adhesive sandwiched between a release paper and a protective carrier sheet. Before pressure is applied, the adhesive is only slightly tacky, so the mounting sheet can be moved and repositioned. When pressure is applied, the adhesive forms a permanent bond.

The steps for using are:

1. Place picture to be mounted face down on a hard surface. Separate the sheets and place the adhesive sheet on the back of the picture. To activate the adhesive, rub firmly over the back of the sheet with a squeegee or hard roller.
2. Remove the adhesive sheet and discard it, then position the print where you want it. It will be slightly tacky due to the adhesive on the back and will tend to remain where you place it.

3. Cover the picture with a protective sheet and apply pressure to the entire surface to activate the adhesive and form a permanent bond with the backing material.

You now have a permanent mount that will not discolor or release from its backing. This type of adhesive is excellent for mounting colored prints (plain or resin coated papers) because no heat is required.

Dry Mounting on Hard Surfaces

The dry mounted visual will remain adhered to its backing material almost indefinitely. This quality makes dry mounting one of the preferred processes for preserving pictures that are valuable or that will be subjected to hard usage. Another advantage of dry mounting is that is can be accomplished with a common household iron, although the dry mount press is the preferred tool for this. Dry mounting can become relatively expensive if a large number of visuals are to be mounted; however, this problem is lessened when the tissue is purchased in roll form rather than in sheets.

Prior to the actual mounting process, you should heat the press to a temperature of 225° F. Next, reduce the moisture in the pictures and boards by placing them in the press for forty-five seconds, then opening the press for a moment and closing it again for thirty additional seconds. This drives the residual moisture out of the materials and prevents blistering. In very dry climates, such as those found in some areas of the West, the drying step is not so crucial. Now, you are ready to mount the picture. Follow these steps:

1. Trim the mounting board to the proper size; trim the picture to approximate size.
2. Tack the tissue to the back of the picture as shown in Figure 2-4. Note: Seal Release Paper can be used to cover the tissue prior to tacking. This prevents the iron from sticking to the tissue.
3. Check to make certain that the tissue is securely in place; you don't want it to shift positions in the press.
4. Trim the tissue and the picture to the exact size.
5. Tack picture to board as shown. Once again, Seal Release Paper comes in handy.
6. Cover the visual with a protective sheet of paper.
7. Place in press for thirty to forty-five seconds. Remove, and while still hot, quickly place under a weight (a cold dry mount press is very good for this). Leave the mount under the weight until it is cool, then remove it to complete the process.

Note: The steps described above are for tissues such as the Seal MT5 variety. When using a low temperature material such as Seal Fotoflat, you should make the following adjustments: (1) Use a temperature of 180° F rather than the higher 225° setting. (2) Place pressure on the mount immediately upon removal from the heat press since Fotoflat is removable when hot. Other than this, the mounting steps are identical to those given above.

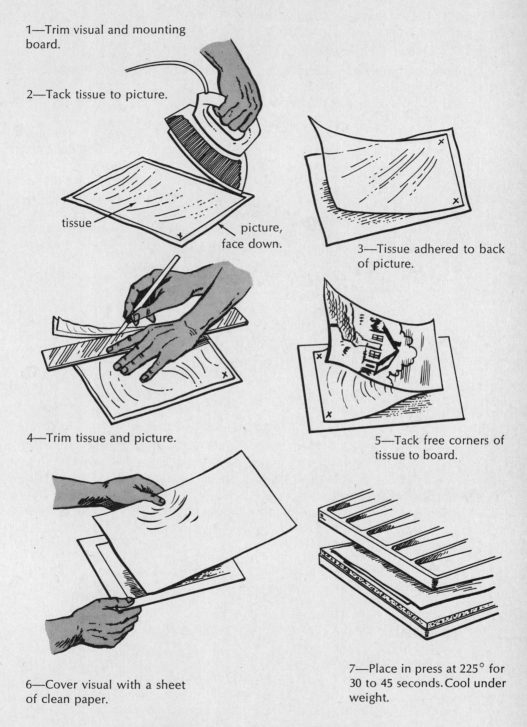

1—Trim visual and mounting board.

2—Tack tissue to picture.

tissue

picture, face down.

3—Tissue adhered to back of picture.

4—Trim tissue and picture.

5—Tack free corners of tissue to board.

6—Cover visual with a sheet of clean paper.

7—Place in press at 225° for 30 to 45 seconds. Cool under weight.

FIGURE 2-4 Dry Mounting (MT 5 tissue)

Fotoflat is excellent for mounting fragile materials such as crayon drawings, water colors, and colored prints. Additionally, if you plan to remove the visual from its backing at any time, this can be accomplished in the following manner:

1. Place the mounted material in a press which has been preheated to 200° Fahrenheit.
2. Close (do not lock) the press and let it remain in this position for one minute.
3. Immediately remove the mount from the press, release a corner of the picture, and carefully peel it away from the backing material. You may have to reheat sections of the visual if removal becomes difficult.

DRY MOUNT PRESS
Courtesy Seal Inc.

A versatile dry mounting adhesive that consists of a thermo plastic adhesive sheet (not a tissue) that melts completely during the mounting process is the Seal "Fusion 4000" material. This adhesive can be used to mount virtually any kind of flat visual including such sensitive items as the RC (resin coated) photographic papers. A wide variety of mounting surfaces, metal and wood included, can be used as a base for the visual.

The steps are as follows:

1. Warm the press to a temperature of approximately 200° F. Temperature indicator strips are available that can be used to verify heat levels.
2. Pre-dry materials as described for the standard dry mount process.
3. Place the picture face down, cover the back side with a sheet of adhesive. Place a sheet of Seal Release Paper over the adhesive, then tack one edge of the adhesive to the visual in a continuous line by applying the heat over the release paper.
4. Position the picture, face up, on the mounting board. Repeat the sequence described in step 3 as you attach the free edge of the adhesive to the board. You will now have a situation in which one edge of the adhesive is attached to the picture while the other edge is attached to the mounting board (see dry mounting diagram for illustration of this).

5. Next, bond the picture to the board as follows:
   a. For photographs, cover the materials with a sheet of Seal ColorMount paper. Then cover this with a sheet of Seal Release. Place the materials in the press for approximately forty-five seconds.
   b. For materials other than photographs you should place a sheet of Seal Release or clean craft paper over the visual prior to locking it in the press for approximately forty-five seconds.
6. Cool the materials under pressure.

One last comment about dry mounting might be in order before we move on. It is possible to mount pictures with inexpensive polyethylene plastic bags and sheets. This material can be purchased from a variety or hardware store, or in bag form from a grocery store. It is used somewhat in the same manner as the dry mount tissue, but is normally not tacked into place since it has a tendency to disintegrate under the direct heat from the iron. This material requires a higher heat for adhesion than does the MT-5 tissue.

Dry Mounting on Cloth (Chartex)

Chartex is a heat sensitive cloth material that permits you to mount large visuals on a cloth backing without the necessity of mixing messy pastes and using water. It also takes less time to mount a picture on Chartex than it does to wet mount it; but it costs considerably more. The dry mounting cloth is rather expensive when compared to the muslin used in the wet mounting process, but the extra expense might be worth it when the factor of convenience is considered.

Before proceeding with the actual mounting, you should preheat your press up to a temperature of 180° F, then predry your picture in the manner described for dry mounting on a hard surface. Then follow these steps:

1. Trim the visual and the cloth to approximately the desired size.
2. Place the visual face down on a clean surface, cover with cloth, adhesive side against the visual. Tack one edge of the cloth to the visual. You will find that Seal Release Paper will be useful at this point; it is placed over the cloth, thus protecting it from the tacking iron.
3. Position a protective sheet over the visual (this may be clean butcher paper, newsprint, or the Seal Release Paper mentioned earlier) and then insert the assembled materials into the press. Close and lock the press; leave materials in place for twenty to thirty seconds.
4. Remove visual and immediately apply pressure. You may use a cold dry mount press for this, or a large, flat board such as a wet mounting board. Books can be stacked on the visual, or it can be placed on a table and rubbed down with the hands—a process that is not very satisfactory. The preferred method is to use one of the special flat weights which are manufactured specifically for this purpose.
5. Trim the cloth so that the edges are sharp and even (or hem it) and your visual is complete.

NOTE: A picture can be removed from the Chartex cloth by heating the mount to 200° F and then carefully peeling the sheets apart.

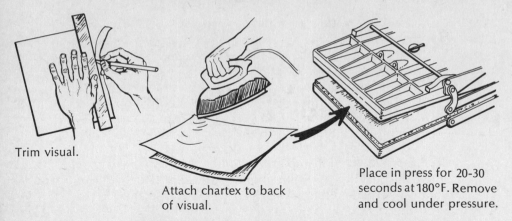

Trim visual.

Attach chartex to back
of visual.

Place in press for 20-30
seconds at 180°F. Remove
and cool under pressure.

FIGURE 2-5   Chartex Cloth Mounting

The Heat Lamination Process (Seal-Lamin)

A visual that is to be handled by students should have its surface covered in some manner. The application of a transparent plastic material such as Seal-Lamin will protect a surface from stains, fingerprints, markers, grease pencils, and so on. Various marking devices can be used on a laminated picture and can then be removed with a damp cloth. This is particularly useful when maps, charts, crossword puzzles and other types of "fill in" visuals are being used. Such nonpicture types of things as leaves and grasses can also be laminated. However, as objects become increasingly three-dimensional, the practicability of this decreases.

There are a number of different ways that you might approach the lamination process. For example, you can laminate small pictures and objects such as leaves directly to the backing material without first securing them in place with a mounting medium. Larger pictures must be mounted before being laminated, otherwise, they tend to bulge in the middle since there is nothing at this point to bond them to the backing. Dry mount tissue is normally used in instances such as this. Or you may wish to laminate the visual and then mount it to a board. Virtually any type of mounting material can be used if you follow this procedure. Again, you may laminate both sides of the picture, thus making it unnecessary to attach it to a backing. Other approaches are also possible, but these seem to be the major ones. For convenience, several different thicknesses as well as a gloss and a matt surface are available in this material.

One of the shortcomings inherent in this process has to do with the mechanical requirement: it is necessary to have a dry mount press to laminate successfully; a household iron will not suffice.

Incidentally, don't attempt to laminate visuals that are printed on an excessively rough or textured paper. The film cannot reach the bottom of the depressions in the paper and a mottled effect will result that will be unattractive.

To create a lamination, you should first prepare the press by placing a sheet of masonite board under the rubber pad. This increases the pressure that will be exerted upon the visual. Now heat the press to a temperature of approximately

275° F (for heavier materials, this should be increased). Close the press in order to preheat the pad before proceeding with the process. You may wish to remove the residual moisture from the picture if this is needed (see dry mount process). If the picture has just been dry mounted, this obviously would not be necessary. You are now ready to laminate. Follow these steps:

1. Place the picture face up on a flat surface and position the laminating film over this—the dull (treated) side must be against the picture. Trim the film so that it is just slightly larger than the picture.
2. Place the assembled materials in a folder of newsprint or butcher paper, or use the Seal Release Paper mentioned earlier. Rub with your hands to work out wrinkles and to keep the materials in place.
3. Insert the folder containing the materials into the press. Close and lock for one to one and one-half minutes (longer for heavier materials).
4. Remove the work from the press and cool under a weight. When cool, the visual should be trimmed to size to complete the process.

If you would like an interesting textural effect, simply crumple the sheet of lamination into a tight ball with your hand. The film is then straightened and placed over the picture in the usual fashion. Much of the wrinkled pattern will remain after the bond has been made, but it will be consistent over the entire surface and will give a somewhat antique appearance to the visual.

The steps just described are for the standard types of heat lamination film, that is, those that require high temperatures for bonding. The Seal Company produces a low temperature film that bonds at 225° F.—the same temperature at which dry mount bonds, thus making it possible to use one press at one setting for both processes. When using this material, you should proceed with the steps listed above; however, the press should be adjusted to the lower temperature, and the material should be left under pressure for one minute.

NOTE: When laminating over a dry mounted picture, a white area may form along the edges of the picture during the process. This white effect results when the laminating film does not adhere to the backing board because it is held away from the surface by the raised edges of the picture. To correct this problem, you will find it necessary to rub over the white area with your finger before removing the visual from the press. Wrap a handkerchief around your finger before attempting this because the visual will be very hot, and so will the platen of the press, so don't burn yourself.

If you should desire to laminate a visual on both sides, you can proceed in either one of two ways. First, you can place one sheet of film under the picture and a second one over it (sensitized sides toward the paper) to form a sandwich which is then placed in a protective envelope and inserted into the press. The second method involves laminating one side of the visual at a time. This is the safer of the two approaches, but it takes more time.

During the lamination process, bubbles may develop under the film due to incomplete adhesion. Placing the visual back under the press for a time normally will solve this problem; however, if the bubbles persist, you may find it necessary to prick them with a pin to release the air trapped within them.

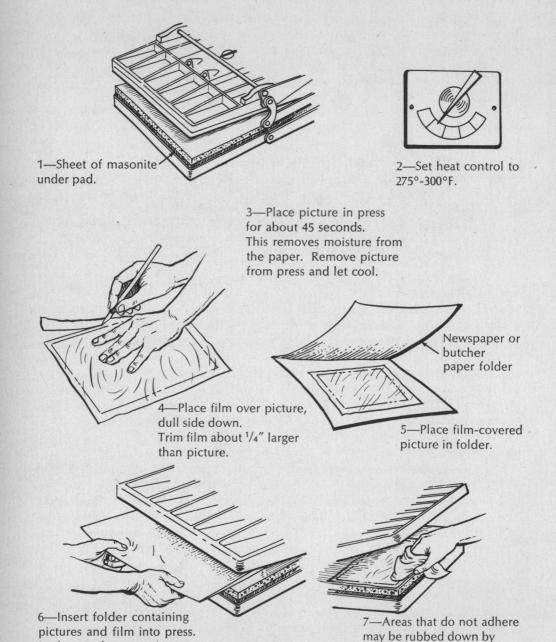

1—Sheet of masonite under pad.

2—Set heat control to 275°-300°F.

3—Place picture in press for about 45 seconds. This removes moisture from the paper. Remove picture from press and let cool.

4—Place film over picture, dull side down. Trim film about ¼" larger than picture.

Newspaper or butcher paper folder

5—Place film-covered picture in folder.

6—Insert folder containing pictures and film into press. Lock press for one minute or longer if needed.

7—Areas that do not adhere may be rubbed down by hand while hot.

8—Remove the visual and trim the edges.

FIGURE 2-6   Heat Lamination (Seal-Lamin Film)

Picture Split. An interesting modification of the traditional hot lamination process is the picture split. Often a magazine page or calendar sheet will have an excellent picture on either side of it. This process enables you to preserve and mount both pictures and gives you the latitude of displaying both of them at the same time. To make a picture split it is necessary to laminate both sides of the page as outlined above.

Then the four edges are trimmed until the paper is entirely exposed on all edges. Separate one corner by carefully inserting a razor blade between the two sheets of laminating film. Now grasp the two corners of the film and begin to pull them apart. The laminating film will adhere so tenaciously to the surface of the visual that it cannot be pulled away. The weak point in the "sandwich" is in the core of the paper sheet upon which the pictures were printed—this is where the separation will occur. Complete the peeling process and the result will be two nicely laminated pictures that can be mounted to sheets of poster board or made into transparencies using the "lift" process as described in the chapter on transparency production.

Mechanical Lamination

Mechanical laminators such as those which are manufactured by the General Binding Corporation make the process simple and rapid. These consist essentially of a pair of powered shafts upon which the rolls of film are secured, a stage upon which the material to be laminated is placed, a heating element, and some controls. The heat source is thermostatically controlled and is activated by a preheat switch. The "run" switch starts the machine so that pictures can be fed into it and through it. A continuous flow of double-laminated pictures emerges from the output side in an unbroken belt of plastic. The rollers and the heat are turned off with the same switch; then, all that is left is to cut the pictures apart to finish the process.

A second approach involves the small, compact laminating machine called "The Wizard," which is produced by the Seal Company. Pictures and other sheet materials are inserted into special Seal-Lamin pouches which are then fed into the laminator. Upon being heated within the machine, the plastic pouches adhere to either side of the visuals, thus protecting them permanently.

Self-Adhering Laminating Film

If a press is not available and you wish to laminate a picture, you may resort to the use of self-adhering or "sticky-backed" film. It is rather difficult to apply a sheet to a picture without developing a wrinkle or bubble in it; however, this problem takes care of itself after a little practice.

This material consists of clear (or colored) plastic with a sticky adhesive on one side. A backing sheet is furnished with the film in order that the sticky side will be protected until the material is used.

1. Trim the plastic to fit the surface to be covered. Do this with the backing sheet in place.
2. Place the visual on a flat surface with the picture side up.

3. With the fingernail or a razor blade, separate the plastic from the backing at one corner only.
4. Peel the backing from the plastic along one end of the sheet; place the exposed sticky surface against the upper edge of the picture. As you rub the plastic into position, continue to peel the backing away from the plastic a little at a time. This procedure of rubbing and peeling should enable you to adhere the laminating film to the visual without trapping air bubbles under the film. If air bubbles do result in spite of everything, prick them with a pin and rub the spot down with a spoon or the back of a pocket comb.

Machines in the form of motor driven or hand cranked rollers can be purchased for use in the cold lamination process. One such machine is the Transeal laminator, a relatively inexpensive yet efficient device. Incidentally, the rollers used by custodians for wringing water from mops do an excellent job of adhering the plastic to the visual.

NOTE: The clear, plastic shelf covering that is sold in rolls in most variety stores makes a good, inexpensive self-adhering laminating film.

Wet Mounting

The wet mounting process is an old standby that is extremely useful when large visuals such as maps and posters are to be preserved. An advantage of this process is its modest price, both for the adhesive and the cloth. Regular wheat paste makes the best adhesive, although it is possible to create a wet mount with flour-and-water paste. The cloth can be new, bleached or unbleached muslin (the latter is best), old bed sheets, pillow cases, flour sacks, or other similar material. Although this process can be a bit messy, with proper planning and care, this turns out to be a minor consideration.

To wet mount a visual, you must first make certain that it is not printed on clay-coated paper. The clay-coated test is a simple one: merely moisten your finger and rub it over a corner of the paper. If the surface dissolves and leaves a white residue on your finger, the paper is clay-coated and cannot be used for a wet mount. Now follow these steps:

1. Wash the surface of the mounting board. A piece of shellacked plywood will do. It must be ⅝" or equivalent, overwise it will warp.
2. Soak the cloth thoroughly in water, then wring it out.
3. Mix wheat paste to a creamy consistency (add paste to water, not water to paste). A small amount of a casein glue such as Elmer's, or a glue size may be added to the wheat paste to strengthen it. Add one or two tablespoons to each pint of paste mix.
4. Stretch wet cloth evenly over the surface and tack it around the edges with thumb tacks. Make certain that it is stretched tightly.
5. Lay the visual on the cloth and make pencil guide marks on the cloth corresponding to the corners of the visual.
6. Soak the back of the visual by placing it face down on a clean surface. Continue adding water (use a sponge) until all wrinkles are removed from the paper and it lies flat.

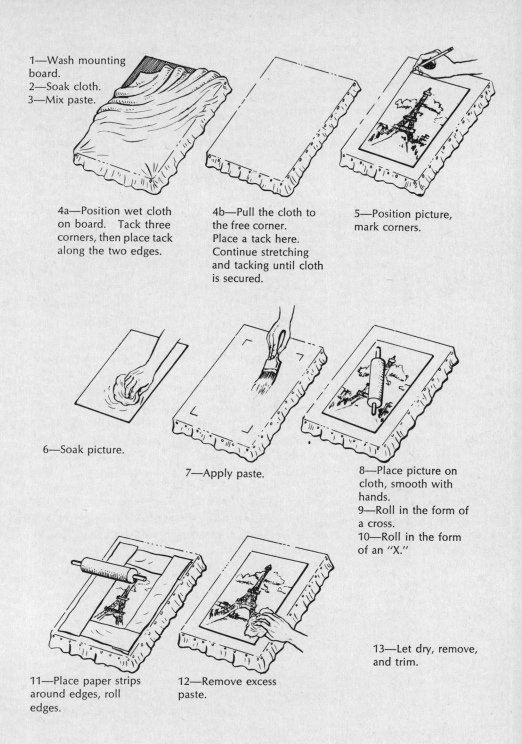

1—Wash mounting board.
2—Soak cloth.
3—Mix paste.

4a—Position wet cloth on board.   Tack three corners, then place tack along the two edges.

4b—Pull the cloth to the free corner. Place a tack here. Continue stretching and tacking until cloth is secured.

5—Position picture, mark corners.

6—Soak picture.

7—Apply paste.

8—Place picture on cloth, smooth with hands.
9—Roll in the form of a cross.
10—Roll in the form of an "X."

11—Place paper strips around edges, roll edges.

12—Remove excess paste.

13—Let dry, remove, and trim.

FIGURE 2-7   Wet Mounting

7. Apply an even coat of paste to the cloth. The paste should extend slightly beyond the area delineated by the pencil marks because the picture will often stretch somewhat when it is moistened.
8. Position the visual, printed side up, on the cloth. Smooth it from the center out toward the edges with your hands.
9. Now roll it with a rolling pin. Roll from the center out to the edges in the form of a cross or a plus (+) sign. Do not press too hard on the rolling pin or you will force out the paste.
10. Now lift each corner to relieve the stress and roll once more . . . this time in the form of a times sign or an "X".
11. Lay strips of paper around the edges of the visual. The paper will absorb the excess paste that will be forced out from under the visual by subsequent rolling. Now roll all around the edges.
12. Remove the strips of paper and carefully wipe away the excess paste that may have collected on the visual.
13. Place the mount in an out-of-the-way place that will afford it protection while it dries. After drying for about four hours, the mount should be ready for removing and trimming.

Passe Partout Mounting (Glass or Plastic Covered Mounting)

This is an excellent method for preserving materials of all kinds, particularly if these materials might be used for some other purpose at a later time. Pictures can be displayed in a passe partout envelope and can then be removed and passed through the transparency maker to create a transparency. Three-dimensional materials, such as fishing flies, a display of coins, or different kinds of sea shells can be exhibited for a time in this type of mount and can later be removed for other purposes.

One of the shortcomings of the passe partout method, however, is that it is quite time consuming and relatively expensive to make. If the open-ended variety is created, this problem is minimized because one mount can be used to display any number of pictures over a period of time.

There are two basic kinds of passe partout mounts: the open-ended variety and the one that is bound on all four sides. Both varieties are similar, with the formation of the open end being the major difference. It should be sufficient to describe the open-ended variety in detail, and the closed kind just to the extent that the differences are emphasized.

The materials needed to make the passe partout mount include a roll of book-mending tape such as Mystik tape (although virtually any kind will work), a sheet of glass or plastic, a piece of heavy cardboard (corrugated cardboard from a packing box will do), some mounting board, and masking tape. If you plan to create the open-ended mount, an extra sheet of the mounting board will be needed.

The process for creating an open-ended mount is as follows:

1. Trim the glass or plastic, the backing board, and the mounting boards so that they are all the same size and so that all the sides are square and

even. If glass is to be used, the simplest procedure is to purchase it in the right size at the onset; this makes cutting unnecessary.

2. With a straightedge and a soft pencil, mark an outline around one of the sheets of mounting board. The outline can be any distance in from the sides; however, a measure of about one inch is about right.

3. Next, using a metal straight edge and a sharp blade, cut along the lines that you have just drawn. Make several cuts along each line; do not try to penetrate the heavy material with one stroke.

4. After a clean cut has been made completely around the card, remove the center piece and set it aside (it will not be needed for this process but may be used later for lettering or some other purpose). The resultant mask will become the front of the open-ended passe partout mount.

5. The second piece of mounting board will serve as the back portion of the mount that will be visible through the opening in the mask. Some people omit this card, but it makes the mount more attractive when there is no picture being displayed in it. This card is now attached to the heavy cardboard with one strip of tape. The tape should be placed along the short side and should overlap equally on the front and back of the two cards.

6. With a straightedge and a grease pencil, mark a guideline for the tape on the film or glass. This mark should be about ¼" or ⅜" in from the edge.

7. Cut four pieces of tape from the roll and attach them to the side of the table so that they hang downward out of the way. These tapes should be longer by about 1" than the sides of the mount that they will bind. With the masking tape, attach each end of the binding tape to the table; the sticky surface should face up. By attaching the tape to the table, you will find that it will be much easier to handle. Carefully position the plastic or glass over the first strip of tape. When the edge of the tape is aligned with the grease pencil line, press the plastic or glass onto the tape and adhere it securely. Note that the first pieces of tape to be attached are long ones. Note also that the grease pencil lines must be on the side of the plastic or glass that faces away from the tape.

8. Attach the other strips of tape in the manner described above. Remove all grease pencil lines at this point.

9. Now place the mask on the plastic. The "best" side should face the plastic because this is the side that will be seen.

10. You will note that a seam has been formed on both sides of the mount by the strips of tape. Make a cut along this seam on both sides of the end that will become the open end (see diagram).

11. Fold the resultant tab over to bind the mask and plastic together.

12. Cut the corners so that a "sling" results. This requires three cuts on each corner (see diagram). The sling should be as wide as the total thickness of the mount because it will be folded over the corner to seal this part of the mount. Before cutting the slings, stack all elements of the mount together and determine what the thickness of the finished mount will be. Use this measurement to determine how wide to cut the slings. Make your first cut so that it is an extension of the long side of the mount. The

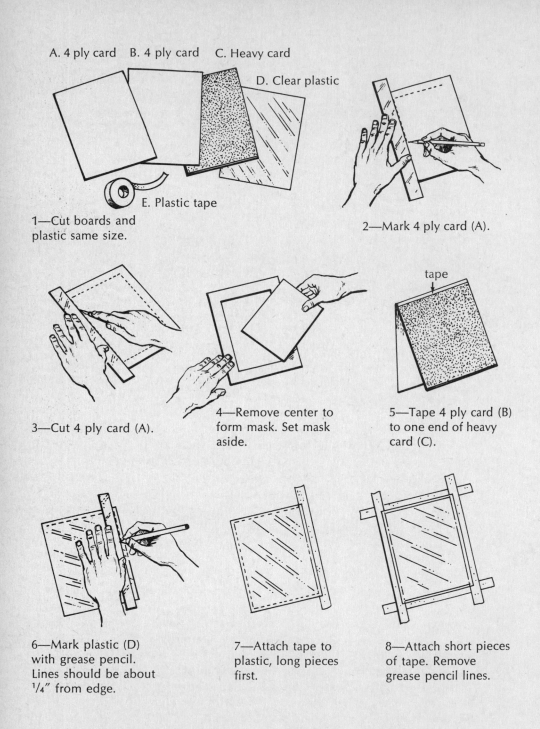

A. 4 ply card   B. 4 ply card   C. Heavy card

D. Clear plastic

E. Plastic tape

1—Cut boards and plastic same size.

2—Mark 4 ply card (A).

3—Cut 4 ply card (A).

4—Remove center to form mask. Set mask aside.

5—Tape 4 ply card (B) to one end of heavy card (C).

tape

6—Mark plastic (D) with grease pencil. Lines should be about 1/4" from edge.

7—Attach tape to plastic, long pieces first.

8—Attach short pieces of tape. Remove grease pencil lines.

FIGURE 2-8   Passe Partout (Plastic Envelope)

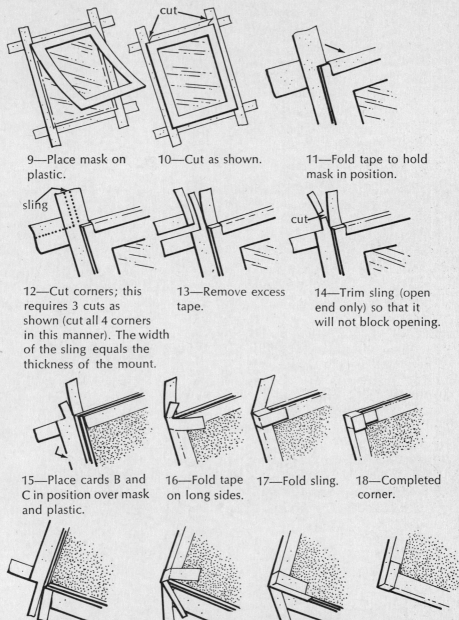

9—Place mask on plastic.

10—Cut as shown.

11—Fold tape to hold mask in position.

12—Cut corners; this requires 3 cuts as shown (cut all 4 corners in this manner). The width of the sling equals the thickness of the mount.

13—Remove excess tape.

14—Trim sling (open end only) so that it will not block opening.

15—Place cards B and C in position over mask and plastic.

16—Fold tape on long sides.

17—Fold sling.

18—Completed corner.

19—The corners for the closed end are cut in the same manner as for the open end. (If all 4 sides are to be closed, treat all corners as in sequence 19-20-21-22.)

20—Steps 10 and 14 are omitted, however.

21—The sling is folded over the corner; the strip of tape is folded over the short end.

22—Completed corner.

second cut is exactly like the first one, but over from it a distance that is equal to the thickness of the mount. The third cut is at right angles to the first and second ones.

13. After all three cuts have been made, a small piece of excess tape will remain; this should be discarded.
14. The sling on the open end must be trimmed in order that it will not partially block the opening.
15. Now place both front and back units together. Line them up carefully.
16. With the plastic facing down, begin at the center of one of the long sides and fold the tape over, adhering it to the back as you move out to the corners.
17. You will find that the slings will stand up on their edges as a result of folding the tape along the sides; fold the slings over the corners on the open end.
18. Fold the tabs over the slings to complete the corners on the open end.
19. The corners for the closed end are cut exactly like the corners for the open end. If the mount is to be closed (all four sides bound with tape, no opening), it will not be possible to change pictures at intervals; the closed passe partout is therefore much less versatile than the open-ended variety.
20. When creating a closed mount, it is not necessary to cut a mask or to make the cuts described in step 10. Also, do not trim the slings as described in step 14.
21. The corners on the closed end are folded in the same manner as those on the open end. Be sure to fold the slings in **first** before folding the short sides of tape over.
22. After the mount is complete, you may wish to add a stand. Several types of stands are illustrated in the section on nonprojected visuals. If you plan to attach several separate passe partout mounts together to form an "accordion," you should join them when they are face to face (in the position that they will assume when folded). Otherwise, insufficient room will be provided for folding the various units together.

BIBLIOGRAPHY

Arnheim, Rudolf. **Visual Thinking.** London: Faber and Faber, Ltd., 1969.

Gibson, James J. "The Information Available in Pictures." **Viewpoints** 47, no. 4 (1971): 73-95.

Hochberg, Julian. "The Psychophysics of Pictorial Perception." **AV Communication Review** (Sept.-Oct. 1962): 22-54.

Kemp, Jerrold E. **Planning and Producing Audiovisual Materials.** New York: Thomas Y. Crowell Company, Inc., 1975.

Williams, Catharine M. **Learning from Pictures.** Washington, D.C.: Department of Audiovisual Instruction, National Education Association, 1963.

Wittich, Walter A., Schuller, Charles F., Hessler, David W., Smith, Jay C., **Student Production Guide to Accompany Instructional Technology.** 5th ed. New York: Harper and Row, 1975.

3

ILLUSTRATION

INTRODUCTION

The term "illustration" is used in this instance to describe any kind of tracing, enlarging, drawing, or coloring that is undertaken in an effort to modify or construct a visual to satisfy a particular set of requirements. Frequently, originals that are available are the wrong size, are not reproducible, lack color, have too much detail, or need accents in certain areas. When this is the case, some type of modification is necessary—generally, this must be accomplished by hand. This chapter is devoted to the description of ways in which such modifications can be made. Also included are directions for creating simple freehand cartoons that can be useful when figures are needed for bulletin boards and posters.

Hand-drawn illustrations are flat pictures just as a page from a magazine is a flat picture. They are employed in much the same manner as the magazine picture or the photograph, but they are generally much less "realistic." If a high degree of correspondence to the actual object is desired, the hand-drawn picture is probably not the best choice—a photograph will be better. However, if certain details need emphasizing, or if simplification is necessary, then the hand-drawn picture can be excellent. Again, when an attention-getting device is needed, the drawing of a cartoon character can be very good. Additionally, some illustrations are not suitable for reproduction in a transparency format and must be drawn or at least outlined and detailed with ink or pencil.

Frequently, published materials of various kinds become the basis for illustrations, transparencies, handouts, and other kinds of media that will be used for instructional purposes. The recent copyright law states that materials can be reproduced (including multiple copies) if they are to be used in the classroom. However, they may not be reproduced for profit-making purposes without the explicit permission of the copyright holder. This means that if you decide to publish some educational media that you have assembled and copyrighted materials are included among these, you must obtain permission for your publishing venture. A good rule to follow is that if you are in doubt about the legality of your use of materials that are in print, you should write to the owner of the copyright and ask for permission to use them. Most publishers and others are quite cooperative where this matter is concerned and generally respond favorably to a reasonable request.

THE PASTE-UP

Various pictures, lettering, borders, etc., can be collected from different sources and formed into a composition on a sheet of paper or card. Most generally, such materials should be rendered in a line technique (that is, they should be like a cartoon, with no shadows). Booklets of line illustrations can be purchased from suppliers such as the Harry Volk Company which are perfect for paste-up work. Or, you might use illustrations from coloring books, cartoons from various sources, prints made from high-contrast line negatives (described in the chapter on photography). as well as drawings that you have created yourself.

The finished paste-up can be processed in a thermal machine or photocopier to make a transparency. Paper copies can also be made using various copying machines, or a thermal spirit duplicating master might be created from which handouts can be made.

Such paste-ups can also be copied on a machine such as a Xerox, or they can be photographed onto a negative film for conversion into a photographic print. The end result is a copy that can be used as the master for duplicated handouts, transparencies, offset plates, and so on.

Photographing such originals as the line paste-up on color film is not a satisfactory technique due to the fact that color film "sees" every trimmed outline, smear of rubber cement, or pencil guide line. Paste-ups for color work can be created, however, but the approach is somewhat different from that just described. Illustrations to be pasted to a background must be carefully contoured so that trim lines follow the outlines of the objects. Lettering must be done directly on the surface of the card or paper. It cannot be applied in strips or blocks as with the line-copy paste-up. Such lettering as LeRoy or dry-transfer varieties work well for direct application. All guide lines, rubber cement residue, and other unwanted elements must be completely removed before the visual is suitable for copying onto color film.

Guide lines are normally drawn lightly with a blue pencil (blue pencil does not pick up on most line films or on most copy papers). The elements to be pasted to the surface are trimmed and then are coated on the back with an adhesive. If a wax coater is available, this is an excellent way in which to prepare the visual for use. The wax coater is a device which contains a supply of wax and a heating unit. When the visual is inserted into the unit, a roller distributes a thin layer of the wax to its back side; it is then positioned and pressed into place. Spray adhesive is a popular and relatively inexpensive material for adhering the

Illustration   45

visuals. However, the most common technique is to use rubber cement for this. A satisfactory method is to coat the area on the card first so that this has a chance to dry. Then the back of the visual is coated with the cement. Before this can dry, the visual is positioned properly—the fact that one surface is wet while the other is not permits the manipulation of the elements. If both surfaces were dry, this would not be possible. After the cement has lost its tackiness any residue is cleaned up with a ball cf dried cement or a commercial "pick-up" to complete the paste-up.

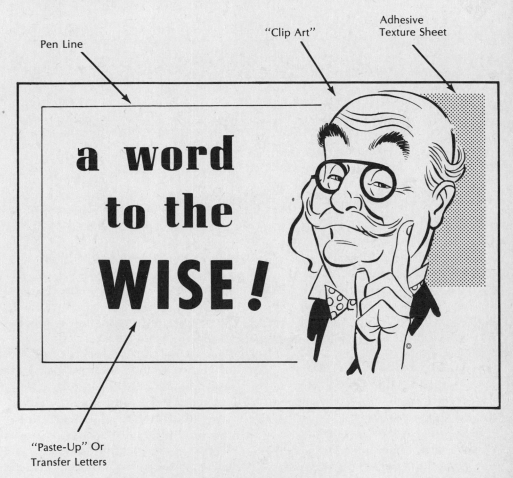

FIGURE 3-1   A Paste-Up

TRACING TECHNIQUES

When the picture that you plan to use is in a book or magazine that you wish to preserve, or if it must be rendered in line for processing in a transparency maker, you may have to make a tracing of it. When making a tracing, begin with a good grade of paper such as that used by artists for layout work. Never tape the paper to the picture to be traced; use paper clips so that the original will not be damaged when the paper is removed. If you plan to ink the tracing, it should first be drawn in pencil, then removed from the original and inked with pen or brush. The pencil may then be erased. If you plan to use the drawing as a master for transparencies, you may want to make the initial sketch in light blue pencil. This marking medium will not reproduce on the transparency, so it need not be erased. Black pencil must be erased completely, particularly when the thermal transfer process is to be used.

If you wish to use the tracing as the basis for a finished illustration, you can transform it into a kind of transfer paper by coating the back evenly with pastel or soft pencil. Or, use a commercial transfer paper such as Saral. The tracing with the transfer material on the back is positioned on the paper or board upon which the final illustration will be rendered. It should be held in place with tape, clips, or pins to keep it from slipping. As you trace over the desired lines with pencil or ballpoint pen, the pastel or soft pencil on the back of the sheet will transfer onto the board or paper, thus replicating the original. Finish the illustration using any of the many techniques available for this purpose.

ENLARGING AND REDUCING TECHNIQUES

Very often pictures will be located that are precisely right for the job at hand, except for the fact that they are either too large or too small to be utilized. There are a number of techniques that can be used to change the size of these pictures. In addition to the photographic process (which is an excellent way of modifying sizes except for the fact that it requires dark room facilities), the squared, pantograph, and projected techniques are commonly used. Let us examine the three latter processes in detail in this chapter. The photographic technique will be covered in another section of this book.

The Graph Method

When creating an illustration with the squared or graph method, it is necessary to draw grid lines a given distance apart on the original and on the enlarging paper or cardboard. Make these lines with a soft pencil so they might be erased at a later time. In case it is not desirable for some reason to draw lines directly on the surface of the original, you can clip a piece of tracing paper or plastic over the original and draw the lines on this. The spaces between the lines should be uniform throughout. The distance from line to line is dependent upon the enlargement desired and will vary from picture to picture. For example, if the lines on the original are drawn one-fourth inch apart and an enlargement of four times the original size is required, then the lines on the material upon which the drawing will be rendered should be one inch apart. These lines should be numbered or lettered so that reference to the appropriate points on the visual can easily be made. Once the proper preliminary steps have been taken, it is relatively easy to reproduce the small original onto the larger format. Simply match the intersections of the lines on the original with the equivalent

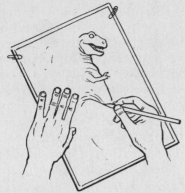

1—Clip a sheet of tracing paper over the original and trace outlines.

2—Turn tracing over. Cover back of sheet with pencil, pastel, or charcoal.

3—Rub substance into surface of tracing paper. This will prevent unwanted transfer to drawing paper.

4—Turn tracing over so coated side is down. Clip to drawing paper or cardboard. Trace over lines.

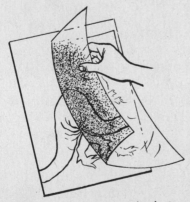

5—Where pressure is applied during tracing, the carbon will transfer to the art paper thus duplicating the figure.

6—Add final embellishments, then erase unwanted lines to complete the visual.

FIGURE 3-2 Tracing and Transferring

intersections on the enlarging paper and sketch the appropriate details in this area. Continue in this manner until the pencil drawing is completed and then ink it in or use some other method for making it permanent. Finally, erase all unwanted pencil lines, including the graph lines, and add any additional embellishments, such as color, that you consider necessary.

To reduce a picture with the graph method, it is necessary to reverse the process, that is, to draw the lines on the reducing paper or board closer together than the lines on the original. As a general rule, you will seldom find it necessary to reduce visuals because they are almost always too small rather than too large. However, if you plan to resize a large visual to fit a transparency or a duplicated hand-out format, you will find this to be a useful technique.

The Pantograph Method

The pantograph is a handy, compact, inexpensive device that is much less time consuming to use than is the graph method of resizing pictures. Initially, this machine may seem a bit awkward to manipulate, but with practice, you will find that it can be a fascinating instrument with which to work.

To use the pantograph for enlarging, you should follow these steps:

1. Check the device to be sure that sufficient lead is in the holder; make certain that all articulations are tightened so that random movement is controlled; be sure that each of the four arms is adjusted to the same setting (if you wish to enlarge three times, all four arms must be set on "3").

2. To change the amount of enlargement, unlock the arms and align each one of them to the new setting.

3. Position the pantograph to your left, then place the original in front of you; finally, put the enlarging paper on the table to your right (Figure 3-4).

4. Hold the foot in your left hand so that the pantograph will not slide about, then grasp the lead clutch in your right hand and move it until the tracer pin rests on the extreme upper dimension of your original. Check the position of the lead; if it is too high, or off to the side, you will want to move the paper, original, or pantograph until the position of lead corresponds with the point that will serve as the top of your enlargement when it is drawn. You must repeat this process for the two sides of the drawing as well as for the bottom. You should now have four pencil marks on your paper that indicate the top, bottom, and side extremes for your drawing.

5. Securely tape all components—original, pantograph, and paper or cardboard—to the table.

6. Proceed to make your enlargement. After it is finished, you will want to render the lines in some permanent medium such as ink or felt marker; the pencil lines may then be erased.

In order to reduce with this machine, it is necessary to remove the tracer pin and the lead holder or clutch from the arms. These two parts are then

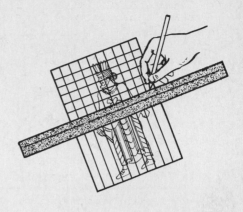

1—Position a piece of tracing paper over the original and make a tracing.

2—Draw graph lines on the tracing.

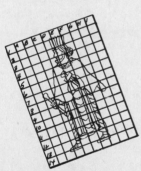

3—Number the lines (it is simpler to locate inter-sections of lines if one set is identified with numbers while the other is identified with letters).

Note: After the enlargement has been completed, it should be rendered permanent by tracing over the lines with ink or marker. All pencil lines should then be erased.

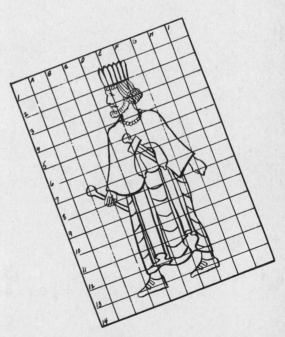

4—Draw graph lines on the enlarging sheet or card-board; number these. Proceed to make the enlargement.

FIGURE 3-3 Squared or Graph Enlarging

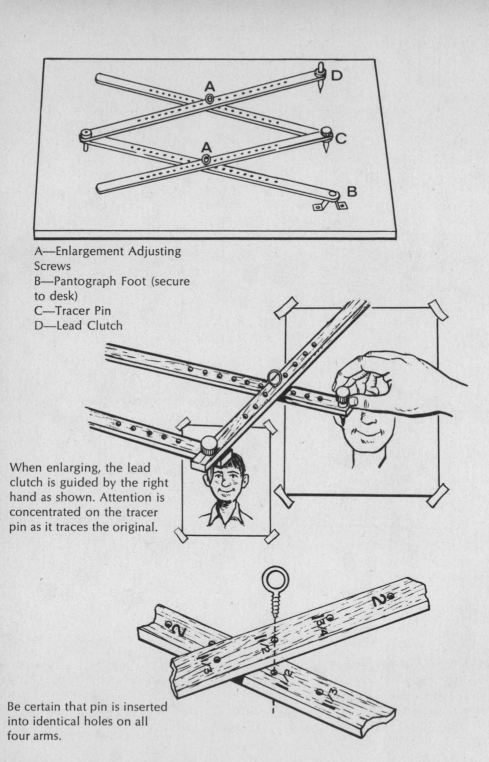

A—Enlargement Adjusting
Screws
B—Pantograph Foot (secure
to desk)
C—Tracer Pin
D—Lead Clutch

When enlarging, the lead
clutch is guided by the right
hand as shown. Attention is
concentrated on the tracer
pin as it traces the original.

Be certain that pin is inserted
into identical holes on all
four arms.

FIGURE 3-4 The Pantograph

Illustration 51

interchanged, that is, the lead holder is substituted for the tracer pin, and the tracer pin for the lead holder. This modification necessitates changing the original to the extreme right and the paper or board to the center position on the table. Now proceed as you did before when you were enlarging (note, however, that instead of manipulating the lead with your right hand, you are now manipulating the tracer pin with that hand—a slight modification that you will get used to after a little practice).

The Projected Method

Just about any kind of projector—including motion picture and slide varieties— can be used for enlarging purposes. Because such machines as overhead, slide, filmstrip, and motion picture projectors require that the original to be enlarged be on a transparent format (film), they are not as frequently used for this purpose as is the opaque projector. To enlarge with this machine, place the original on the stage, move the projector backward or forward until the desired size is obtained, and then focus the lens until the image is sharp. Next, position the enlarging paper or cardboard and tape it to the wall. Now stand off to the side so that you do not block the light and trace the image onto the paper.

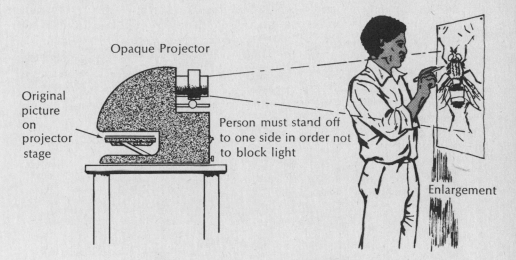

FIGURE 3-5 Opaque Projector Enlarging

Greater flexibility in altering the size of the projected image can be obtained by releasing the set screw that holds the lens barrel in position and then moving the lens in the mount until the image is sharp. The screw should then be retightened in order to safeguard the lens.

As before, the pencil sketch is merely a start. You will want to ink the lines with something permanent prior to erasing the unwanted pencil marks.

To reduce with the opaque projector, it is necessary to place the picture to be reduced on the board or wall and then to illuminate it with a light source such as a photoflood or a lamp. Turn the room lights out for the best effect, although this is not entirely necessary. Open the back of the projector—assuming that you have the kind that has this capability—and you will see the original reflected onto the stage in reduced form. Place a clean piece of paper or cardboard on the stage and proceed to trace the picture with pencil. If the image is not sharp, move the projector or the lens until it appears to be statisfactory.

INKING AND OUTLINING TECHNIQUES

After your pencil rendering has been completed, you will probably want to go over the lines with a permanent medium of some kind. You might also wish to add some color for effect. The following techniques are useful for outlining, detailing, adding texture, and otherwise adding a finished touch to an illustration.

1. Pens and ink are excellent for drawing lines of varying character. Speedball pens, such as the "B" type, will give a line of uniform thickness and a mechanical character. Other pens will give a thick-thin line; the "C" type is chisel-shaped and will produce such a line. Technical fountain pens such as the K and E LeRoy and the Rapidograph are useful when fine lines are desired. These are also excellent for free-hand sketching and for ruling straight lines. The pens that are used with scribers (see section on lettering) can be secured in special holders and used for drawing purposes as well as for straight-line rendering. Finally, ruling pens, such as the cross-hinge variety, are useful when mechanical lines are desired. These are not suited to general drawing and sketching techniques, however.

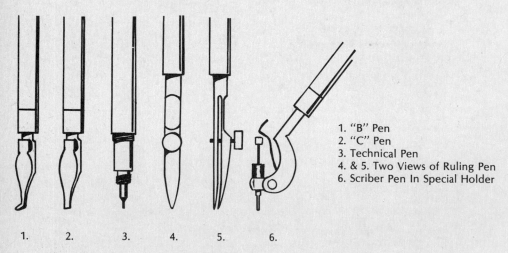

1. "B" Pen
2. "C" Pen
3. Technical Pen
4. & 5. Two Views of Ruling Pen
6. Scriber Pen In Special Holder

1.   2.   3.   4.   5.   6.

2. Brushes and inks are used when a free effect is desired. Push down for a bold area; lift up and exert light pressure for a very fine line.

Illustration   53

3. Felt markers are an old standby and come in all sizes and nib shapes. You will feel a certain confidence with the felt marker that may be lacking when you pick up a brush that is loaded with ink. It is true that ink can be smeared and smudged, whereas the felt marker is relatively free from this problem. However, the felt marker lacks the versatility that the brush displays. If you plan to wash over your line illustration with water colors, be certain that your markers (as well as your inks) are of the waterproof variety, otherwise they will dissolve when the water comes into contact with them.

4. Crayons, grease pencils, and other such materials can be used for outlining and detailing pictures; however, they do not permit the pencil lines to be removed because they will smear when the eraser is passed over them. Of course, if you wish to completely cover the pencil lines and perhaps blend these mediums into the picture, no erasing will be necessary.

5. Charting and drafting tapes are colored or patterned tapes of varying widths that are adhesive on the back side. They are very useful when lines of a mechanical nature are needed. Obviously, it is difficult to manipulate tape around contours and for this reason they are normally used where straight lines are called for. Tapes as narrow as 1/64 inch and as wide as ½ inch, and wider, are available. Use these for charts, graphs, maps, borders, business forms, and so on. (Note: Regardless of which outlining technique you employ, remember that when you enlarge a picture, you must also enlarge the width of its lines correspondingly.)

COLORING TECHNIQUES

Color can be used as a means of attracting attention to a specific part of a visual, or it can be used as an overall embellishment. In either case, the selection of the appropriate medium for a specific situation will make the creation of a satisfactory visual more certain.

Some of the coloring mediums that are suitable for use in the production of teaching materials are the following:

Transparent water colors. Water colors are available in semi-moist cakes or pans, tubes and bottles. They can be painted directly over pen-and-ink and permanent marker outlines without obscuring them. Water colors have a tendency to cause lightweight papers to wrinkle and they tend to streak when used on hard-surfaced papers and cards; heavy absorbent papers are best.

Poster paints (Tempera). Poster paints are opaque; they cannot be used to wash over inked lines in an illustration because they have a tendency to obscure such lines. Typically, poster paints are used on rather heavy cardboard and are applied in broad, flat areas. After the paints have dried, the desired details can be added with inks, markers, or other colors of poster paint.

Felt markers. Felt markers in all colors can be obtained from virtually any variety store or art store. They are easy to use, last a long time, and are relatively inexpensive. It is best to add dark colors over the light ones rather than vice versa because the solvents in the inks have a tendency to dissolve other colors with which they come into contact. So, if you outline a picture in black marker and then attempt to color a portion of it with yellow marker, the yellow will partially dissolve the black which will be carried over into the lighter color as a dark stain or smudge.

Pastels. Pastels are sticks of dry pigment that are highly concentrated and varied in hue. The most common kinds are similar to chalk, but they are less inclined to powder and smudge than is the softer chalk. Permanence is a problem with pastels and chalks but this can be overcome in part by blending the pigments into the surface of the paper with a napkin or paper towel. A further aid to permanence is the plastic spray that can be used to coat the surface of the visual after the color has been applied.

An interesting variation of the traditional pastel is the oil pastel. This coloring stick is a blend of concentrated pigment mixed with some type of oil to make it an effective, if somewhat messy, medium.

Wax crayons. Wax crayons are common items in virtually every school and are therefore familiar to everyone. Crayon should not be plastered over a drawing in a heavy layer, but should be applied in light, successive layers for best results. It is difficult to achieve a smooth, blended effect with crayon when more than one color is being used. The individual hues are generally identifiable in the mixture; however, this effect can be quite pleasant.

Colored pencils. Colored pencils, although excellent for some purposes, are not suitable for coloring large illustrations such as those to be used on the bulletin board. Because of the restricted nature of the coloring surface of the pencil, the time required for filling in large areas is too great to be practical. Use pencils for small visuals such as transparencies or "pass around" pictures. They may also be useful for adding accents to restricted sections of larger visuals.

Colored papers. Areas of large visuals can be filled in rapidly with colored papers of one kind or another. Make your drawing on paper such as butcher paper, then cut the various parts out and trace them onto sheets of colored paper. The colored paper outlines are now trimmed and the parts reassembled on a background of some kind. When glued together, a colored replica of the original illustration will be formed. This is an excellent way to achieve broad areas of smooth, bright color with an economy of time and expense.

Pressure-sensitive colored film. Although expensive, pressure-sensitive colored film is unsurpassed for its even passages of saturated color. The sheet of film is backed by a heavy protective paper that is removed prior to applying the film to the art work. Care must be taken that air bubbles are not trapped between the film and art during application, particularly when the visual being covered is a transparency—bubbles become very noticeable during projection. After the film has been positioned over the visual, it is carefully trimmed to the desired shape with a sharp artist's knife. The unwanted material is removed and placed on the backing sheet for future use. The material that is to be adhered to the art is then rubbed down with a burnisher to effect a permanent bond.

Illustration 55

Many other coloring mediums are available (such as oil paints and acrylics) that are excellent for some kinds of art work but are not well-suited to the production of most instructional materials for reasons such as cost and drying time (for the oils).

SIMPLE CARTOONS

At times, a need arises for some kind of illustration which will have personality and character and will do a "selling job" for you. The cartoon may be the answer. An easy way in which to create your own cartoons is to use the system called the "rule of halves."

The steps in this system are illustrated in the plate on drawing the cartoon head. Note that the divisions are somewhat arbitrary and can be modified to suit your taste. So, if after a little practice you feel like changing things around a bit, remember that in cartooning you can get away with just about anything.

Frequently, cartoons can be located that seem to be just right for the job at hand, but they may be the wrong size. This problem is readily solved through the use of one of the enlarging techniques described elsewhere in this text. Also, cartoons may be traced directly onto acetate for use on the overhead projector by merely placing the plastic over the original and following the lines with an appropriate marker or pen and acetate ink. Cartoons may be passed through the thermal-transfer machine to create excellent transparencies. The black outline will be the only thing that will transfer onto the sensitive film; the colors, if there are any, will simply drop out. You may then add colors as desired directly to the surface of the film (see section on transparency production).

It helps to begin the cartoon with simple circles and lines. These should be drawn freely with a soft pencil. The next step is to pencil in all of the desired details as well as any lettering that is to be included in the design. Now use some type of permanent marking medium such as india ink or a felt marker and fill in all of the lines that are to be retained on the finished drawing. Permit the ink to dry and then "clean up" the unwanted pencil with an art gum eraser. Your cartoon now could be considered to be finished; however, if you wish you can add color (use transparent color such as water color; the ink lines will show right through it), textures (with lines, dots, cross hatching, etc.), or solid areas (just fill in the shoes, hat, or anything else with the solid black marker or ink . . . it will add impact to your cartoon).

ORIGINALS FOR REPRODUCTION

The teacher who wishes to illustrate an idea will have access to many different kinds of visual materials. He may wish to enlarge or reduce a picture using the pantograph or the opaque projector. He might cut pictures from magazines and then mount and display them. Then again, he might run a line illustration through a thermal transfer machine to create a transparency, or he might photograph a flat picture onto a 35 mm slide format.

Pleased

Thought

Anger

Fright

Grief

Innocence

Happy

Mischievous

Anguish

Stern

Shy

Surprise

FIGURE 3-7 Cartoon Expressions

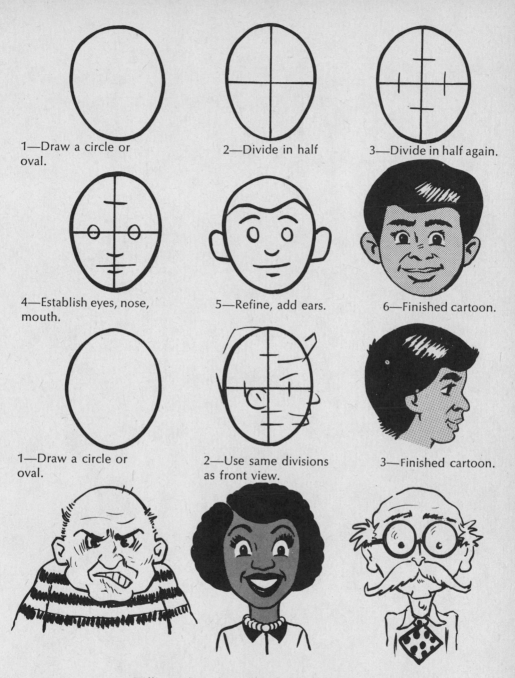

1—Draw a circle or oval.

2—Divide in half

3—Divide in half again.

4—Establish eyes, nose, mouth.

5—Refine, add ears.

6—Finished cartoon.

1—Draw a circle or oval.

2—Use same divisions as front view.

3—Finished cartoon.

Different faces based on above technique.

FIGURE 3-8 Drawing the Cartoon Head Using the "Rule of Halves"

1—Begin with 5 lines, these can all be the same length.
2—Add "Shoulders" and "hips."
3—Add two of the lines to the shoulders for arms.
4—Add the two remaining lines to the hips for legs.
5—Add the head.
6—Add lines around the stick figure to give fullness to the body.
7—Complete the figure and the face (See "Rule of Halves" for details on drawing faces).
8—The side view body uses the same five lines.
9—But a "peanut" shape is added to give a basic body form.
10—Add lines around the arms and legs for fullness.
11—Complete the figure and the face.

FIGURE 3-9 Drawing the Cartoon Figure

All of the figures shown here are based on the "Stick and Peanut" system described in the prior plate.

FIGURE 3-10 Figures in Action

1—Create the pencil sketch.

2—Fill in desired lines with a permanent medium.

3—Erase all pencil lines with an art gum eraser.

4—Add textures, details, colors, etc., as desired.

FIGURE 3-11 Steps in Creating a Finished Illustration

All of these processes require that an original illustration of some nature be available as the basis for the finished product. "Originals" as a group are divided into three basic categories—line, halftone, and continuous tone. Each of these has certain characteristics that make it unique; each is useful for a specific purpose and each is readily available from various sources.

Line

Line illustrations have no shadows as such. They are typically black and white, like cartoons or pictures in coloring books, but they might be printed or drawn in any color and still be line illustrations. A sketch made with pen and ink, an illustration in felt marker, a drawing made with a brush and undiluted opaque paint are all examples of line illustrations. This book contains many diagrams that are printed in line from "line plates."

Halftone

Halftone illustrations are typically found in books and magazines as well as on many calendars, posters, and other types of printed materials. They appear to have shadows and form as opposed to the line illustration that generally looks as if an artist created it with a brush or pen. Actually, the halftone has no shadows as such; it is made up of thousands of tiny dots that are not normally visible to the unaided eye.

In order that a picture might be printed, it must first be "screened" by a process that involves photographing it through a glass or plastic sheet that has precise lines scribed on its surface. This has the effect of breaking down the tonal patterns of the original picture into tiny dots of varying sizes. The effect that is achieved when this type of plate is printed is an illusion of blending values that looks very much like the original from which the plate was made.

Illustration   61

It is possible to see the dot pattern in a halftone if a magnifying glass is used; or, if you look closely at a newspaper picture, you should be able to discern at least some of the dots that make up the printed matter. Newspaper pictures employ a coarse screen because they are printed on a poor quality paper; high quality papers such as those used in some magazines, many calendars, posters, etc., make it possible to employ a much finer screen and, consequently, smaller dots.

Continuous Tone

A picture which is printed on photographic paper using photographic processes, or a Polaroid camera—in other words, a photograph in your album—is a good example of continuous tone. A pastel drawing, a charcoal sketch, a water color rendering, an oil painting are all examples of continous tone. This type of illustration has no dots; shading is represented by lightening or darkening the medium, not by breaking it down into dots. Water color is lightened by adding water; oil paint by adding white. Dark pastels are blended into light ones in order to darken the value; more charcoal is applied to the paper surface for a shaded efect.

Uses of the Three Types of Originals

Although a certain amount of versatility is built into the various originals that are commonly used to create finished visuals, within limits, each has its own specific principal uses. Let's examine a few of these:

(1) **Line illustrations** are useful for creating thermal transparencies. They also work well for spirit and mimeograph masters; that is, the type that are created with the thermal transfer machine. When line drawings are rendered on tracing paper, they may be used for the creation of diazo transparencies; also, line drawings are much simpler to enlarge by hand than are the other two types of originals. Some line illustrations are also suitable for mounting and displaying, but this is not their major application.

(2) **Halftone illustrations** work well as photocopy transparency originals because their dot pattern is generally compatible with the capability of this type of machine. The photocopy process is sensitive enough to "see" the minute dots and to replicate them satisfactorily. This type of original makes an excellent "lift" transparency if it is printed on clay-based paper; the colored originals are particularly popular for this. Additionally, flat pictures of this type are commonly copied onto slides using various types of slide cameras. Most generally, however, halftone pictures are mounted and displayed as nonprojected visuals either alone, in a series, on a bulletin board, or in combination with other types of visuals.

(3) **Continuous tone illustrations** can be mounted and displayed, or rephotographed onto the slide format and projected. They do not lend themselves to transparency production except through photographic means because transparency machines are unable to "see" the subtle grays in continuous tone materials and merely resolve them all into the blotches of black or white. This type of original is therefore much less useful as a basis from which to create other types of visual materials than are line and halftone illustrations.

BIBLIOGRAPHY

Garland, Ken. **Graphics Handbook.** London: Studio Vista, 1969.

Minor, Ed. and Frye, Harvey R. **Techniques for Producing Instructional Media.** New York: McGraw-Hill Book Co., 1970.

Schlemmer, Richard M. **Handbook of Advertising Art Production.** Englewood Cliffs, N.J.: Prentice- Hall, Inc., 1966.

Wills, F. H. **Layout.** New York: Sterling Publishing Co., Inc., 1966.

Wright, Andrew, **Designing for Visual Aids.** New York: Von Nostrand Reinhold Co., 1970.

4

LETTERING TECHNIQUES

INTRODUCTION

The verbal or digital symbol is such a widely used tool in communication that it is imperative that the person who is in the communication business— such as the teacher—have some knowledge as to how these symbols may be selectively formed and employed.

There is a problem related to the use of verbal symbols—words—that might be worth emphasizing at this point. As was stressed in the section on words and pictures in Chapter 1, words are all too often used in an effort to develop concepts within the minds of students who are not fully prepared for this approach. Unless students have had experiences—either actual or simulated—with the things to which the words refer, any amount of verbal description will not suffice to form the desired concepts. Words are useful when ordering percepts into concepts. They are indispensable as recall devices that trigger a response based on a concept that is already learned and in storage. Words aid us in categorizing concepts, in restructuring them, in describing them, and in synthesizing larger concepts from lesser ones. But words alone are not sufficient for the formation of basic concepts and must be coupled with other kinds of stimuli if concept formation is the teacher's principal objective.

Aside from the typical lecture and some books, most teaching materials consist of a combination of iconic and digital stimuli. Verbal labels on pictorial materials result in greater understanding and learning if the labels add to the information presented by the pictures. Also, significant improvement in assembling the parts of an object into the finished project can result when the students are required to learn the names of the parts. Nomenclature can be employed effectively when its cueing properties are utilized—in assembling the parts of an object, the student orders the parts by naming them sequentially while manipulating the actual parts physically. Paired-associates types of materials are commonly used in the teaching of reading; these involve an iconic symbol and its identifying verbal symbol. Posters, bulletin boards, transparencies, and so forth, generally have both pictures and words built into them.

A verbal display can be attractive and legible or it can be unattractive and even confusing depending upon how skillfully the designer manipulates his elements. Not only must the message make sense, but it should also be pleasing and interesting to look at from a design point of view. It is helpful, in composing a verbal message, to know something about the kinds of lettering that are available along with some of the techniques that can be employed in forming the letters.

Lettering may be grouped into three principal categories: (1) handmade letters, (2) premade letters, and (3) mechanically made letters. Handmade lettering includes such techniques as steel pen lettering, felt pen lettering, and cutout lettering. Premade or available letters include die cut letters such as the sticky backed paper, plastic, and cardboard varieties; dry transfer or rub-on letters, paste-up letters, and other less commonly used kinds such as three-dimensional wood, ceramic, and plastic letters. Mechanically made lettering includes those kinds formed by devices such as scriber and template systems (Leroy), rubber stamps, stencils, including the pen and guide system (WRICO), and modifications of these.

LEGIBILITY STANDARDS FOR LETTERING

Projected Materials. Standard typewriter sizes in capitals and lower cases are generally a bit small for use on a transparency. If the typewriter is to be used, it is best to type everything in capitals if possible. Many schools and district level resource centers have a primer typewriter available. This type is excellent for the production of transparencies for use on the overhead projector as well as for 35 mm slides.

Photographing typed copy generally requires that close-up attachments be used with the camera; without such attachments, the lettering will be so small that it will not be legible on the screen. A clever way of producing slides for use in slide projectors such as the carousel is to type the desired material in small blocks about the size of the opening in a 35 mm slide mount. Pass this copy through a thermal transparency maker or a photocopier to reproduce it on film. Next, cut the blocks from the film, and then mount them in cardboard slide mounts. You are now ready to project some legible and very inexpensive slides.

Eastman Kodak, in their publication on legibility, recommends that the height of a letter be at least 1/25th the height of the total information area. This should be considered as a minimum. Actually, up to a point, the larger the letters, the better they will be seen. A system that works well for determining a suitable size for letters is the "8 H System." Essentially, this involves measuring the height of the projected image (this might be the size of the projection screen) and then multiplying this by eight. If a screen is four feet in height, it can be viewed satisfactorily from a distance of thirty-two feet. That is to say, if the

1/25th rule stated above is observed when producing the art to be copied, the visual when projected to fill a screen which is four feet tall will be legible to an individual seated thirty-two feet away.

In the final analysis, the real test of the legibility of projected materials is whether or not they can be read from the back of your classroom. Make a sample slide or transparency using the kind of lettering that you plan to employ in the finished product. Project this on the screen and then walk to the back of the room and see if it is readable without strain. If it is, proceed to complete your visuals; your students will be able to read them.

Nonprojected Materials. Lettering which is used on many nonprojected visuals must be of such a size that individuals can readily read if from the maximum viewing distance. This might seem redundant because this is precisely the point that was made when lettering for projected materials was discussed. Note, however, that a certain amount of enlargement potential is inherent in the projected visual due to the fact that projectors can be moved back from the screen to change the size of the image if it is not satisfactory. There is no enlargement capability built into the nonprojected visual so the lettering must be the proper size from its very inception.

As a general rule, letters that are to be viewed by the entire class at any given time should be no smaller than one inch in height. A one-inch letter can be clearly seen by a person with normal vision from a distance of thirty to thirty-five feet, the depth of most typical classrooms. To be on the safe side, you may wish to create letters that are larger than this; however, certain constraints such as the size of the cardboard or bulletin board and the amount of verbal material in the display will dictate maximum sizes to a large extent.

As a double check, you should create or obtain some sample letters which should be positioned where the finished display will be assembled. These may then be viewed from the maximum viewing distance to determine whether or not they are satisfactory as far as size and boldness are concerned. If they are legible, then the display can be finished with the assurance that it will be visible from all parts of the room.

Remember, though, that bulletin boards and other such nonprojected materials do not always require that all elements of the composition be visible to every member of the class at any given time. One of the inherent advantages of such displays is their "self-paced" nature—students can walk up to them and study them whenever they wish. Therefore, the use to which a nonprojected visual will be put must be considered when selecting the sizes of letters to be used.

THE FAMILIES OF LETTERS

It is a virtual certainty that we will never know precisely how the first alphabets were developed and by whom, but whatever the source, there can be no question as to the great significance of this event. It is true that the ability to communicate through the use of digital symbols has had much to do with the ways in which peoples and societies have evolved. Yet, as we observe the incredibly diverse styles of letters used in printed and lettered materials, we may feel that very little in the way of organization exists relative to the design and classification of these letters. On the one hand, great, bold letters are used in newspaper headlines, while on the other hand, graceful and light letters are used on the printed page. We see one kind of letter on a diploma and an entirely different kind on a billboard.

In spite of all the apparent confusion, it is possible to classify the lettering styles into categories that vary slightly from one classification system to another. One of the more useful classification schemes—because of its simplicity—is the one which groups all the lettering styles which we commonly use into five main categories as follows:

Roman
thick and thin,
serifs (embellish-
ments on the
ends of strokes)

Gothic
uniform thick-
ness, no serifs

Cursive
letters joined,
"handwriting"

Text
fancy, elaborate,
contrasting thick
and thin strokes

Novelty
unusual
creations

FIGURE 4-1   The Five Families of Letters

The Roman Letter. This type of letter has strokes that alternate between thick and thin. It also has small extensions on the ends of the strokes called "serifs." Most body copy—such as that in books and newspapers—is printed in Roman style. The Roman letter is easy to read. Its thick and thin configuration makes each letter distinctive and each word easy to assimilate at a glance. Most typewriters utilize this style of letter.

The Gothic Letter. Gothic letters have strokes that are of uniform thickness throughout. Additionally, this kind of letter has no serifs on the end of the strokes. This is the most useful letter form for the media designer; it is bold, carries well and is often used in advertising for headlines and captions although it is now being used more extensively for body copy. Incidentally, the elementary school teacher who is engaged in the process of training the students to form letters will recognize this style of letter as the one which is commonly referred to as "manuscript."

The Cursive Letter. This style might best be described as a form of handwriting. The letters are joined together, but, beyond this, little can be said about them. They may be thick, thin, bold, fine, rough, smooth, expanded, condensed, etc. The cursive style is used mainly in advertising and it is used with discretion here. Too many cursive words can be difficult to read and the media designer would do well to use this style only when a special effect is desired.

The Text Letter. This letter has a look of antiquity about it. It is picturesque, decorative, and elaborate. This beautiful but difficult to read style is most often found on bulletin boards about "Merry Old England," knights in armor, Charles Dickens, and Christmas.

The Novelty Letter. If the letters that you are classifying do not fall into one of the four main groups listed above, place them in the novelty group. This style is used only when a certain unusual effect is desired. Usually it is used in an attention-getting manner and most generally only one or two words are involved. Words may be made to look like wood, rope, animals, plants, etc.

HAND LETTERING TECHNIQUES

Although rather demanding from the standpoint of the discipline and effort that are needed for an attractive effect, hand lettering is one of the most useful methods for creating verbal messages. Hand lettering techniques enable the teacher to form letters of any size without having to resort to the use of templates, slides, or patterns. When handmade letters are used, there is no need to worry about running short of a particular letter or number. Additionally, no special equipment beyond a pair of scissors or an inexpensive pen is needed for the creation of these letters.

Among the useful techniques that can be employed are drawing from a basic pattern, cutting from blocks of paper, drawing with pens, and drawing with felt markers. These represent but four of the many techniques that can be used in the area of hand lettering. The alert teacher will always be on the lookout for additional ideas that will assist him in the creation of attractive verbal displays.

A Hand-Drawn Alphabet. Teachers find this alphabet to be very simple to make and economical from the standpoint of both the time and materials necessary to create it. Students in the primary grades can do an excellent job once they know the basic formula for these letters and once they have access to the two basic patterns.

To create the two basic pattern forms, first decide on how high you want your letters to be and then mark this measurement on a piece of light cardboard such as oak tag. The patterns should have a ratio of two units wide to three units high; so, if you desire a letter that is six inches tall, its width will equal four inches. You may wish to vary this ratio for wider or thinner-looking letters, but the two-to-three measure is good for most purposes.

You should cut two rectangles of your chosen size from cardboard. The next step is to decide how wide you would like to make the strokes that form each letter. Dividing the width of the pattern by four, six, or eight will result in a bold, medium, or light stroke. If we divide our four-inch block by four, a one-inch stroke will result; if we divide it by six, our stroke will be just under three-fourths of an inch in width. Now, cut a thin strip of cardboard the width of the stroke that you have chosen. This strip should be longer than the longest side on your pattern block. Place the strip along one of the edges of the pattern block, and, using it as a straightedge, draw a line across the block; repeat this on all four edges (See Figure 4-2). Find the horizontal center of this block, and, using the strip once again, draw a pair of lines across the center. You should now have two rectangles within the original rectangle.

The second block should have lines drawn from corner to corner in the form of an **X.** Use the pattern strip for this, making certain that the oblique lines run directly through the corner as shown. Now, using a razor blade or sharp knife, cut out the two patterns.

To form letters, simply draw a guide line and then select the appropriate pattern and trace the portions needed. At times, it will be necessary to combine portions of both patterns, as in the **K, M, N, R, W, Y,** and **Z.** The rest of the letters can be formed by using one or the other of the patterns exclusively. Note that the corners of such letters as the **C, G, O,** etc., are rounded by tracing over a coin or a button that is held in place over them.

Your letters may be cut out of interesting material, outlined with pen or marker, colored with pencils or paint, made into stencils, and so on. Opaque paints, inks, etc., will cover most of the pencil lines that were used in the formation of the letters; however, it may be necessary to erase any visible pencil lines that might detract from the appearance of your handiwork.

A Cut-Paper Display Alphabet. In order to create the letters in this cutout display alphabet, you will first need to create a "master" pattern as follows: (1) Decide on the height of the letters that you wish to create. (2) Cut a square of paper that has sides the same height as your letters. That is, if your letters are to be eight inches high, you would cut a square of paper eight inches high by eight inches wide. (3) Now, divide this square into five equal spaces in both the vertical and horizontal dimensions. This is easy to do regardless of the initial dimensions of the square. Merely place a ruler on a diagonal across the paper so that the end of the ruler touches one side of the paper and a number divisible by five touches the other side. Now, place pencil marks at the appropriate places (on 2", 4", 6", and 8" in this case). The result will be five equal divisions across the paper. Fold the paper at these marks and then do the same thing with the other dimension of the paper. (4) Unfold your pattern, it should look like Figure 4-3.

It is necessary to make one pattern that is used over and over to form each and every one of the letters in the alphabet. After you have created a few of the basic letters, you will find that it will be a simple matter to create them all using this system. First, decide on the width of the letter that you wish to make. The widths can be the same as those for the hand drawn letters described above, or you can determine your own widths or make your letters conform to the appearance of the ones illustrated. Next, fold the pattern to a width that is equivalent to the width of the letter that you plan to create. For example, an **A** is square, so do not fold the pattern; an **E** is about three spaces wide, so fold the pattern to this width, etc. (Note that the number above the first figure on the diagrams of cut-out letters represents the width of the letter.) Next place the folded pattern on a blank piece of paper and cut around it. This will give you a block of blank paper that will be exactly the size of the letter that you plan to make. Now fold the pattern to one space wide; this is the width of every stroke of every letter. Place the folded pattern in positions on the blank paper that duplicate the positions of the strokes in the letter. Finally cut along the edge of

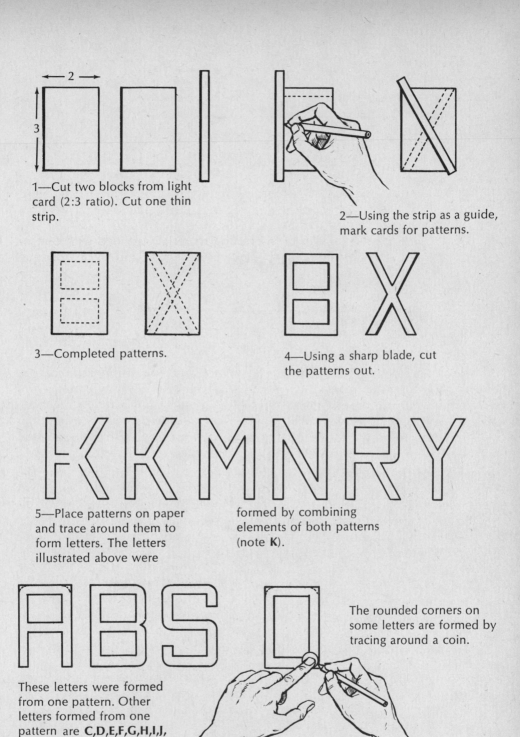

1—Cut two blocks from light card (2:3 ratio). Cut one thin strip.

2—Using the strip as a guide, mark cards for patterns.

3—Completed patterns.

4—Using a sharp blade, cut the patterns out.

5—Place patterns on paper and trace around them to form letters. The letters illustrated above were formed by combining elements of both patterns (note **K**).

These letters were formed from one pattern. Other letters formed from one pattern are **C,D,E,F,G,H,I,J, L,O,P,Q,U,X.**

The rounded corners on some letters are formed by tracing around a coin.

FIGURE 4-2   Hand-Drawn Alphabet

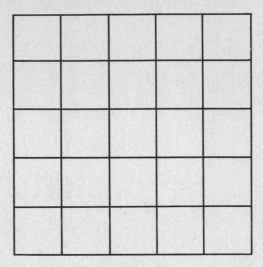

FIGURE 4-3

the pattern to form the desired letter. Note that each one of the small squares on the pattern is exactly equal to the width of each part of every letter. If you will keep this in mind as you create this alphabet, the letters will turn out to be uniform and very attractive. In the diagrams that accompany this description, the gray parts represent the folded pattern in each case, while the unshaded areas represent the paper from which the letter is cut.

A Hand-Drawn Pen Letter. Many different types of lettering pens are available from different sources, but one of the old favorites is the Speedball series which has been in use for as long as many of us can remember. When lettering with the Speedball pen, expect your product to look handmade and rather unmechanical. After all, this is one of the charms of the handmade letter and one of the reasons that it continues to be popular in spite of many innovations in the field of lettering.

Five basic styles of Speedball pens are available. The **A** pen will form a Gothic letter with a blocky look; **B** pens are the easiest of all to use and form Gothic letters that have rounded ends. You will find the **C** pen to be a challenge; it makes the beautiful thick and thin Roman and text styles that we all enjoy looking at, but which take considerable practice to master. The **D** pen is a combination of B and C styles and is used to make rather bold Roman-looking letters. Finally, the **E** pen is a very large "steel brush" that is chisel shaped. It is used in the formation of large letters that have a Roman or text character.

When lettering with the Speedball pen, it is a good idea to use an ink that has been formulated especially for use in pens of this type such as Higgins or Pelikan india inks. Fountain pen inks and those thin varieties which are used in felt-tipped marking pens are not satisfactory because they lack the body necessary for the formation of bold, intense lines such as those required in lettering. After a lettering session, the pen should be washed thoroughly in water and then wiped off so that the residual ink does not dry and clog the pen.

After the master pattern has been created, the letters are formed as follows:

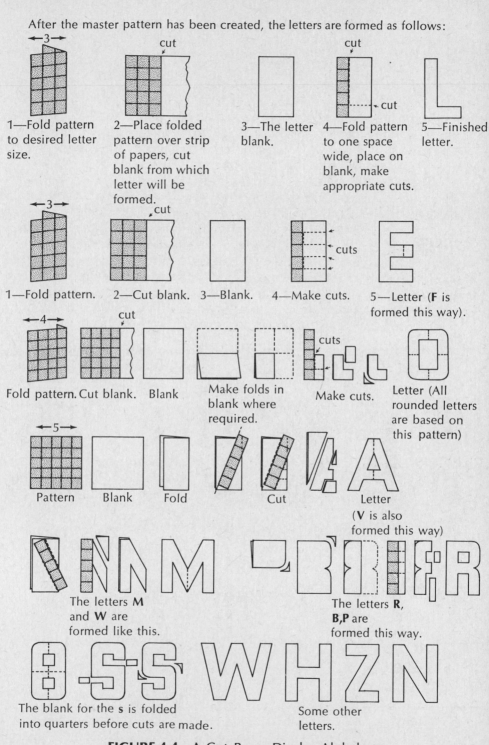

1—Fold pattern to desired letter size.

2—Place folded pattern over strip of papers, cut blank from which letter will be formed.

3—The letter blank.

4—Fold pattern to one space wide, place on blank, make appropriate cuts.

5—Finished letter.

1—Fold pattern.

2—Cut blank.

3—Blank.

4—Make cuts.

5—Letter (**F** is formed this way).

Fold pattern. Cut blank. Blank

Make folds in blank where required.

Make cuts.

Letter (All rounded letters are based on this pattern)

Pattern   Blank   Fold   Cut   Letter

(**V** is also formed this way)

The letters **M** and **W** are formed like this.

The letters **R**, **B,P** are formed this way.

The blank for the **s** is folded into quarters before cuts are made.

Some other letters.

FIGURE 4-4 A Cut-Paper Display Alphabet

Before you start to letter, you should draw appropriate guide lines on the paper in light pencil. You should also plan to sketch a rough approximation of each of the letters in the word while paying special attention to the spacing of the letters.

Prior to inking the letters, a certain amount of time should be spent in gaining some proficiency with your pen. Draw guide lines on your paper or card before you begin your practice session, Remember, one of the most essential lettering tools is the ruler or straight edge. Now load your pen and try creating a series of basic strokes such as vertical, horizontal, oblique, and rounded lines. These represent the raw materials from which the letters will be formed.

As you make the various strokes, if you discover that your pen lines are ragged rather than smooth and sharp, it is probably because the nib of the pen is not in complete contact with the surface of the paper. To correct this, look at the pen as you hold it in position to see if the nib is flat on the paper. You may have to observe the nib from a side view in order to determine this. With your eye on the nib, pull the pen along for the distance of a full stroke and observe what is happening. An aid to keeping the pen in constant flat contact with the paper is to letter with the arm, not with the fingers. The wrist should be held stiff and the lines should be made by pulling the entire arm toward the body. After this motion has been mastered, it is an easy matter to turn the paper to form the other strokes.

The technique just described applies to pen lettering in general. However, the use of different pens will automatically result in the formation of different

FIGURE 4-5   Practice Pen Strokes - "B" Pen

When the nib is maintained flat against the paper a uniform stroke will result.

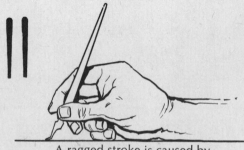

A ragged stroke is caused by an improperly held pen.

FIGURE 4-6

styles of letters. For example, if you use the C pen rather than the B variety, your letters will appear alternately thick and thin rather than uniform in thickness due to the characteristics of the pen. If you are using a chisel pen, such as the C or E varieties, you should maintain a constant angle of about 45° (see illustration) throughout the formation of each and every letter—this angle doesn't

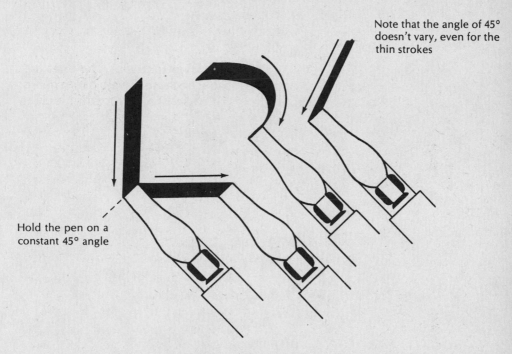

Note that the angle of 45° doesn't vary, even for the thin strokes

Hold the pen on a constant 45° angle

FIGURE 4-7   Basic "C" Pen Strokes

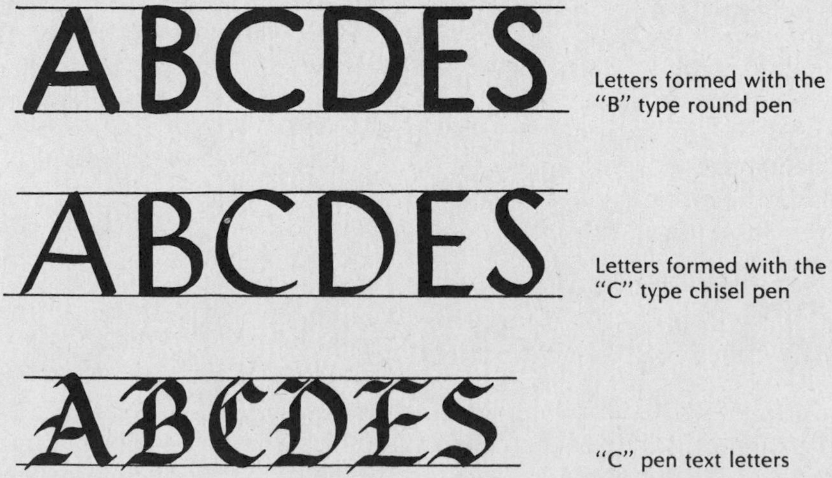

ABCDES

Letters formed with the "B" type round pen

ABCDES

Letters formed with the "C" type chisel pen

ABCDES

"C" pen text letters

FIGURE 4-8   "Speedball" Pen Letters

Hand Lettering with the Felt Marker. Select a marker that is relatively new and has a sharp chisel nib when you wish to create this type of letter. Old markers that have rounded nibs will make lines that are rough and lack precision. These worn nibs are fine for drawing purposes but are unsuitable for lettering. As with any lettering technique, the drawing of guidelines on the paper or card is a necessary prelude to the actual formation of the letters.

The secret of creating attractive verbal messages with the felt marker is simply one of determining the proper angle at which to hold the instrument and then staying with this position throughout the process of forming every letter—this is similar to lettering with C and E pens.

1—The nib is held on an angle.

2—Only the sharp edge should contact the paper.

3—An up-stroke gives a thin line.

4—A down-stroke gives a thick line.

5—All strokes are made with the pen held on the same angle.

BCDE abefn

some sample letters

FIGURE 4-9   Lettering with the Felt Marker

Essentially, the angle of the nib is determined by creating an inverted **V** shape, or an **A** without its cross bar. Hold the marker so that one of the sharp edges is in contact with the paper. Now, push it upward toward the top of the paper to form one leg of the **A**—this should be a thin line. Without removing the marker from the paper and without changing its angle, pull it toward the bottom of the paper to form the other leg of the **A**—this should be thick. You have created a basic thick-thin (Roman) letter configuration. You have also established the angle at which the nib should be held in order to form attractive and legible letters.

MECHANICAL LETTERING TECHNIQUES

Letters that are formed with mechanical lettering devices are uniform and precise in appearance. When such devices are properly employed, the effect can be very professional looking. However, this type of lettering equipment is often expensive to buy and may not always be available locally.

A decided advantage that the mechanical devices have over premade letters is that you never have to be concerned about exhausting any of the letters or numbers; you simply form new ones as they are needed.

Mechanical devices have the letters "built" into them; there is very little latitude for modification possible with a template or a stencil. Handmade letters can be made larger or smaller, but mechanically formed letters generally must conform to the size and shape of the master on the guide although there are exceptions to this.

A wide array of mechanical devices is on the market today, but those commonly used in the classroom or media center seem to fall into one of the three categories covered in this section: stencils (including pens and guides), stamps, and templates and scribers.

Stencils

Typically, stencils are made from heavy paper, although there are varieties that are plastic or metal. A modification of the standard sheet-type stencil is the pen and guide (Wrico) system which produces a cleaner, more professional looking letter than does the other kind. Stencils are available in many styles and sizes. They are useful when large, bold letters are required, but they produce rather crude letters that typically have a fragmented appearance due to the "bars" or supports that are needed to maintain the centers of lobed letters in position. The letters that are formed with this method generally have an irregular edge which results when the markers or brushes that are used do not exactly conform to the sharp edges of the stencil. On the other hand, stencils are inexpensive, readily available, and require no special skills for utilization.

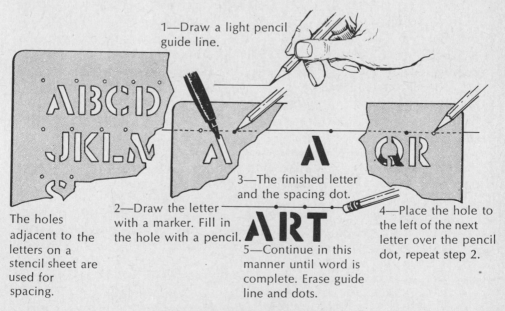

1—Draw a light pencil guide line.

2—Draw the letter with a marker. Fill in the hole with a pencil.

3—The finished letter and the spacing dot.

4—Place the hole to the left of the next letter over the pencil dot, repeat step 2.

5—Continue in this manner until word is complete. Erase guide line and dots.

The holes adjacent to the letters on a stencil sheet are used for spacing.

FIGURE 4-10 Stencil Lettering

The pen and guide system—as typified by the Wrico system—consists of a special flat-nose pen, which comes in a number of different widths, and a plastic lettering guide with letter forms cut through its surface. Many of the pen and guide sets also include a guide holder which serves to support the guide in a manner that assures the alignment of the letters as they are formed. The sizes of letters that are available in this system are numerous, but the styles are quite limited and consist mainly of Gothic letters of varying degrees of boldness. In addition to the restricted choice of styles, the pen and guide system also has the added disadvantage of being somewhat expensive if a complete selection of pens and guides is desired. Essentially, though, a basic set consisting of a couple of guides, a holder, and a pen can be a relatively modest investment and can serve as the basis for building a larger collection a bit at a time. These letters will be very attractive, sharp, and clean if properly formed. They are excellent for use in creating large visuals such as posters, charts and bulletin boards. The procedure for using this system is as follows:

1. Select a piece of smooth, hard-surfaced paper or board upon which to letter. Tape this to the table or drawing board.
2. Place the guide holder along the bottom edge of the paper in such a way that when the guide is placed in its holder the letters will be positioned where you want them to be. You may wish to tape the holder in position but this is not necessary since its cork base will generally keep it from slipping.
3. Adjust the pen. The fluted rod which is located inside of the pen barrel may be adjusted in and out by turning the adjusting shoulder at the top of the pen body. Move it in or out until it is exactly even with the end of the barrel. Check the flutes in the rod to make sure that they are clean. If they are choked with dried ink, the pen will not function well and imperfect letters will result.
4. Load the pen by depressing the plunger and placing the extended fluted rod into the ink well. When pressure is released from the plunger, the rod will retract into the barrel of the pen and loading is complete.
5. Try a few strokes on a piece of scrap paper; if the strokes look even and black, you may proceed with your lettering.
6. The pen must always be held in a vertical position; little pressure is needed to cause the ink to flow but an effort should be made to maintain the pen in contact with the outer edge of the letter form in order that the line which is formed does not become irregular (particularly on "hollow" letters such as **O, Q, D,** etc.).
7. Space optically or "by eye." Simply slide the guide back and forth until the proper letter on the guide is in the correct position in relation to the letter just formed and then ink the new letter.
8. Permit the ink to dry thoroughly, trim the card or paper, and the word or words are ready to go up on the bulletin board or on your poster.

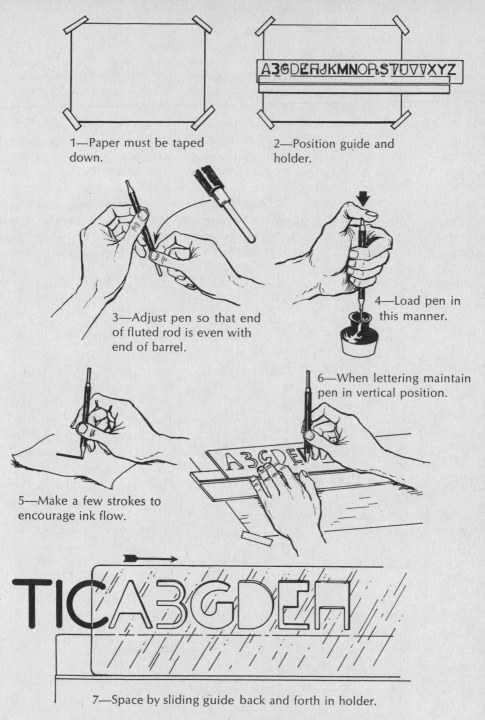

1—Paper must be taped down.

2—Position guide and holder.

3—Adjust pen so that end of fluted rod is even with end of barrel.

4—Load pen in this manner.

5—Make a few strokes to encourage ink flow.

6—When lettering maintain pen in vertical position.

7—Space by sliding guide back and forth in holder.

FIGURE 4-11 Pen and Guide Lettering System (Wrico)

Scriber and Template

This system—as typified by the LeRoy— consists of a scriber and a template which has the letters recessed into its surface but not perforated all the way through as in the Wrico. The scriber has a pointed tracer pin which fits snugly into the letters on the template. A tail pin, which is blunt on the end, fits into the tail pin slot which runs the length of the template. This extension on the end of the scriber maintains the scriber on a left to right path that does not vary from a straight line. In this way, all of the letters are accurately aligned as they are formed. A pen—or pencil lead—extends from the scriber in such a way that it is unencumbered by the template. As the tracer pin traces the letter, the pen—or lead—duplicates it on the paper. Once again, spacing is accomplished optically.

Professional models of the scriber and template system are expensive and probably would best be used in a media center where the need for a considerable amount of this kind of lettering might justify the large initial expenditure. It should be mentioned, however, that inexpensive versions of many kinds are available which place this system within the reach of virtually any school that would care to acquire a modest basic scriber and template capability.

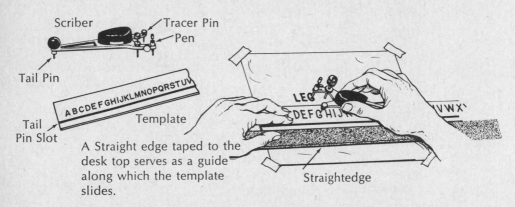

FIGURE 4-12 Scriber and Template Lettering

A certain amount of practice is needed before competence is achieved with the scriber because it is a sensitive device that requires rather sensitive handling. Here are the steps involved in lettering with the scriber and template system:

1. Select a piece of smooth, hard-surfaced paper or cardboard. Tape this to the table or drawing board.
2. Tape or fasten a straightedge along the bottom of the paper; place the template on the top edge of this.
3. Select the proper pen size and position it in the scriber; lock it in place by tightening the knurled screw.
4. Load the pen by dropping a few drops of ink into the reservoir. Work the pin up and down in the barrel of the pen until a globule of ink forms at the tip; wipe this off on a piece of scrap paper.

5. Try a few strokes with the pen; if it forms an even, black line you may proceed with the task at hand.
6. Place the tail pin in the tail pin slot and the tracer pin in the letter that you wish to form; touch the pen to the paper and carefully guide the tracer pin around the letter on the template. You should use as little pressure as necessary to cause the pen to function. As a matter of fact, if the pen is positioned slightly above the surface of the paper, the ink will flow more adequately through capillary action and a more dense letter will result. This positioning of the pen above the paper surface may be accomplished by adjusting the screw on the scriber which is provided for this purpose.
7. As the lettering proceeds, you will find it necessary to slide the template back and forth in order that the required letters might be formed. Spacing becomes a matter of checking the position of the letter to be formed by holding the pen slightly off of the paper so that no marks are made while manipulating the template slightly to the left or right as needed.
8. After the lettering has been completed, permit the ink to dry thoroughly and then trim the card to the proper size. It is now ready to use as a picture caption, a paste-up, or any other kind of visual display that requires professional looking legible letters.

Rubber Stamps

The rubber stamp set is a common item in virtually every elementary school and many secondary schools. It is readily available, uncomplicated, and easy to use. The letters that are formed are bold and legible, but they often appear grayish due to improper inking of the pad or unequal pressure on the letter. Also, even under the best of conditions, it is difficult to keep the letters from "bouncing," or falling out of alignment as they are printed.

To use the rubber stamp system, it is first necessary to establish a line upon which the letters will be placed. Most stamp sets contain a special aligning ruler that can be taped in position on the board or paper and used to line up the letters so they do not "bounce."

The stamp pad should contain plenty of fresh ink and should be soft and pliable. Select the desired letter and press it into the ink pad; a rocking movement will often ink the letter more adequately than will a simple, direct pressing movement.

Now, place the letter on the aligning ruler or the guide line and press down on it. Once again, a rocking motion will transfer more ink than will a direct, flat pressure. To space the letters, it will be necessary to judge the distance between the letter that has just been formed and the stamp that will form the next letter. To accomplish this, hold the inked stamp against the ruler or guide line, but maintain the inked portion just off the surface of the paper. When it is determined that the spacing is correct, the inked stamp is permitted to come into contact with the paper and pressure is applied to form the next letter.

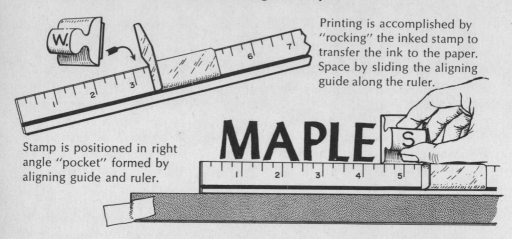

Stamp is positioned in right angle "pocket" formed by aligning guide and ruler.

Printing is accomplished by "rocking" the inked stamp to transfer the ink to the paper. Space by sliding the aligning guide along the ruler.

FIGURE 4-13   Rubber Stamp Lettering

PREMADE LETTERING TYPES

A wide assortment of this popular letter type is to be found at your local art or school supply outlet. Many variety stores as well as media materials vendors will also carry certain kinds of premade letters. One of the problems inherent in using a set of letters of this kind is that there is a limit to the number of each of the letter forms that is included in any given set; therefore, it is common to run out of **E**s or **S**s or something else. Then the only alternative you have is to purchase another sheet, or set, of the same style of letter that you have been using—a rather uneconomical, but necessary, procedure.

Some of the larger letters—particularly the three-dimensional variety—can be acquired singly as needed, but virtually all of the smaller letters must be purchased in sets. Although this is a disadvantage, the advantage of having beautiful, perfectly formed letters that can easily be positioned in place is certainly worth considering.

We may group the various types of premade letters into four basic categories, namely, two-dimensional die cut letters that do not require a support sheet, dry-transfer or rub-off letters, paste-up letters, and 3-D letters.

Die Cut Letters

This kind of letter is generally made from adhesive-backed paper, cardboard, or thin plastic, although other kinds of materials are sometimes used. For example, letters punched from felt or letters backed with flock or velure are available for use on the felt or flannel board.

Cardboard letters in all sizes and styles are relatively inexpensive and widely available. Paper letters are among the least expensive of all the die cut forms. Some have an adhesive on the back which must be moistened prior to use. Others have pressure-sensitive backs and are merely pressed into position. Thin plastic letters are tough and serviceable. Most of them are pressure-sensitive and are made ready for adhering by peeling off the paper backing that protects the sticky surface.

When using the die cut letter, a straightedge such as a yardstick is taped in position across the paper or cardboard or other material that will serve as the support for the letters. The letters are then aligned on the straightedge and adhered to the support. It is best never to use pencil lines for guide lines because these cannot be erased from along the bottom of the letters due to the three-dimensionality of even the thinnest of the die-cut forms.

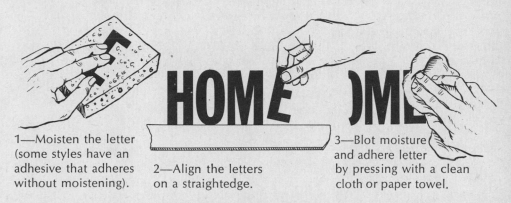

1—Moisten the letter (some styles have an adhesive that adheres without moistening).

2—Align the letters on a straightedge.

3—Blot moisture and adhere letter by pressing with a clean cloth or paper towel.

FIGURE 4-14   Die-Cut Letters

Three-Dimensional Letters

For special uses, this type of letter is unsurpassed. Wooden cutouts are used when letter recognition is being stressed. The top side is identified with some kind of tactile code which encourages the child to touch and manipulate the various forms. If a tack board is available in the room, a set of ceramic or wooden letters with pins in the back will be handy. Magnetic letters can be acquired for use on magnetic boards; or, standard letters can be made magnetic by attaching a small section of strip magnet to their backs. Molded plastic letters can be used as they come in the package or they may be sprayed with spray enamel if a different color is desired.

Bell and Howell has a set of gum-backed ceramic letters on the market that is excellent for movie and slide titling. These can be adhered to a hard-surfaced material, such as glass, and can then be removed for re-use.

Dry Transfer Letters

Dry transfer letters are printed on the back side of transparent plastic sheets. They are prevented from transferring randomly by a protective cover sheet that is removed when they are to be used. There are several advantages to dry transfer types including the fact that they are so simple to use. A guide line of some kind will be needed in order that the letters can be properly aligned—a piece of paper with a straight edge or a light pencil mark will do the job. Merely place the paper in a position so that the edge will serve as the guide, then tape it down and proceed to transfer your letters. Note that the letters have a light black line printed just below them on the sheet; this permits you to position them in a straight line just above the pencil line which then can be erased without damaging the words that have been formed. Transferring is achieved by rubbing with a dull pencil, a ball point pen, an orangewood stick, or something similar. Letters may be removed by erasing them or by picking them up with a piece of masking tape.

Dry transfer letters are excellent for finished display work such as labels on pictures, captions, titles, posters, and charts. They are also useful if verbal materials are desired on hand-made transparencies. They are not satisfactory for creating masters for transparency production that will be subjected to any kind of intense heat—such as that encountered in some transparency-making equipment.

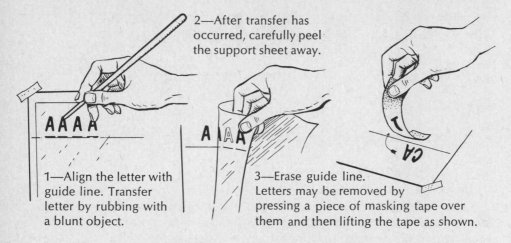

2—After transfer has occurred, carefully peel the support sheet away.

1—Align the letter with guide line. Transfer letter by rubbing with a blunt object.

3—Erase guide line. Letters may be removed by pressing a piece of masking tape over them and then lifting the tape as shown.

FIGURE 4-15 Dry-Transfer Lettering

Any excessive amount of heat will cause the dry transfer letter to melt or to peel off of the master sheet thus damaging or destroying the master. For this type of work, the paste-up letter is suggested as the best alternative.

Paste-Up Letters (Letters on Plastic)

Unlike the dry transfer letter, this variety must be cut from the sheet upon which it is printed. The paste-up letter sheet is actually two sheets—one of plastic, the other of waxed paper—that are sandwiched together into a unit. To use this type of letter, a guide line should first be drawn or a piece of paper may be used as a straightedge. A razor blade is used to carefully score around the letter that is to be lifted off of the waxed paper backing sheet. The guide line is located just below the letter.

Slip the blade just under the edge of the block of plastic containing the letter and the guide line and carefully lift it off of the backing sheet. Now position this block on the pencil line or along the edge of the piece of paper that you are using as a straightedge. As with the transfer letters, the guide line on the plastic is aligned with the guide line on the paper. Rub the letter into position and then go on to the next one, and the next, until the word or line of words has been formed. Carefully cut through the plastic between the guide line and the letter form and peel away the strip of guide lines that were formerly attached to the letters. Now erase the pencil lines, or, if the edge of a piece of paper was used as a guide line, simply remove the paper and dispose of it.

You will notice that the plastic base upon which the letters are printed is somewhat visible. This is particularly true when colored backgrounds are used.

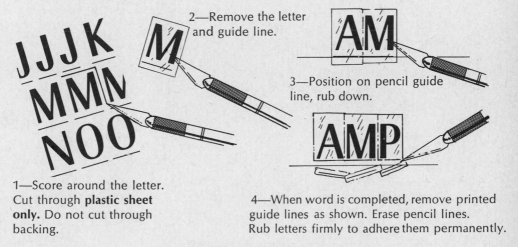

2—Remove the letter and guide line.

3—Position on pencil guide line, rub down.

1—Score around the letter. Cut through **plastic sheet only.** Do not cut through backing.

4—When word is completed, remove printed guide lines as shown. Erase pencil lines. Rub letters firmly to adhere them permanently.

FIGURE 4-16   Paste-Up Lettering

Obviously, this characteristic of the paste-up letter makes it less desirable than the precut or the dry-transfer varieties as a form for use on finished work such as posters and transparencies. However, this letter is excellent for the production of "masters" that will then be photographed or passed through a transparency maker to create the finished visual. Remember that this letter is not sensitive to heat and therefore is not damaged or destroyed when it is subjected to the heat that is produced by certain transparency makers such as the thermal transfer machine.

SPACING LETTERS

The satisfactory spacing of letters in a word can only be achieved with practice. This is a vexing problem to say the least and causes the conscientious designer no end of grief and frustration. Essentially, the basic problem is that spacing does not lend itself to any kind of mechanical solution—you cannot use rulers and dividers with words and letters. In order that a feeling of uniform spacing might be achieved, it is necessary to space optically—a technique that is referred to as "eyeballing" by lettering professionals.

To "eyeball" successfully, you must work with a "chunk" of space rather than with a linear measurement. The total space between each pair of letters in a word must be consistent throughout the word (note that we are referring to the total space, not just the distance between two letters). With this in mind, you should be able to squeeze the block of space here and stretch it there in order to compensate for the variety of letter shapes in the alphabet. Think of the space as being something like clay. You only have so much of it and this amount must fit between the letters and fill the spaces completely.

1—Because of the different shapes that letters have, it is not practical to space them mechanically. Although the straight-sided letters **N** and **H** seem to be well spaced, the slanted **A** and **V** seem to be too far apart.

3—When letters are positioned according to space area instead of linear measure, the effect will be much more acceptable.

2—Although the linear measure is the same between all letters, the total space area varies considerably.

4—Note how the finished "word" holds together. Compare this figure with 1.

FIGURE 4-17   Spacing

You will find it necessary to overlap letters such as **A** and **V** in order to make your "clay" fit. You will have to pull the **T** very close to slab-sided letters like the **H**. **O**s can be placed close together and **M, N,** and **H** can be moved apart. Your words should read as units with no obvious breaks in them. This effect can be accomplished through careful spacing.

BIBLIOGRAPHY

Adams, Sarah, Rosemier, Robert, and Sleeman, Phillip. "Readable Letter Size and Visibility for Overhead Projection Transparencies," **AV Communication Review** 13, No. 4 (1965): 412-17.

Anderson, Charles R. **Lettering.** New York: Van Nostrand Reinhold Co., 1969.

Craig, James. **Designing With Type—A Basic Course in Typography.** New York: Watson-Guptill Publications, 1971.

Croy, Peter. **Graphic Design and Reproduction Techniques,** 2nd ed. New York: Hastings House Publications, 1972.

Garland, Ken. **Graphics Handbook.** London: Studio Vista, 1966.

George, Ross F. **Speedball Text Book,** 17th edition, Camden, N.J.: Hunt Pen Co., 1956.

Longyear, William. **Type and Lettering.** New York: Watson-Guptill Publications, 1966.

Minor, Ed, and Frye, Harvey R. **Techniques for Producing Instructional Media.** New York: McGraw-Hill Book Co., 1970.

Planning and Producing Slide Programs. Rochester, N.Y.: Eastman Kodak Co., 1975.

5

VISUAL DESIGN

Pictures and other kinds of materials are typically combined to form displays such as bulletin boards, posters, and charts. On a lesser scale, pictures, words, and various embellishments are used in combination in the creation of overhead transparencies, slides, layouts for pages, and so on. Bringing these diverse elements together to form a related whole can be a problem that is difficult to solve at best and one that is often resolved in a haphazard fashion simply because few guidelines are available on the composition of mediated experiences. Because the emphasis in this book is on those kinds of visual materials that can readily be created in the average school, the following information will emphasize this aspect of composition. With a little imagination, however, these suggestions can be utilized in the creation of just about any kind of mediated learning experience. Balance, emphasis, unity, etc. are as important in a self-instructional slide-tape package as they are in a bulletin board or a chart.

Rules for composition are difficult to establish, and once established, tend to become quite restrictive if blindly adhered to. Often an exciting visual will evolve through sheer good luck or a "happy accident." Unfortunately, these successes are difficult, if not impossible, to replicate because they have resulted from an accidental combination of things rather than through a systematic approach to a problem.

It may be that the outstanding designer has what could be referred to as a "sixth sense" which enables him, without being bound by any formal rules, to come up with excellent designs time after time. Fortunately, very few classroom teachers need to worry about this level of endeavor. The basic problem that the teacher faces is simply one of making his visuals attractive enough, and explicit enough, that the desired message gets through to the students with as little ambiguity as possible. Essentially, what the teacher needs is a basic set of loose directions and rules that will assist him in the establishment of the fundamental design; beyond this, the sky is the limit.

In this chapter, we will begin by considering the elements and principles of design in a rather general manner. Then we will look at composition in more specific terms and in greater depth. Next, an excursion into the fascinating world of color will be taken. And, finally, we will examine some of the information relative to visual design that has derived from research in this field.

THE DESIGN ELEMENTS

The elements of a composition can be likened to a collection of different kinds of building blocks. These will constitute the "things" in the composition. We may subdivide the elements into (1) space, (2) line, (3) shape, (4) form, and (5) surface—which includes texture, color, and value.

Space. Space may be thought of as being either negative or positive. The most common kind of negative space is to be found in the background or "unused" areas of a composition. For example, the portions of the bulletin board that are not covered by pictures, captions, or other materials would be considered as negative areas. The parts of a slide that serve as a "foil" for the dominant subject material would be considered as negative spaces. Negative spaces are frequently employed as part of the total composition, much as pauses between notes are employed in a musical selection. Without negative spaces, a visual display would appear packed and cluttered.

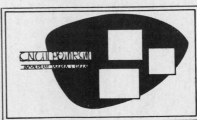

An empty bulletin board, a sheet of paper, a fresh piece of film represent negative space.

The distribution of negative space is as important as the placement of the postive elements in a design.

The unused portions of a design are referred to as negative space.

FIGURE 5-1   Space

Line. For our purpose, we may consider line as being one-dimensional, that is, its important dimension is its length, although it does have width. Lines represent the simplest elements available to the designer. Primitive man probably first drew with simple lines; modern man finds them to be indispensable to the expression of graphic concepts. A tracing of a figure made with a fiber marker on a sheet of acetate is a good example of a line in a space. Often yarn, rope, colored string, and cord are used as integral parts of a bulletin board design. All of these materials have length as their most important dimension and may therefore be classified as examples of line. Poster drawings, enlargements for the bulletin board, charts, and graphs are frequently line illustrations that have some color added to them for clarification and interest.

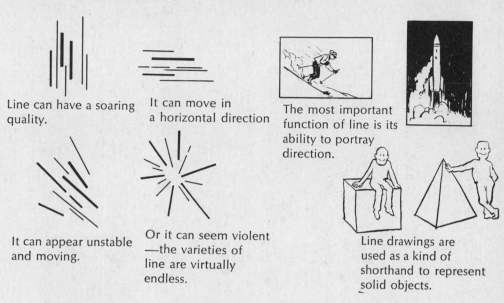

Line can have a soaring quality.

It can move in a horizontal direction

The most important function of line is its ability to portray direction.

It can appear unstable and moving.

Or it can seem violent —the varieties of line are virtually endless.

Line drawings are used as a kind of shorthand to represent solid objects.

FIGURE 5-2   Line—This element is one-dimensional. It has length.

As a line twists, turns, wiggles, soars, and otherwise describes different movements, it displays what is known as "direction." Lines can display an unlimited variety of directions, each with its own characteristic and personality.

Shape. A shape may also be referred to as a "plane." Shapes have two distinct dimensions—height and width. A sheet of colored paper, a piece of cardboard, a section of wooden panel, a piece of plastic would all be examples of shape. These flat materials are typically cut into varying configurations and are then often detailed with line to form many of the visual designs found in the classroom. Felt board figures are excellent examples of shapes; so are the colored paper cutouts that embellish many bulletin boards. Big, blocky display letters and the colored poster board upon which pictures are mounted also represent examples of shapes.

Form. Form may be apparent or actual. Apparent—or simulated—form is found in shaded drawings such as charcoal or pencil sketches. A most common type of apparent form is the halftone photograph which is found in books and magazines. This type of illustration displays a certain "depth" and roundness because of the manner in which the lights and shadows are distributed over the surfaces of the objects which are pictured.

Actual form can be found in sculpture, cut and folded paper, wood constructions, formed metal, natural objects, etc. Objects having actual form dis-

1—Geometric
shapes.

2—Abstract
shape.

3—Representational
shape.

FAMOUS VIOLINISTS

The Three Types of Shapes

Shapes
in
posters.

HOLLAND

The cards upon which
pictures are mounted are
generally geometric shapes.

FIGURE 5-3   Shapes or Planes (Two Dimensions: Height and Width)

play the dimension of depth in addition to those of height and width—they are "3-D." Objects having simulated form are two dimensional in actuality but are three dimensional in appearance.

Form is three-dimensional—it has depth. Objects in nature display actual form. Many pictures and photographs have simulated form.

A mask and a vase have actual form. So do the children for that matter.

A photograph, a shaded drawing, and many magazine and book pictures have simulated form.

Drawings and photographs appear to have three-dimensional form mainly due to shading.

FIGURE 5-4   Form (Three Dimensions)

Surface. All of the elements display a surface, although line elements typically display less of a surface than do the other elements. Most generally, the surface of a line is dependent upon the surface character of the space or shape upon which it is drawn. If a crayon line is drawn upon a coarse paper, the line will appear roughly textured. The same line drawn on a sheet of plastic-coated paper will appear as a smooth line, and so on.

Surface treatments include:

a. Color (or gray, black, and white, called "neutrals")—the "hue" of a surface
b. Value—the degree of lightness or darkness of a surface
c. Texture—the roughness or smoothness of a surface

The concept of surface can be illustrated using a piece of colored burlap for an example. The burlap, which comes in small pieces or in large rolls, is excellent for covering bulletin boards, display panels, or tack boards. It has a roughly woven "texture." The "colors" range from bright yellow to black. The "value" range extends through light straw colors which are light (high) in value, through orange which is medium in value, to very dark blues and blacks which are dark (low) in value.

COLOR
Is it red? Blue? Green?
Or some combination?

VALUE
Is it light? Is it dark? Or
something in between?

TEXTURE
Is it rough? Is it
smooth?

FIGURE 5-5   Surface—All surfaces have the qualities of color, value, and texture.

THE DESIGN PRINCIPLES

The principles are the "rules" by which the elements are assembled into a design. Actually, the term "rule" is not a good one, for it implies a kind of law or regulation that is binding to a large extent. Principles are not meant to be this restrictive. At any rate, a knowledge of the design principles can be quite helpful in many cases where the objective is to compose an interesting and effective visual display. The principles covered in this section are (1) balance, (2) center of interest, (3) emphasis, (4) unity, (5) contrast, and (6) rhythm.

Balance. Balance has been described as a kind of equilibrium within a composition. Two kinds of balance are normally defined. These are formal, or bisymmetrical, and informal, or asymmetrical. Often the see-saw or teeter-totter analogy is used to demonstrate the two kinds of balance—the fulcrum is equivalent to the vertical center of the composition. If equal weights are placed at equal distances from the fulcrum, the see-saw will balance. In visual design parlance, if two pictures that are of equal size and value (among other things) are placed at equivalent distances from the vertical center of the visual, the design will be in balance.

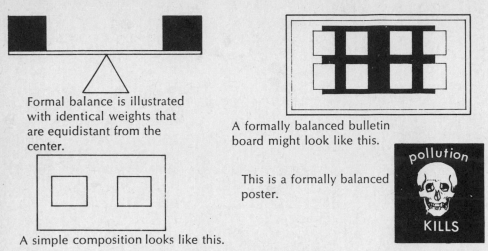

Formal balance is illustrated with identical weights that are equidistant from the center.

A formally balanced bulletin board might look like this.

This is a formally balanced poster.

A simple composition looks like this.

FIGURE 5-6   Formal Balance

The fact that this approach works as far as the formal mode is concerned is quite evident when the many examples of bisymmetrical layout are considered. However, that the informal concept is equally viable is subject to question. When the beginning designer tries to apply the idea to a practical layout problem, he or she often finds that the results are less than desired. For example, according to the see-saw method, it should be possible to place a large man near the fulcrum and a small girl out near the end of the plank to achieve balance. In practice, this is feasible, but when a large and a small picture are substituted for the man and girl respectively, something frequently goes awry. The small picture might be brightly colored, while the large one is drab, or vice versa, then the concept of equivalent "weightiness" breaks down. In other words, a pound of small girl is equal to a pound of large man, but the establishment of an unequivocal weight standard for pictures seems to elude us.

In the final analysis, unless you lack all confidence in your design ability, a good approach is to use your own good taste or intuition when arranging elements in an informal way. Of course, the other principles listed here have much to do with the manner in which this is done. For example, you can still feel secure most of the time in arranging a picture of an individual so that the gaze is directed into the picture rather than out of it. And mergers, which are covered in the section on further design considerations, are undesirable under virtually any circumstances.

For an additional discussion of informal balance, refer to the "the division of space" on page 100.

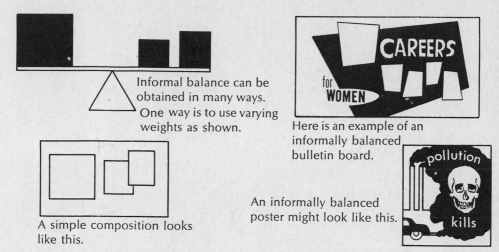

FIGURE 5-7   Informal Balance

Center of Interest. The center of interest is the **raison d'etrê** of a design. It is the main theme. the statement for which everything else serves as a foil. A center of interest might command attention due to its bulk, or it might be diminutive in size, yet so compelling in other ways as to demand attention. Center of interest and emphasis are intimately, often inseparably, interrelated. Lines that lead to the center of interest help to emphasize it. Pointers, such as roads, that diminish in width as they move into the photograph, or arrows that direct attention in a poster, serve to emphasize a specific portion of the composition.

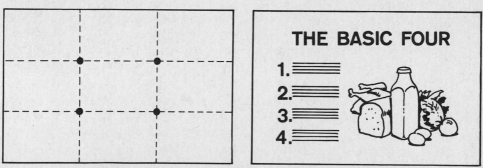

Divide the space as shown. Center of interest can be located at any intersection. In this example, the lower right intersection was selected.

FIGURE 5-8   One Way to Locate the Center of Interest

A useful technique for locating the center of interest, particularly in a photograph, is the "rule of thirds." This system, which is well covered by Eastman Kodak in their publication on composition, is based on a grid pattern that consists of two equidistant vertical lines and two equidistant horizontal ones which dissect the picture surface into thirds. Four points are formed by the intersections of the lines that serve as optional positions for the placement of the center of interest. Although usually placed off-center, a strong center of interest might be located close to the middle of the picture. However, in the final analysis, intuition is often the best "rule" to follow when attempting to come up with the most effective placement.

Emphasis. Frequently, the elements in a composition are so similar that they seem to run together, thereby giving the viewer some difficulty in iden-tifying the main theme. When the key part or parts of a display are emphasized in some way, the viewer knows just what to look for and can get down to the business of learning about the concept immediately.

Emphasis can be achieved through a number of techniques, among which are the following:

a. Use an arrow or some other directing device.
b. Make the most important item brightly colored if the other items are drab. You may wish to mount the main visual on a backing of brightly colored cardboard to accomplish this effect.
c. Make the main element larger than the others.
d. Direct attention through placement of the items on the surface.
e. Use contrasting values to direct attention to the item that you wish to emphasize.
f. Use a shape which contrasts with the other shapes. A circle in an array of squares will stand out.
g. Place the item to be emphasized at a point at which lines intersect. This will cause attention to be directed to it. Once again, emphasis is inex-tricably related to the center of interest. However, the term "emphasis" is used in large part to describe ways in which we can make the center of interest—which is often thought of in terms of subject matter—stand out from the rest of the display.

Unity. Many compositions lack unity even though this principle is among the simplest to understand and the easiest to achieve. Often a bulletin board display consists of a number of pictures scattered in a random fashion over the surface of the board. The total effect is one of disorder. When we look at such a display, we seem to perceive a number of pictures rather than **one** composition. This is the test of a good bulletin board: Does it seem to "hold together" as a unit, or does it scatter attention and dissipate interest because of its randomness?

Unity is easily achieved through overlapping. This principle is borrowed from nature—trees overlap mountains and one another; mountains overlap clouds in the sky; buildings overlap other buildings; grasses and shrubs in the foreground overlap objects in the background and middle ground. The total

 Emphasis has to do with making the key item stand out.

Arrows or pointers are effective.

A contrasting value can emphasize an area.

 The placement of an item can cause it to be emphasized.

Size can be used.

Note: One of the best ways to achieve emphasis is with color.

FIGURE 5-9 Emphasis

feeling that nature displays is that of "oneness." This same effect is achieved in the classroom through overlapping pictures and other elements of the composition over a background of some type. The background on a bulletin board might be a large, irregular piece of burlap trimmed to look like the silhouette of an object; it might be a piece of colored butcher wrap or cardboard; it might be the actual material such as a fish net or a colorful shawl or rug. The background material should relate to the subject of the display, e.g., fishnet—commercial fishing or the sea. This same idea can be utilized in the production of transparencies, posters, and other kinds of media.

For example, a transparency that pictures a number of related figures, such as the presidents of the United States, or a visualization of the Dewey Decimal System, may employ an underlay of color or texture which can effectively unify the several figures.

Another method of achieving unity is to place a border around the elements of the display in order to "fence them in" so to speak. Or the parts of the display that are of secondary importance may be tied to the part or parts of major importance by utilizing lines of various kinds. Use interesting materials such as rope, colored yarn, crepe paper streamers and lengths of ribbon for the "lines."

The repetition of a given shape, such as a rectangle, can result in a certain feeling of unity; a group of pictures which are mounted on sheets of construction paper of a common shape will look unified to a certain extent. The same can be said of color. A color which is repeated again and again, either in the pictures themselves, or in the mounting boards upon which the pictures are placed, will result in a limited feeling of unity.

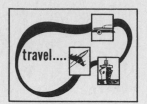

Unity involves "one-ness" or a "tying together."

1—A "border"can be used to achieve unity.

2—Another technique is to use lines to unify.

3—Perhaps the most effective method is to overlap a common shape.

FIGURE 5-10   Unity

Contrast. Contrast refers to the characteristic of an object that causes it to stand out in an array of objects. Contrast is closely related to emphasis; however, a total portion of the display might contrast with the background but only one aspect of the display (a single important picture, a title) should display emphasis. Contrast can be achieved in many ways. Perhaps the most common variety is the differentiation between the figure and the ground that is accomplished through the use of contrasting dark and light values, for example, a background of black with figures of white, yellow, light green, etc., superimposed upon it. Contrast is also created when colors that display different

CONTRAST

The important parts of a display can be made to stand out (contrast) mainly through the use of color, size, value, and shape.

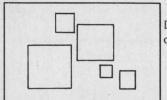

When light and dark values are used, contrast results.

An unusual shape will contrast.

Differences in size can create contrast.

When contrast is lacking, a visual lacks "punch."

FIGURE 5-11   Contrast

characteristics are used in combination. Complementary colors contrast most—reds and greens, oranges and blues, violets and yellows, etc.—and can be used for creating maximum visual stimulation and excitement. Shapes and forms also may differ radically and may be used to create a feeling of contrast. Textures, lines, and even the composition itself may be manipulated to cause one part of the design to stand out and become what is known as "figure" and another part to recede into the background and become what is referred to as "ground."

Rhythm. Rhythm in visual displays, as in music, derives from repetition with variety. Rhythm has to do with a certain regularity within a design that can be identified and anticipated—once again, as in a musical piece. However, if the theme is repeated over and over without some departure, even though very slight, from the standard, then monotony sets in.

In a painting, rhythm may be expressed by a row of trees, each one being much like all the others, but just different enough to break the monotony. Part of the difference in such a scene will come from the fact that linear perspective causes the trees to appear to diminish in size as they recede from the eye.

In a bulletin board, repeating the shape of the mounting cards while varying the sizes a bit will result in a kind of rhythm. The manner in which the cards are placed in relation to each other is also important.

FIGURE 5-12   Rhythm Results When an Element is Repeated
in Some Systematic Manner

You should not expect to find each and every one of the principles listed above in every visual design that you see. Nor should you worry too much about incorporating every one of them, or even the majority of them, in any given composition that you assemble. The final test for any kind of visual is whether or not it successfully accomplishes what it is supposed to. To totally ignore the principles of design, however, is to virtually insure that the efficacy of the message will be diminished, or even destroyed. In such an instance, ambiguity takes over and the information derived might well be false or irrelevant.

FURTHER DESIGN CONSIDERATIONS

A number of useful ideas are covered in the following discussion that were not included under the heading of "Principles." This is not because they could not be made to fit in one or another of the categories, but rather because their importance suggests that more emphasis be given to them than would be the case if they were merely mentioned as aspects of a larger category.

Eye Movement. The movement of the observer's eye tends to be directed through and about the picture by a number of devices. If the fact that the eye can be guided along certain pathways with considerable precision is observed, it is possible for the person designing a visual to get the maximum amount of mileage out of his efforts.

For example, it is a well-established fact that the gaze of the person looking at a visual will follow the direction in which the subjects in the picture seem to be looking. If a profile is being used and it is placed near one or the other side margins, the eyes should face away from the margin and into the picture.

Lines which are suggested by such features as fences, roads, streams, and pathways tend to lead the eye along their length. By carefully arranging such features, the artist and photographer can control the manner in which a person views their work. Abstract painters use pure line to direct eye movement, while the graphic designer uses a combination of representational and abstract elements to do this.

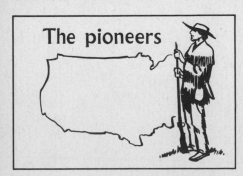

The viewer's eye is directed into the display through the orientation of the figure.

The viewer's eye is directed out of the picture in this example.

FIGURE 5-13   Eye Movement is Determined by the Design of the Visual

Mergers. A merger is formed when two disparate objects seem to come together in such a way as to suggest a physical joining. An example is the picture of the girl who appears to have a tree growing out of her head, or the basketball player who appears to have two arms on the same side of the body (one of which actually belongs to a second player who is obscured for the most part). Another kind of merger occurs when the subject seems to blend in with the background. This variety has important implications for the graphic designer as well as the photographer, while the other is most important where photography is concerned.

FIGURE 5-14   One Kind of Merger

Techniques for correcting the problem of mergers should be self-explanatory. Merely make certain that they do not appear in the viewfinder and they won't appear on the film. Select backgrounds that contrast with the subject or element that is to be superimposed over them.

Cropping. Though most appropriate in photography, cropping can be useful in many situations. A picture or photo is cropped by cutting away certain portions of the periphery in order to modify the composition. A picture that is cropped too drastically will appear crowded and cramped. A good job of cropping can eliminate much that is superfluous in a visual and emphasize that which is important. A particular case in point involved a picture of a craftsman who was working on a small, intricate object which he held in one hand. By cropping away everything but the expressive hands and then enlarging these, the visual was greatly enhanced. Most cropping jobs will not be this drastic, but many pictures could be improved considerably by a certain amount of cropping.

Simulated movement. Although actual movement is not possible in a still picture, that is, unless special techniques such as polarization are employed—simulated movement is quite practical and readily achieved. A sequence of still pictures can show apparent movement through the changes that occur in each succeeding picture. A blurred image in a photograph implies movement as does a blurred background (achieved through the technique of "panning"). Straight lines that are drawn behind a figure imply movement, as does a cloud of "dust." A picture of a person or an animal with the legs up off the ground suggests that movement is occurring. An airplane or bird that is in the air must be moving because it is difficult to remain suspended unless there is some forward movement in most instances.

FIGURE 5-15 Simulated Motion

The Division of Space. In constructing your design, whatever it happens to be, you will begin with the base material—paper, card, display surface, or plastic—and will arrange the other elements upon this. We should probably say "within this," since the base material constitutes the "space" part of the design and you will be working within the confines of an area that is delimited by its edges.

Each of the elements to be arranged within this space should be thought of as an abstract example of "pure" line or shape, that is, a caption is not considered from the standpoint of verbal content, but from the standpoint of configuration and perhaps value. The caption, then, becomes a rectangular gray shape in the most abstract sense. A picture becomes a larger, middle-value rectangle; a border line is thought of as a low-value line, and so on. With all representational aspects of the various elements done away with, it should be possible to consider the design from a strictly abstract point of view.

The elements can be arranged within the space in a formal sense, in which case, the two halves of the design will appear as mirror images of each other. Creating a formal arrangement is much less challenging than is creating an informal one. However, such an arrangement is also less desirable, as a rule.

When combining the elements in an informal manner, you should manipulate them in such a way that no two areas are exactly alike. That is to say, the space is bisected in such a manner that each resultant division is slightly, or markedly, different from every other division. A good way in which to manage this is to plan the layout on a reduced scale with lines and shapes of some kind. Pencils or markers will serve for the lines and blocks of construction paper of varying sizes are excellent for the shapes.

Create the "dummy" on a sheet of scratch paper—if things don't work out, this can be discarded and another start can be made. Eventually, a nice pattern will evolve that you feel comfortable with. You might then adhere the shapes with spray adhesive or rubber cement to preserve the design until you can translate it into the finished product. The pictures, blocks of lettering, backgrounds, lines, margins, etc., are then combined into the bulletin board, poster, or other composition using the dummy as the guide.

COLOR

Color characteristics. Colors are divided into two large categories which are labelled "chromatic" and "achromatic." Chromatic colors possess the qualities of hue, brightness or value, and intensity or saturation. Achromatic colors possess the qualities of brightness and intensity, but lack hue.

a. **Hue.** This term is used to describe a specific "color," that is, red, green, and so forth. Achromatic colors such as gray, black, and white lack this attribute.

b. **Value.** This is how light or how dark a color appears. The lightest color, or the one which possesses the highest value is, of course, white. Among chromatic colors, it would be yellow.

c. **Intensity or chroma.** Intensity is used to describe the strength of a color, i.e., a bright red or a dull red. The more foreign color that a particular pigment contains, the less intense will be the effect.

The color wheel. In order that we might better understand the relationship of one color to another, a diagram called the "color wheel" has been devised. The colors are so arranged around the circle that those highest in value (brightest) are located at the top and those lowest in value are at the bottom. The intervening colors form a scale that ranges from light to dark. The hues also possess a logical relationship as arranged on the wheel. An infinite number of hues might be created by continuing to mix the adjacent ones together, but, for our purpose, it should be adequate to consider just a few of the possibilities.

a. **The primary colors.** In pigments, these are red, yellow, and blue (or, to be more precise, magenta, yellow and cyan). These cannot be mixed from any combination of existing colors and must therefore form the minimal basis for any kind of colored graphic work.

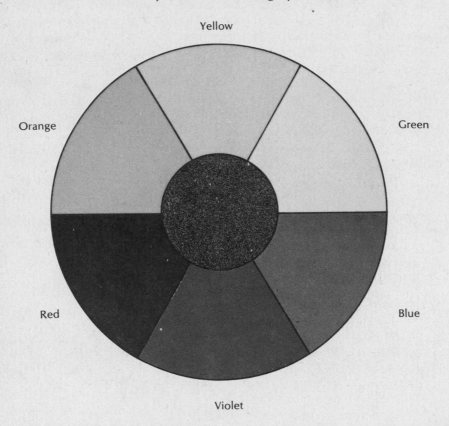

FIGURE 5-16   The Color Wheel

b. **The secondary colors.** These are composed of mixtures of the primaries. Red and yellow produce orange; blue and yellow give us green; and red and blue produce violet. Most basic paint sets include both the primary and the secondary pigments plus black, brown, and sometimes white.

c. **The intermediate colors.** When a secondary color is mixed with its neighboring primary, an intermediate results. An intermediate will carry the names of both of its parents, that is, yellow-green, blue-violet, and so on.

d. **The tertiary colors.** Such colors are formed by mixing any two of the secondaries together. Tertiary colors do not possess hue names as do the others. For example, a mixture of orange and violet produces a warm, brownish-looking color. The orange-violet mixture has been termed "russet" by some designers, but this uncommon label is virtually unknown by most individuals, who would probably refer to the new hue as "reddish-brown." Tertiaries are beautiful, soft colors that afford a welcome change-of-pace from the saturated primaries and secondaries that are so commonly used.

When all of the colors on the wheel are intermixed equally, an achromatic color results. This is often indicated by drawing a smaller circle in the center of the larger wheel and then filling this space with the grayish-looking color mixture.

Other mixtures. Not only can the chromatic colors be intermixed, but the achromatic ones also can be involved.

a. **Tints.** These are created by mixing white with a hue. For example, white and red produce a tint known as pink.

b. **Tone.** This term is sometimes used to describe the admixture of gray and a hue.

c. **Shade.** A shade is merely a hue mixed with black.

In addition to the feature of color relationship that is built into the wheel, the characteristic of "color temperature" is also involved. This has nothing to do with the measurement that is used in photography, but rather with the fact that some hues tend to look either warmer or cooler than some other hues. Red appears hot, while blue seems cool. The colors on one half of the wheel are the warm (advancing) ones, while those on the other half are the cool (receding) ones.

Complementary colors. Finally, it is possible to refer to the wheel when various kinds of color schemes are desired. Several colors that sit next to each other are referred to as "analogous colors." Those that are placed directly opposite across the wheel are "complementary colors." Many other kinds of schemes can be identified, but this brief explanation should suffice for our purposes. If you will refer to the diagram of the color wheel, you will note that the pairs of complements consist of a warm and a cool color. Red and green make a pair as do orange and blue and violet and yellow. If additional colors had been added, the rule still would apply; so red-orange and blue-green would be complementary as would yellow-green and red-violet.

A practical application for the complementary color scheme involves the mounting of pictures among other things. If you desire the greatest possible color contrast, mount your picture on a color that is as close to a direct complement as you can find. If the picture is a summer scene that is predominantly green, select a red card upon which to mount it. Remember, if you do not want contrast, use one of the other approaches described.

Another application is to be found in the area of graphics. When designing a poster or a bulletin board, for example, the same principle can be applied—a yellow caption on a dark purple ground will jump right out at you.

In the mixing of pigments, the complementary pairs also play an important role. If complements are mixed in equal proportions, an achromatic, grayish color will result. Adding just a small quantity of one complement to another will tend to gray the dominant hue. If you are using a red which is too bright for your taste, mix a small quantity of green with it to tone it down. A bit of orange will kill a garish blue, a touch of violet will make the yellow more somber.

Selecting backgrounds. The use of the complementary color approach was mentioned as a practical way in which to select a background for a picture. Also mentioned was the fact that such an approach will result in a contrasty combination that might not be suitable in some instances. Another technique that leads to a much more harmonious result involves the use of a color that is not dominant in the picture. In using this approach, you should determine the dominant color of the visual, then discard this as a possibility for the mounting board. Now search for a color that exists in a recessive way in the visual and match the board to this. You will be pleased and surprised at the beautiful, harmonious combinations that result from this approach.

Of course, if you prefer the analogous look, you may mount the picture on a board that replicates the dominant color. You most certainly will achieve a feeling of unity through this approach.

Finally, let us consider the role of the achromatic picture and card in the mounting process. An achromatic visual can be mounted on an achromatic (black, gray, or white) card if the goal is to maintain this effect. Or, a colored visual can be mounted on an achromatic card, thus making it unnecessary to worry about whether or not the hue combination looks right.

Still another possibility is to mount an achromatic picture on a colored card. In this instance, the selection of the mounting board might be made on the basis of "psychological color," that is, you might consider the kind of feeling that the visual projects and then find a color that is compatible with this. For example, a teacher had a powerful black-and-white picture of a grief-stricken girl who was holding her hands up to her face. The emphasis was on the long, expressive hands; the rest of the picture was played down. A blue card was selected because this color is often associated with sadness, although other cool colors might also have been used. The end result was a tastefully mounted visual that conveyed just the feeling that the teacher desired.

Psychological colors. Colors are such an important and integral part of everyone's life that an individual's personality can conceivably be determined to an extent on the basis of the colors that he or she prefers. A European psychologist, Dr. Max Luscher, believes so firmly that personality can be revealed through color that he has devised a test which is so highly regarded in many parts of the world that it is used by various organizations and even hospitals as a diagnostic and prescriptive aid. This test, the Luscher Color Test, has received considerable notice in this country also. Perhaps you have seen articles relating to it in the magazine section of certain newspapers as well as in a popular monthly magazine.

Whether or not you believe that personality and color preference are interrelated, there is some pretty firm evidence that different colors evoke different kinds of feelings from individuals. This is never more evident than when you enter a room for the first time. The general color effect will undoubtedly influence the way you feel. Other examples can be listed. However, you should be able to think of any number of situations in which you were involved personally where colors had a profound effect on how you felt.

Following are a few notes on color that might be of some help as you plan and produce your teaching visuals. It is difficult to make statements that are unequivocal due to the very personal nature of color, so think of this information as being suggestive, not prescriptive.

a. A color cannot be accurately judged unless its surrounding hues are also taken into account. Red looks more brilliant on a green background than it does on an orange one. For the purpose of this discussion, we will consider colors in conjunction with an achromatic (gray) background.

b. A specific color seems to have many connotations. However, the reds and yellows are typically described as being exciting and stimulating.

c. Red is an aggressive color. It also represents courage and agitation. It is considered as the "hottest" of the hues and advances or comes forward when viewed in conjunction with achromatic and cool colors.

d. Yellow is associated with vitality. However, it is also used to suggest envy and cowardice ("He's a yellow coward"). It is the lightest in value of the chromatic hues and contrasts maximally with black and the low-value hues. Signs are often painted on a yellow ground with a dark color for increased carrying power.

e. The blues and greens are the cool, receding colors. They convey an opposite effect from the reds and yellows.

f. Blue is the coolest of the colors and denotes peace, calm, serenity. It is also associated with sadness and grief.

g. Green is the color of spring and therefore of hope and renewal. It also symbolizes jealousy. Green and blue are universally considered the most pleasant colors.

h. Purple denotes two rather unrelated feelings, those of rank and authority on the one hand, and that of depression on the other. It is also considered in conjunction with rage at times.

i. Black is associated with darkness and death. It makes a good foil for the brighter colors. Black is considered as the "heaviest" of the colors.

j. White is purity; it is also stark. It is the lightest of the colors and is used with darker ones when contrast is desired.

RESEARCH AND VISUAL DESIGN

The section on the elements and principles of design dealt in a broad way with those kinds of things that can assist the teacher in composing an attractive and unified visual display. It does not necessarily follow, however, that a display that is pleasing to the eye will automatically teach the concepts that it is supposed to teach. It most definitely will project a feeling of harmony, unity, etc., if well designed, but we seldom desire that our students interact with teaching materials on this level only. There must be a certain content built into them and this will vary according to the objectives that have been established and the subject that is being emphasized.

Getting the students to identify content and learn about it is one thing; getting them to do this selectively and economically is another. Most students can readily determine what a presentation is about and they will generally pick up some information along the way. But all too frequently this information isn't accurate, organized, or adequate for the formation of useful concepts. How can we, as educators, take steps to insure that at least part of what we wish to have the students learn is learned? How can we decrease the ambiguity and ran-domness of a presentation while increasing its effectiveness and clarity?

A considerable amount of research has been conducted on such problems as those mentioned and the results have been rather widely published in various books and periodicals. Admittedly, many of the findings that have accrued cannot be applied directly to the design of teaching materials at the classroom level. However, others, such as those described below, are more readily utilized, and with a little imagination can be built into much of the material that is produced in the school.

Attracting and maintaining attention. Numerous strategies have been em-ployed in an effort to accomplish this. The suggestions listed below represent a cross-section of these.

a. To attract attention to a particular word, make it a bright color; to attract attention to a picture in an array of pictures, mount it on a contrasting colored board. To attract attention to important details of a map, make them darker in value (if the map is light) or lighter in value (if the map is dark), or color them if the map is in black and white.

   However, the addition of colors, etc., to embellish a visual in order to attract attention can be overdone. If the materials become too fancy, the students may pay more attention to the fancy decorations than to the things to which they should attend.

b. Visuals which tend to hold attention for the longest period of time are those which incorporate variety in their designs. This includes variety of line, shape, color, and value as well as variety in subject matter.

c. Novelty kinds of things tend to attract attention. It takes imagination to continually come up with ideas that are different, but the effort pays off in increased attention and interest. The tendency to pay attention to unusual types of phenomena seems to be closely related to the need of the individual to be aware of the environment in order to adequately function in that environment.

d. Another way that attention can be directed to a particular aspect of a visual is to use motion, such as pointing or drawing on a transparency or chart. Polarized material (see section on transparencies) can be used to build motion into a projected visual. Moving a piece of cardboard or paper down a transparency to reveal one feature at a time is an effective way to attract attention. The use of arrows, circles, lines, etc., that appear spontaneously on a motion picture frame is another way of varying the visual to add interest to it as well as to point out important features.

e. Designing teaching materials around subjects and people that are of current interest most certainly helps to attract and maintain attention. Using popular cartoon characters, politicians, movie stars and sports figures in your displays will increase the tendency for students to attend to them.

Learning about relationships. This is an important aspect of concept development.

a. It is possible to facilitate this generalizing or organizing skill by creating visuals that emphasize the similarities of a family of objects through the grouping of several diverse examples that all display the attributes that make them members of this group. For example, the first class lever can be illustrated on a chart or a transparency in several different formats such as a balance, a pair of tin snips, a pump handle, and a see-saw.

b. Size relationships in media materials such as pictures, slides, transparencies and other two-dimensional visuals are often misleading to the student. It is possible to build size cues into a visual that will serve the same function as the actual cues would serve in the real world. For example, if a dinosaur is being pictured, it would assist the student greatly if a man were pictured standing alongside of the giant lizard. The vast size of a modern jetliner might be emphasized by comparing it to a multi-storied building. A miniature camera can be compared to a box of matches; an insect to the size of a pin head, and so on.

c. The differing relationships of various items can be displayed graphically by using graphs of different kinds. A longer bar denotes a greater amount, while a shorter bar indicates a lesser amount.

Learning to discriminate. This is another important aspect of concept development. Identifying the attributes that are peculiar to a particular concept, discriminating between an example and a nonexample, and generalizing this knowledge to other instances constitutes concept development.

a. One of the ways in which the ability to discriminate can be fostered is through the use of teaching materials that incorporate contrasting components in their designs. Related objects should be grouped together in logical arrangements (sets) when the initial encounters with the new concept are being arranged.

b. It is also good strategy to contrast items that are examples of a particular concept with those that are not examples. A case in point might involve a lesson on spiders in which a spider is displayed and the characteristic features pointed out (four pairs of legs, cephalothorax, etc.). The spider is contrasted with a typical insect, and the differences emphasized—a very good method of teaching identifications. An effective way of testing for the skill of discrimination is to present visuals that utilize ungrouped items that must be selectively grouped by the student.

c. Contrast in the sizes of the headings used on a printed page helps to group related materials together. Varying spaces on the page might accomplish a similar objective.

Simplicity and complexity. Determining the amount of information that should be built into a visual can be a real problem. Often, too much is included while at other times the amount is insufficient. The age of the child has much to do with how simple or complex a visual should be.

a. The preschool child is particularly prone to become preoccupied with a specific detail in a complex visual and to disregard the other features of the visual. However, the older child is able to synthesize the various parts of a complex picture into an integrated whole and to interpret it on the basis of a total entity. At about age twelve, the child is able not only to synthesize but also to make generalizations and to draw conclusions.

   Where preference studies are concerned, it appears that as children grow older, their preference for more complex pictures increases. Younger children (six-seven years old) prefer simple, flat, pictures of familiar objects. Older children (ten-eleven years old) prefer sketchy, complex pictures. This change in preference may be related to a change in the artistic skills of the child, that is, to the kinds of visuals that the child might produce.

   It seems that visuals to be used with young children should be kept simple and uncomplicated. Children avoid complex visuals until they reach a stage at which they are able to cope with them. Older children might benefit from more complete and detailed types of visuals, but these should not be overburdened with irrelevant embellishments.

b. Children in the lower elementary grades often lack the sophistication to successfully cope with the stylized artwork of many artists. Children prefer pictures that are accurate form and color representations of things encountered in the natural world. If pictures are too abstract or stylized, or are colored inaccurately, or with an eye for design rather than for fidelity to the actual object, the child may not comprehend them adequately and the degree and kind of learning that has resulted from this encounter with the visuals will be suspect.

c. Diagrammatic visuals should be supplemented with other kinds of materials in order that the child might develop a broad understanding of the concept being taught. The use of simplified diagrams alone might result in a type of learning that would not be generalizable to the real situation when it was encountered. Additionally, a simplified, diagrammatic approach might include only the relevant features of the task and none of the irrelevant so that the correspondence between the contrived and the real experiences would not be adequate.

d. The development of the student's perceptual abilities tends to evolve from the concrete to the abstract, from the simple to the complex. When creating teaching materials, it is good policy to take advantage of this principle. Media should be structured in such a manner that the concept is illustrated initially with a considerable economy of detail and embellishment. As the students' knowledge increases, they will be able to handle more complex and more varied representations; these should be provided for them.

e. Visuals should be simplified to the extent that they do not show complex information that is totally unrelated to the concept being taught. It is one thing to include trees, roads, lakes and streams in the visual being used to teach the concept of dams, but it is another thing to show the population concentrations on a map designed to teach about geological features.

Remember that cueing devices can be used in a complex visual to direct attention to those aspects that are deemed essential to the learning experience. Such things as arrows, circles, colors, etc., can be used as cueing devices.

Using cues. Cueing devices are used to attract attention to a characteristic of a visual that is considered important. The cueing device seldom adds additional information to the visual, but it does direct attention to important information that is already a part of the visual.

a. Some of the more commonly used cueing devices are the underlining of words, pointing, adding color to important words or areas, calling attention to something with verbal narration, arrows (these might flash on and off in a motion picture, or be static in a transparency), colored overlays on transparencies, etc.

b. In some cases, distortion might be an effective method of emphasizing important features in the visual. Distortion involves the accentuation of desired features through an increase in size, an alteration of color or value, or a modification of the basic structure of the object. Distortion may also involve a decrease in the size, etc., of those features deemed to be unimportant or of lesser importance. Exaggerating the identifying features of an object or person, if skillfully accomplished, can aid in directing attention to these features; this technique is related to caricature drawing.

Use the technique of caricature in the diagrammatic drawing of such things as the parts of flowers and animals, rockets, laboratory equipment, poster illustrations, and so on. It is well that the learning experience not end with the distorted visual, however. Actual objects, or good pictures, or other surrogates for the objects should be employed in order that the student might develop a complete and accurate concept of the object.

c. The transfer from the simulated (mediated) classroom situation to the real situation will be better if both relevant and irrelevant cues are incorporated in the visual design. The relevant cues should be identified through the use of cueing devices. For example, if dams are being discussed, it would help the student to better understand the concept of dam if the lakes, mountains, trees, roads, and other features associated with dams are displayed as part of the visual. The dam itself could be emphasized through use of a cueing device such as a colored arrow.

d. Cueing devices are not needed in every visual. They are required only when the visual is so complex or the irrelevant cues are so powerful that confusion exists on the part of the student as to precisely which aspect of the visual should be attended to.

Embellishments. Embellishments are decorations that are added to a visual for one of several reasons. Embellishments might be added to a design to make it more appealing, that is, to stimulate interest in it. They might also be used as cueing devices. If this is the case, they might take the form of arrows or other such functional embellishments. At times, they might take the form of memory aids (mnemonics).

a. When embellishments are added to a design as an afterthought, they tend to detract from the important features thus causing less learning to occur than would have been the case if they had been left off.

But embellishments such as cartoon figures that are related to the concept being taught might not only make the material more attractive, but might also result in increased learning through the addition of reinforcing information.

b. It is desirable to use color where the discrimination between colors is important in the learning of a concept. For example, in learning to identify minerals, color can be all important. In chemistry, the color of a flame can be extremely critical; in biology, colors of specimens often are important as aids in their identification.

c. The differentiation of materials in graphs and charts can be accomplished quite readily through use of contrasting colors. Color coding, as in anatomical studies, can be useful when various obscure items need to be emphasized and identified.

d. It seems that color in a picture renders it more "real" and more adequately duplicates the real world which is dynamic in nature. Younger children are assisted in the accurate "reading" of the picture through the addition of color to a much greater degree than are the older (upper elementary and above) children who tend to see motion in a picture whether or not it is colored.

e. A majority of children in the lower grades favor colored rather than uncolored visuals. Older children prefer uncolored pictures depicting "reality" over pictures of the same objects that are colored but not realistically rendered. In the case of older children, it seems that whether a picture is colored or uncolored is not as important as whether or not it conforms in shape, detail, and form to the real object.

f. As a final note on embellishments, it is interesting that all embellishments need not be visual in nature. The addition of music to a presentation might be construed as a kind of embellishment. Many kinds of sounds that are introduced to add a dimension of reality to a presentation might be identified properly as embellishments. Often these kinds of aural additions detract from the effectiveness of the message; however, well-chosen aural embellishments can often add considerably to the appeal of the message as well as to its ability to transmit information effectively.

BIBLIOGRAPHY

Clements, Ben and Rosenfeld, David. **Photographic Composition.** Englewood Cliffs, N.J.: Prentice-Hall, 1974.

Composition. Rochester, N.Y.: Eastman Kodak Company, 1975.

Dwyer, Francis M. "Adapting Visual Illustrations for Effective Learning." **Harvard Educational Review** 37 (Spring 1967): 250-263.

_____. "Visual Learning: A Critical Analysis." **Proceedings First National Conference of Visual Literacy.** Edited by Clarence M. Williams and John L. Debes. New York: Pitman, 1970.

Fabri, Ralph. **Color, A Complete Guide for Artists.** New York: Watson-Guptill Publications, 1967.

Fleming, Malcolm L. **Perceptual Principles for the Design of Instructional Materials.** Washington, D.C.: U.S. Department of Health, Education and Welfare, Office of Education, Bureau of Research, 1970.

French, J. E. "Children's Preferences for Pictures of Varied Complexity of Pictorial Pattern." **Elementary School Journal** 53 (1952):90-95.

Friend, David. **Composition.** New York: Watson-Guptill Publications, 1975.

Gerritsen, Frans. **Theory and Practice of Color.** New York: Van Nostrand-Reinhold Company, 1975.

Gibson, James J., ed. **Motion Picture Testing and Research.** Army Air Forces Aviation Psychology Program Research Reports, No. 7. Washington, D.C.: Government Printing Office, 1947.

Girard, Robert. **Color and Composition.** New York: Van Nostrand-Reinhold Company, 1974.

Gropper, George L. "Learning from Visuals: Some Behavioral Considerations." **AV Communication Review** 14, No. 1 (1966)37-39.

Ketcham, Howard. "The Last Word in Visual Communication." **Proceedings First National Conference of Visual Literacy.** Edited by Clarence M. Williams and John L. Debes. New York: Pitman, 1970.

Kuppers, Harold. **Color.** New York: Van Nostrand-Reinhold Co., 1972.

Lumsdaine, A. A., Sulzer, R. L. and Kopstein, F. F. "The Effect of Animation Cues and Repetition of Examples on Learning from an Instructional Film," **Student Response in Programmed Instruction.** Washington, D.C.: National Research Council, 1961.

Luscher, Max. **The Luscher Color Test.** Translated and edited by Ian Scott. New York: Pocket Books, 1971.

May, Mark A. **Enhancements and Simplifications of Motivational and Stimulus Variables in Audiovisual Instructional Materials.** Washington, D.C.: U.S. Department of Health, Education and Welfare, Office of Education, Government Printing Office, 1965.

_____, and Lumsdaine, A. A. **Learning from Films.** New Haven: Yale University Press, 1958.

Mellinger, B. E. **Children's Interest in Pictures.** New York: Bureau of Publications, no. 516, Teachers' College, Columbia University, 1932.

Plack, Jerelyn J. and Shick, Jacqueline. "The Effects of Color on Human Behavior." **Journal of the Association for the Study of Perception 9, no. 1 (1974):4-15.**

Rudisill, M. "Children's Preference for Color vs. Other Qualities in Illustrations." **Elementary School Journal** 52 (1951):444-51.

Travers, Robert M. W. "The Development of Dynamic and Static Interpretations of Pictures," **Proceedings First National Conference on Visual Literacy.** Edited by Clarence M. Williams and John L. Debes. New York: Pitman, 1970.

Travers, Robert M. W., ed. **Studies Related to the Design of Audiovisual Teaching Materials.** Washington, D.C.: U. S. Department of Health, Education and Welfare, Office of Education, Government Printing Office, 1966.

Vernon, M. D. **The Psychology of Perception.** Baltimore: Penguin Books, 1962.

Wills, F. H. **Layout.** New York: Sterling Publishing Co., Inc., 1966.

Wright, Andrew. **Designing for Visual Aids.** New York: Van Nostrand-Reinhold Co., 1970.

6

POSTERS, CHARTS, AND GRAPHS

INTRODUCTION

Graphic teaching materials such as posters, charts, and graphs are typically rendered on a large scale and exhibited as nonprojected visuals; however, at least in the case of charts and graphs, the slide or overhead transparency formats are frequently used. This chapter will emphasize the nonprojected approach although much of what is covered could easily be generalized to the creation of projected materials.

POSTERS

Posters are meant to function in the affective domain, that is, in the realm of the emotions. There was a time when posters were instrumental in causing people to do all manner of things that ranged from marching off to war to purchasing chewing gum. In recent years, the impact of television has had much to do with the diminished effectiveness of the poster. Most people require a medium that is more persuasive and perhaps more "real" than is the poster in order to change their habits and attitudes— this is where television comes in. In spite of this, there still exists a need and a place for such visuals. Billboards, advertisements of various kinds in newspapers and magazines, some of the still visuals used on television, cards placed in store windows and in front of movie theaters, etc., are often nothing more than variations on the standard poster theme.

In the classroom, presentations that stress affective or value-oriented concepts frequently include a mix of affective-oriented media of which posters are a part. Although concepts such as "honesty," "valor," "loyalty," and "democracy" cannot be learned through interactions with posters alone, this medium can serve to activate appropriate feelings if the concept has already been learned.

Posters are useful for effecting modest kinds of behavior change. For example, a poster can encourage the students to throw their refuse in the trash can—a rather useful kind of behavior. A poster over the sink in the art room can stress the importance of leaving a clean area; it might not always work, but it sometimes does.

Of course, there are those posters that merely inform and can't be said to do much else. This type of poster is close to being a sign and may, indeed, be nothing more than this. There is a thin line separating the various kinds of visuals and a point at which a merger seems to occur, but this should be of little concern to us since we are most interested in how well something works rather than with how we should classify it.

The important thing to consider is that students often "get the message" more adequately if it is presented in a light, cartoon poster form than they do if they are "preached to." So, posters do have a place, and they can be very important if some kind of message is to be communicated or if something is to be advertised. They may not be too useful in the development of concepts, in the teaching of principles, or in the solving of problems.

Creating a Poster

An effective poster evolves from the role that it is meant to play in the communication process—this is a perfect example of form following function.

As mentioned earlier, posters can be used to inform, but their major function is to persuade and exhort. The billboards along our highways are posters, although many do nothing more than clutter the landscape. They are there for the express purpose of convincing you that you need something. In other words, posters **sell,** at least they are supposed to. And they will sell if care is taken in their design and production and if other factors, such as audience, distribution and posting are carefully considered.

In order to be effective, posters must "carry" with a punch. They must be seen from a distance, and the impact should be immediate and unambiguous. Posters communicate at a glance. Because the audience is seldom a captive one (as with children in a classroom), this type of visual must stand on its own ability to draw the potential viewers' attention away from a multitude of other types of visual stimuli in the environment.

A poster should have "staying power." Long after the poster is no longer visible, it should remain as a vivid image in the viewer's mind. Novel kinds of material attract attention. Clever design and unusual, intriguing approaches to composition will cause people to be aware of the poster and to attend to it. Skillful rendering of letters and pictorial content will make the poster more attractive than the crudely produced variety. Lettering is particularly important in poster making. It is much better to have a poorly drawn picture and good lettering than the other way around. Because of the wide variety of drawing styles, people tend to accept illustrations that may be quite unprofessional in nature. Lettering, on the other hand, is fairly well standardized, and poor lettering is immediately associated by the viewer with ineptness or a lack of sincerity.

Excellent lettering is possible through the use of the Wrico lettering system. This technique results in letters of many sizes that are legible and clean looking. Cutout display letters are easy to make and are very attractive; they can be made in any color or combination of colors for special effects. The pre-made letter comes in paper, cardboard, plastic, and other materials. The range of sizes and types is virtually limitless but the cost for the larger styles may influence the poster maker to rely on some of the other types of available letters.

Simplicity is another attribute of the effective poster. Once again, the ephemeral quality of the poster requires that the message be imparted at a glance. A poster should say what it has to say in the simplest, most direct manner and then it should say no more. There should be no unnecessary embellishments.

Use one of the enlarging techniques to create the iconic portion of the poster. The picture should be rendered in some medium that is fairly permanent, bold, and contrasty. India ink is excellent; so is felt marker. For color, try sticky-backed color sheets, colored markers, poster paint, stencils and spray paint, or cut paper. The last two mediums deserve more than a brief mention because they lend themselves so well to the classroom production of multiple posters.

In both instances, the poster layout is made on paper such as butcher wrap. In the case of the stencil, a separate cutout is made for each of the major areas using the original layout as the pattern. These stencils are then registered over the base material and spray paint is used to color the exposed card or paper. Each succeeding stencil is registered and the colors added to build up to the finished product.

The colored poster paper approach is just the opposite of the stencil. In this case, the pieces are cut from the layout and are then positioned like patterns over the appropriate color of paper. They are then traced and the resulting figures are cut out. By assembling the different colored pieces and gluing them to the base material, the poster is assembled bit by bit. Either of these techniques will enable the students to produce any number of posters of the same kind through repeated use of the same basic patterns and templates.

Although it is conceivable that a poster might sometimes be constructed of pictorial material only, the typical approach involves the use of both words and pictures. As far as the verbal portion of the poster is concerned, it should be so constructed that all nonessential material is excluded. Make the most important word or words stand out from the rest of the verbal message (this is emphasis). Do this through the use of color, size, or contrast. Position your words so that they read logically from left to right; words that run up and down the page are contrary to the manner in which people normally read. Words that slant toward the corners will lead the eye out of the poster and part of the impact will be lost.

Make several rough sketches before beginning the actual work. Sometimes, ads in magazines will give ideas for compositions. Merely substitute your materials for those in the ad, but use the same basic structure. Arrange the elements of the design on the floor or table before attaching them permanently to the backing materials. This will prevent many of the design problems that are frequently encountered in visual construction. As you arrange the parts of the design, keep in mind the principles of composition: balance (does the poster seem to be in equilibrium?), contrast (do the various parts stand out?), emphasis (can you tell at a glance what the message is?), unity (does the poster "hold together"?).

For additional information on the use of lettering in a visual such as a poster and on the applied principles of composition, refer to the chapter on composition.

FIGURE 6-1   Examples of Student-Designed Posters

Silk Screen

Silk screen is a rather specialized technique that makes the production of multiple copies of a poster a relatively simple matter, that is, after the "make ready" has taken place.

A silk screen is a wooden frame (generally made of two x two lumber) which has a sheet of fabric such as organdy or silk tightly stretched across it. Frames, fabric, and other necessities can be purchased from virtually any art supply store. Ready-made printing frames with the fabric already in place are available, but these are more expensive than the ones that you stretch yourself. You should soak the fabric in water for a time prior to attaching it; shrinkage will cause it to set up like a drum, which is the way it should be.

Simple stencils can be cut from materials such as newsprint and butcher paper. These are taped to the underside of the screen (the side that will be in contact with the base material upon which the print is to be made). Silk screen ink is pulled over the stencil with a squeegee to cause the stencil to adhere to the screen. A considerable number of prints can be made from a single paper stencil. For a poster that requires more than a single color, additional stencils are made. These are registered with the other stencils so that the finished effect will be one in which each color fits in the proper place.

A better way in which to make stencils is to use one of the special films that are made for this purpose. Silk screen masters may be cut from film by hand or they may be made with a photographic process which utilizes a light-sensitive film (Ulano is a common brand name). To create the hand-cut master, a sheet of the film is placed over the original and the outlines of the areas to be printed are cut with a blade or sharp knife. When the film is removed from the areas that have been outlined with the blade, the resultant openings will represent the areas which will print on the paper or fabric when the screen is completed. The film is backed by a sheet of sturdy plastic, which is removed after the film has been adhered to the silk screen either by moistening it with water (water-based films) or lacquer (lacquer-based films). Any unwanted open areas may be covered with glue, paper, tape, or any other paint-block material. The ink or paint is placed on top of the silk screen and a squeegee is drawn across the screen. The ink or paint is forced through the openings of the stencil to create the silk screen print.

The photographic stencil is created from an original master which is drawn or photographed onto a transparent or translucent material such as acetate or tracing paper. This master is placed over the film and ultraviolet light is passed through it. The solid or opaque areas of the master block the light while the clear areas permit it to pass through and to impinge upon the surface of the light-sensitive silk screen film. The film is then processed in a developing bath and then rinsed in hot water. This removes the unwanted emulsion from the areas that will print and form the images. The moist, sticky film is adhered to the silk and is allowed to dry completely. The plastic backing sheet is removed from the stencil, the open areas around the stencil are blocked, and the ink is placed on the screen. The print is made by drawing the squeegee over the screen, thus forcing the ink through the stencil and causing it to deposit on the surface of the paper or card. The prints are then placed on racks or tables to dry and the process is complete except for cleaning up—a very important last step.

CHARTS

Charts differ from posters in several important ways. Basically, however, a chart is calculated to impart information while a poster is meant to affect attitudes. The chart is relegated to the cognitive domain while the poster holds forth in the affective domain. Charts as well as posters present an abstracted rendition of reality—neither one attempts to "show it as it is," so to speak. In creating either of these visuals, the teacher must select only those aspects of the total concept to be presented that are considered to be essential to the projection of the idea.

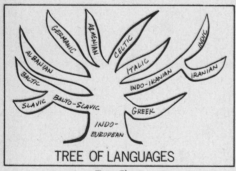

Tree Chart

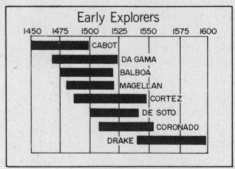

Time Line Chart

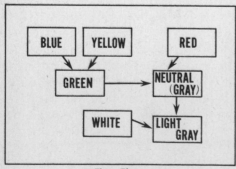

Flow Chart

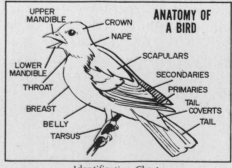

Identification Chart

FIGURE 6-2   Types of Charts

There are several basic kinds of charts. Perhaps the ones most commonly encountered in the schools are the tree chart, the flow chart, the time line chart (used principally in history), and the process chart. Some charts merely identify and label the parts of an object or an organism. A typical example of this type of chart is to be found in the biology department of the school and may consist of a large illustration of a fish, for example, with the various parts identified.

Generally, a chart is most effective when it contains but one idea or concept. The chart should be large enough that the total target group can observe it without undue straining. Obviously, if the target group is small, the chart can be smaller, but for use in the typical classroom, a chart must be at least 22" x 28" (standard size of railroad board) or larger. Make the lines bold and be sure that colors, when used, tend to reinforce and clarify the idea. Don't use colors if they accomplish nothing more than an aesthetic confusion of the concept. Letters and captions must be large and bold—the Gothic letter is good for use on charts and graphs.

Flip Charts

A flip chart is nothing more than a group of pictures (or charts, figures, etc.) that are secured at the top so that they may be flipped back like the pages in a book as the concept unfolds. Usually, the pages are sequential, and almost without exception, the pages in a flip chart are related to some particular single idea or concept.

Flip charts have the advantage of being compact and transportable; the amount and sequence of information is controlled by the manner in which they are constructed. Additionally, they are like a filmstrip in that they never fall "out of sequence." It isn't necessary that a display area be provided for the flip chart. Merely stand it against a chair or place it on an easel and you are ready for your presentation. Also, students enjoy flip charts because they introduce an element of anticipation due to the "revelation" technique that is inherent in their use.

On the other hand, there may be some virtue in displaying a total sequence at one time, as is the case with the bulletin board display. Flip charts are rather limited in the size of group that they can serve and are better suited to small groups than to large ones. Finally, unless used by individuals in a self-instructional manner, flip charts are rigid in their pacing and lack the accessibility of most other nonprojected materials.

Just about any kind of flat material can be used for the pages in a flip chart, but the favorites have been butcher paper, poster blanks (railroad board), illustration board, and cloth (generally muslin).

The method of creating a typical flip chart is as follows:

1. Obviously, you must have an idea. Your idea should either lend itself to a sequential kind of exposition or it should be a pictorial representation of objects that cannot be displayed for some reason. An example of a sequential exposition would be the sequence involved in the taxidermy of a bird; an example of pictorial representation would be the illustration of the water birds of your state.

2. Now, create a flip chart in miniature (i.e., use cards or sheets of paper to outline the sequence that the chart will follow).
3. Using one of the enlarging techniques (squared or graph enlargement, pantograph enlargement, or projected enlargement), transfer your drawing to the larger material. An alternate method involves the use of ready-made visuals such as charts and posters that can be acquired from different companies or purchased from art shops or book stores. These may be mounted on Chartex dry mounting cloth or they may be wet mounted.
4. Often a cover will help to make your flip chart a more cogent visual device. You may want to create a clever one that will help to introduce the material.
5. Hinge the separate sheets together in one of the following ways: For light-weight materials such as butcher paper, it is necessary only to staple the sheets together. Another method involves the use of two wooden slats, one on either side of the flip chart. These slats are attached together with screws or small stove bolts. Another method that works

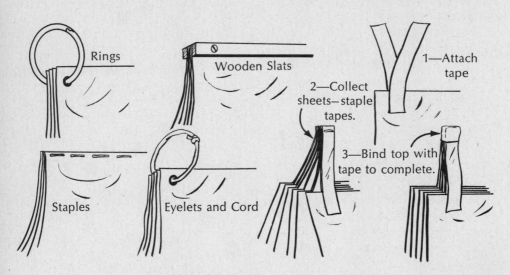

FIGURE 6-3   Hinges for Flip Charts

well for the cloth mounted visuals utilizes large looseleaf rings and holes punched through the mounting cloth. For heavier materials such as poster board, it is best to use Mystik tape for the hinges. The tape is cut into strips about six inches in length and a piece of it is adhered to the front as well as to the back on each of the top corners of the cardboard. The tape should be adhered so that five inches of it extend above the edge of the board. The adhesive side of the tape on the front should be adhered to the adhesive side of the tape on the back. Once every page has had the tape adhered to it, it is then a matter of collecting the pages together and stapling the ends of the tape securely together. The stapled tapes can then be finished with an additional piece of tape wrapped around them. The result of using the tape as mentioned is a flip chart that is hinged in such a way that the pages cannot bind as they are folded back. In all cases, the last page of the flip chart should be a piece of heavy cardboard. This will support the chart regardless of the kind of device that is available for display (often there will be nothing more than the back of a chair).

GRAPHS

Graphs are used to display relationships in a visual fashion. These relationships may be difficult to grasp when verbally presented and the graph is calculated to make the concept of relationships more concise. Almost any numerical comparisons can be reduced to a graphic form of one type or another. Generally, amounts are also combined with time to create an even more meaningful type of visual device. Some common varieties of graphs are described below. They do not represent every subtle modification that graphs might display, but for the purposes of the typical classroom, they are quite adequate.

Line graphs. Line graphs are constructed on two axes, one of which represents time and the other which represents amount. The time axis generally runs horizontally across the bottom of the graph while the amount axis runs vertically up the left side of the graph. Typically, these lines form a grid as they intersect and time-amounts are plotted by placing dots in the appropriate place on the grid. These dots are then connected with lines and the result is a line graph. The single line graph is easier to read than is the multiple line graph which often necessitates the use of lines of differing character (such as solid, broken, dotted) or of differing colors. The line graph is a typical example of the two-scale graph.

Bar graphs. Bar graphs are normally one dimensional in nature, that is, they involve only amount, not time. The bars are lined up horizontally and are used to represent different products, countries, etc. The horizontal direction of the bar is used to indicate amounts. Normally, each bar of the graph shows 100 percent of the amount of the product being measured; however, some bars are subdivided into segments and the resultant graph often is difficult to interpret. An example of a bar graph might be one that compared the naval tonnage of several dominant naval powers at a given point in time (say 1918 or 1941). Each of the bars would represent the total tonnage for a specific country, and the total graph would represent that tonnage for a given year only.

Column graphs. Column graphs are much like line graphs. They typically involve two dimensions or scales as do line graphs, and they are charted in much the same manner, that is, through the utilization of grid intersections. Column graphs are useful when a small number of points are to be plotted; line graphs are best when a large number of closely spaced points are to be used.

Pictographs. The pictograph is popular with casual readers who would prefer not to take time to interpret more complex types of graphs. The pictograph utilizes pictorial symbols which stand for amounts of certain things. A typical example of the pictograph is the one that shows silhouettes of school children that illustrate school population growth. A single figure of a child might stand for 1,000 children; if ten such figures are shown in a line, it follows that the school population for that particular district or for that year was ten times 1,000, or 10,000 children. One of the problems inherent with this type of chart is that we end up cutting children into halves, fourths, etc. In other words, if each child represents 1,000 and the actual population is less than this (say 700), we have no device that will accurately portray this number of school children. Often the exact amount is included along with the symbols so that the graph might be more accurately interpreted.

Some suggestions for making pictographs that are understandable are as follows: Use symbols that can be understood by the target group. Use simple symbols and construct the graph so that it, too, is simple. For the most accurate interpretation of the graph, include accurate figures along with the pictures.

Circle or pie graphs. The circle graph is good for comparing the parts of a whole. The circle graph is represented by a circle in which the 360° of the typical circle have been converted into the 100 percent of the typical graph. The total amount of the item being considered corresponds to the 100 percent of the

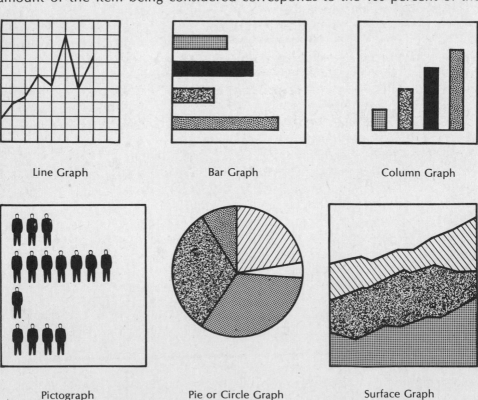

Line Graph   Bar Graph   Column Graph

Pictograph   Pie or Circle Graph   Surface Graph

FIGURE 6-4 Types of Graphs

total graph area. The total amount is broken down into its component amounts and these are graphically displayed on the circle graph by breaking the total space into equivalent percentages. A typical example of the use of the circle graph would be distribution of the tax dollar. Research has discovered that school children can comprehend the circle graph more readily than they can any other type of graph when parts of the whole are being compared. Adding the precise amounts to the parts of the graph aids the viewer in accurately interpreting what the graph is communicating.

Surface graphs. This graph is similar to the line graph. As a matter of fact, the first step in creating a surface graph, after the points have been plotted, is to draw a line connecting them, that is, a line graph. A surface graph, however, has a solid base and in this respect differs from the line graph.

BIBLIOGRAPHY

Biegeleisen, J. I. **Design and Print Your Own Posters.** New York: Watson-Guptill Pubcations, 1976.

Brown, James E., Lewis, Richard B., and Harcleroad, Fred F. **AV Instruction: Media and Methods.** New York: McGraw-Hill Book Co., 1969.

de Lemos, John. **Planning and Producing Posters.** Worcester, Mass.: Davis Publications, 1954.

Department of Defense. **Graphic Presentation.** Alexandria, Va.: Defense Supply Agency, n.d.

Fox, Martin, and Rose M. DeNeve. **The Print Casebooks, 1st Annual Edition, The Best in Posters.** New York: Watson-Guptill Publications, 1975.

Margolin, Victor. **American Poster Renaissance.** New York: Watson-Guptill Publications, 1975.

Zahn, Bert. **Screen Process Methods of Reproduction.** New York: Drake Publishers, Ltd., 1956.

7

COPYING AND DUPLICATING PROCESSES

INTRODUCTION

The term **copying process** usually is applied when one or a few facsimiles are produced directly from the original material. The term **duplicating process** is appropriate when numerous copies are produced in rapid succession from a master of some kind.

The copying processes that will be covered in this chapter include the electrostatic process, the photocopy process, and the thermal transfer process (thermal copy). The duplicating processes include the spirit duplicator process, the stencil process (mimeograph), and the planographic (offset) process. Duplicated materials—"handouts," if you will—are among the most commonly used of all classroom teaching materials. They are simple to create, require no exotic equipment for either their production or their utilization, and they are inexpensive.

Frequently, it is desirable to duplicate an original—such as a typed or printed page, a worksheet, a standard form, etc.—in order that each member of a class or other group might have a copy. The most important advantage of duplicated handouts is that such materials may be taken away from the group session by the individual for study at some later time, also, the handout is dispensible.

Teachers have many choices in the manner in which original teaching materials are duplicated. Often the choices are dictated by what is immediately available in the school; however, they may elect to go outside of the school for certain specialized types of duplication. School work rooms, media centers, and offices almost always will provide a spirit duplication facility. Mimeograph equipment also is found in a number of schools, especially at the secondary level. Certain types of heat transfer machines will produce paper copies in limited numbers, while some schools also provide photocopy capabilities as well as offset services.

Although handouts containing pictorial (iconic) matter are often encountered in the primary grades, the most common type of duplicated handout is the one that is predominantly verbal (digital) in nature. Verbal materials, unless used in conjunction with iconic and actual materials, or unless used to give directions for activities, are not overly useful in the development of concrete concepts.

Verbal handouts can impart all kinds of information rather efficiently, and they can be useful when principles are being developed or when certain problem-solving activities are being stressed.

If simple, labelled illustrations are added to the handouts, they can be used as "maps" in conjunction with the real object. An example of this technique can be found in the science class, where students use labelled diagrams as aids in identifying the parts of frogs or flowers.

Generalizing and grouping skills can be developed through use of handouts. For example, a wide array of shapes might be illustrated on a sheet. The students are instructed to identify all of the shapes that represent obtuse triangles, or perhaps parallelograms, or some other geometric form.

When the children are struggling with the concept of time, a duplicated sheet containing drawings of clock faces minus the hands might be helpful. Given different times, the students are asked to draw the hands of the clock faces to indicate the correct time.

Maps, flow charts, diagrams, color charts, and many other kind of drawings can be incorporated into the design of the duplicated handout to make it a versatile and helpful instructional tool.

If one or two copies of an original are desired, the photocopy process, if available, is suitable. If a limited number is needed, perhaps a half-dozen or so, then the thermal copy process is a good choice. For high quality, small quantity needs, the electrostatic process is excellent. If copies are needed for a class of twenty-five to thirty people, the spirit duplicator probably should be used. And if copies are needed for very large groups—perhaps every student in a particular subject matter area, or the school patrons—the mimeograph or the offset processes would be best.

Thermal spirit masters will produce a maximum of fifty copies before becoming depleted, while the nonthermal units should double this. Handcut paper mimeograph stencils normally will be good for runs of up to 3,000 or 4,000 copies, the thermal units lose their usefulness at about 300 copies. Economy offset paper plates will produce from 500 to 1,000 copies and quality paper plates up to 2,000; foil offset plates will produce up to 8,000 and metal plates 15,000 or more. Your selection of copying or duplicating techniques will be determined by your needs as well as by the equipment and materials that are available to you.

ELECTROSTATIC PROCESS

This is a widely used well-known method of producing single or multiple paper copies and transparencies from almost any kind of original. It is based on the principle that a positively charged particle will attract a negatively charged one. A typical electrostatic copier (the Xerox) has a drum of selenium metal that is the heart of the machine. The electrical conductivity of selenium varies with the intensity of the light to which it is exposed.

To begin the duplicating cycle, the selenium drum is charged positively. Light reflected from the original is conducted to the drum through a series of mirrors where it in effect "washes away" the positive charge from all areas except for the reflected image areas which remain charged. The latent images (the areas that are positively charged) are covered with a negatively charged powder that is cascaded over the drum at this point in the process. The powder does not adhere to the non-image areas of the drum, for they have lost their positive charge through exposure to the light.

A sheet of paper is passed across the drum and the powder is transferred to its surface through the application of a stronger positive charge originating under the paper. The powder (toner) is now fused to the paper surface with heat and pressure to complete the process.

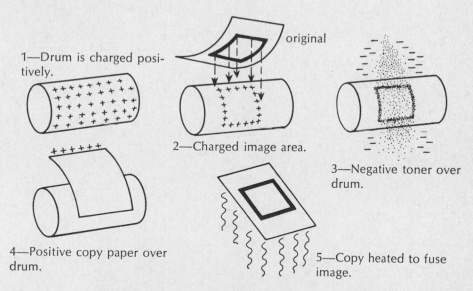

1—Drum is charged positively.

2—Charged image area.

3—Negative toner over drum.

4—Positive copy paper over drum.

5—Copy heated to fuse image.

FIGURE 7-1 The Electrostatic (Xerox) Process

It is also possible to create transparencies using the electrosatic process.

The operation of the typical electrostatic machine is very simple and requires merely that one read and follow the directions posted with the machine. Essentially, the steps are: (1) check the paper tray, or remote "load paper" signal to make sure that the tray is loaded; (2) locate the on-off button or switch and move it to the "on" position; (3) determine the number of copies that are needed and preset this on the machine for automatic multiple production (single copies may be produced by manually pressing the print button).

Some office machines may require that the pressure and temperature levers be adjusted differentially for different originals and for different output. This may require some experimentation for satisfactory results.

The coin operated duplicators that are to be found in libraries are most generally electrostatic copiers. For the most part, these are entirely preset and require that the operator have nothing more than a basic knowledge of which buttons to push and a pocketful of the proper coins.

Most bond papers will work in the Xerox-type machines; however, only films that are specifically manufactured for these machines should be used in the production of transparencies (see chapter on transparencies). It is possible to produce plates for use in the offset (planographic) press with this method. The sensitized units are imaged in the same manner as is paper in general.

PHOTOCOPY PROCESS

Also termed the **diffusion-transfer process,** the wet photocopy approach is gradually being replaced by other machines that do not require a liquid developer. In spite of various shortcomings, the quality of the paper and film copies continues to make this a popular technique with many individuals.

Photocopy machines vary considerably in appearance from brand to brand but they all function in much the same manner in spite of structural differences. The photocopy process is similar to the standard photographic process in that it employs light, a negative and a positive, and a developing solution. It differs from photography in the lack of a potential for enlarging and reducing, the lack of a film negative (photocopy uses paper), as well as in the lack of certain fixing steps in the developing sequence.

To create a photocopy from an original, a negative is first placed in contact with the original to be copied. Photocopy negatives, as has been stated, are paper. They have a treated and an untreated side (or emulsion and non-emulsion side). The emulsion side is typically yellowish in color and has a coated or glazed look. The original-negative sandwich is placed on the light stage with the negative **against** the light source. The light is now activated and the negative exposed. Note that the light passes through the negative, impinges upon the surface of the original, and then reflects back to the negative where a latent image is formed.

It may be necessary to process a test strip in order that the correct exposure setting might be determined. This can be done with strips of negative and positive materials rather than with the complete sheets.

After the negative has been properly exposed, place it against a sheet of sensitized positive photocopy paper. The yellow side of the negative must be against the treated side of the positive— the treated side may be identified by placing the notched corner in the upper right-hand position. If no notch is evident, the paper should have a trademark side, or a side that contains printing. This is not the treated side and should be placed away from the negative; the clear side is treated and should be positioned against the negative.

Separate the two sheets (negative and positive) as they are inserted into the developing unit of the machine. This is made simpler by the construction of the mouth of the machine which incorporates several lateral bars to break up the opening. The separation of the two sheets is essential in order that the developer may contact and activate the surfaces of both the negative and positive. When the sandwich of negative and positive is ejected from the machine, it will be tightly bonded together by the moisture from the developer bath. The image transfer will require several seconds for completion and then the sheets may be pulled apart. If the sheets are permitted to remain in contact for too long, it will be impossible to separate them and they will be useless. Often holding the sandwich up to a light source will permit the operator to ascertain the degree of transfer from the condition of the image. The areas that are not totally transferred will appear light, whereas the areas that are transferred will be dark.

The photocopy process is most successful when the room is in semi-darkness; any ambient light will most likely cause the sensitive negatives to be pre-exposed, resulting in a faint or partial image. Excellent transparencies also may be created with this process. (Note: For a detailed diagram of the photocopy process, see the section on transparency production.)

Incidentally, it is possible to create offset printing plates of good quality with this process.

THERMAL TRANSFER PROCESS

Originals that are to be used with this process must be rendered in a medium that retains heat (faxable). Mediums such as carbon typewriter ribbon, India ink, black pencil, and printer's ink will work satisfactorily. Electrostatic copies, such as those made with the Xerox and the images on photographic films (silver) also retain heat. Originals should be rendered in line for use with thermal papers and most types of film. However, a halftone film is available that makes it possible to create transparencies from the halftone original. You should be aware of the fact that colored images do not retain heat, so are not suitable for use with this process.

To use a belt-type machine such as the Thermofax, proceed as follows:

Adjust the machine to the proper setting before processing the paper. This setting will vary with the machine and electrical output. It may be necessary to run a test sheet in order to determine the best setting for a given machine; however, an average setting is close to the figure "2" on the dial. Place the original face up in the silk screen carrier (if you have one; otherwise, place a sheet of clean paper under the original), then position the reproducing paper over the original.

Most thermal papers will develop an image on both sides (that is, it will show on both sides due to the thin quality of the paper); however, one side will look darker than the other and this is the side to place in an "up" position on subsequent runs.

Insert the sandwich into the machine—the copy comes out almost immediately. Transparencies also may be created with this process. (Note: For a detailed diagram of the thermal process, see the section on transparency production.)

If a flat-stage thermal unit such as the Ditto Masterfax is used to reproduce originals the process would be as follows:

Adjust the exposure to the proper setting—this can be determined by exposing test strips until the ideal result is obtained. Next, position the reproduction paper on the stage of the unit with the sensitive side facing down. The original to be copied is next placed on top of the paper with the side to be copied facing down. The exposure is now made.

Masters for both the spirit duplicator and the mimeograph can be prepared on a thermal machine. Once again, the original must be capable of retaining heat in order to "burn" an image onto the units.

SPIRIT DUPLICATOR (HECTOGRAPH) PROCESS

The spirit duplicator system represents, in actuality, a crude form of planographic printing. It has nothing to do with the complex offset technique because it involves no water and grease combinations, no offset or blanket cylinder, and no addition of printing inks to the printing surface. Actually, the spirit duplicator process is a subtractive rather than an additive process. Every time that an impression is pulled, a small quantity of the carbon ink is removed from the master and is deposited on the paper. After a certain amount of carbon is removed, the impressions begin to lose their brilliance and finally become so light through ink depletion that the master must be discarded and a new one created.

There are several methods available for creating spirit duplicator masters. Perhaps the most widely used is the "handmade" process in which a person works directly upon the surface of the unit with a stylus, ballpoint pen, pencil, or typewriter.

Various colors are available in the master unit, but, the long run purple is the most popular. In addition to the standard purple, such colors as red, blue, green, and black also may be obtained. It is a simple task to create a master that contains several colors on a single surface. You should have a variety of the colored carbon sheets plus one of the white cover sheets that will ultimately become the printing surface. Decide beforehand what color combinations you desire, then begin to draw or type on the white sheet with the appropriate colored carbon beneath it. When all of the material to be represented in this color has been rendered on the master sheet, remove the carbon and replace it with the second color. Now draw or type the material to be reproduced in the second color. Proceed in this manner until all of the desired colors have been utilized. You will note that the colors are all deposited on a single printing master sheet which means that the multicolored copy emerges from the duplicator with one pass through the machine. Other types of multicolored printing, such as offset, require that the paper be passed through the press once for each color—a red, yellow, and blue picture would require three passes through the press to achieve the three-color effect.

appropriate colored carbon beneath it. When all of the material to be represented in this color has been rendered on the master sheet, remove the carbon and replace it with the second color. Now draw or type the material to be reproduced in the second color. Proceed in this manner until all of the desired colors have been utilized. You will note that the colors are all deposited on a single printing master sheet which means that the multicolored copy emerges from the duplicator with one pass through the machine. Other types of multicolored printing, such as offset, require that the paper be passed through the press once for each color—a red, yellow, and blue picture would require three passes through the press to achieve the three-color effect.

A second way of creating a spirit duplicator master is to use the thermal or heat transfer master unit. Different kinds of thermal units are available, but all of them work on the same basic principle.

To create a thermal master, it is essential that the original copy be faxable. The term **faxable** is used to describe drawing and printing mediums that contain carbon, graphite, silver salts as in photographs, or other heat-retaining substances. Also, the original must be rendered in line—continuous tone and halftone originals will not work.

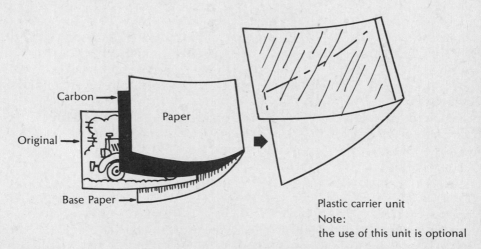

Carbon

Paper

Original

Base Paper

Plastic carrier unit
Note:
the use of this unit is optional

FIGURE 7-2 The Thermal Spirit Duplicator Master

To assemble the unit, merely position the original face up on the heavy backing sheet and let the carbon and the white top sheet fall into place over this. The resultant sandwich will consist of (bottom to top) the heavy backing sheet, the original (facing up), the carbon, and finally the white sheet that will become the reproducing master. You must make sure that the protective tissue between the carbon and the white top sheet has been removed before the sandwich is fed into the thermal machine.

Some people like to insert the assembled materials into a plastic carrier that consists of a sheet of thin plastic which is hinged to a second sheet of thin card stock (see illustration). This is a good way to control excess heat since the plastic acts as a shield over the unit.

If a machine such as the Ditto Masterfax is being used, the spirit master unit will be placed on the stage of the machine with the paper sheet against the glass. If a belt type machine, such as the Thermofax, is being used, this is reversed, and the paper faces up.

After exposure, remove the original from the unit and carefully peel the carbon backing away from the paper master sheet. This sheet is now ready to be placed in the spirit duplicator machine for the printing of multiple copies. Some spirit masters use plastic instead of paper for the printing surface. In this case, the plastic with the carbon impression on its surface is placed in the duplicator and serves as the master from which the paper copies are made. The plastic sheet may then be placed on the overhead projector and used as a transparency.

If any unwanted marks appear on the master unit, they may be removed or corrected before the unit is placed in the duplicator either by cutting them away with scissors or a razor blade or by covering them with cellophane tape.

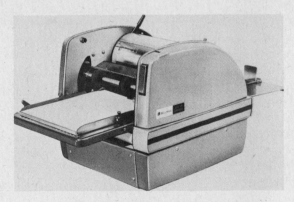

SPIRIT DUPLICATOR

Courtesy Bell & Howell Company

Operating the spirit duplicator. Spirit duplicators are driven electrically or are hand operated. Both work on the same principle, however. The master is placed on the drum and locked into position with the printing side facing up. Paper is loaded in the hopper and the tension is adjusted. The machine is then primed by working the fluid lever up and down in the "prime" position once or twice (some machines have a "prime" position and the lever is simply moved to this position prior to the start of a printing run). Place the lever in the "run" position, then adjust the tension lever to a light or a medium setting. Turn on the automatic duplicator or crank the manual to produce as many copies as you need. As the run progresses it may be necessary to compensate for the depletion of the carbon on the master by increasing the amount of fluid as well as the pressure. When the run is completed, or when the master is depleted, the machine is secured by removing the master and moving the pressure and fluid levers to the "off" position. The fluid tank on some machines is adjustable and should be moved to the "off" position to halt any unwanted flow of fluid into the machine.

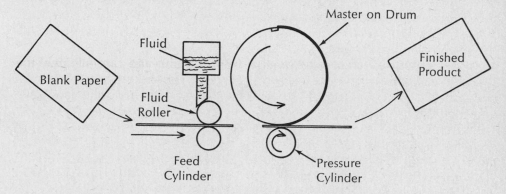

FIGURE 7-3   The Spirit Duplicator (Hectograph) Process

THE MIMEOGRAPH

This is a stencil process in which the areas that print, as in all stencils, are cut through the support material. The mimeograph press consists of a cylinder which has openings on one side for ink passage and a container inside of the cylinder for the ink. An impression roller is located below the cylinder; this roller exerts pressure against the paper as it passes through the press thus causing a satisfactory impression to be formed upon the paper. An ink pad is attached to the cylinder over the ink holes (the diaphragm); this pad controls the distribution of the ink through the openings that have been formed in the stencil. The stencil is attached over the ink pad prior to the start of the printing process.

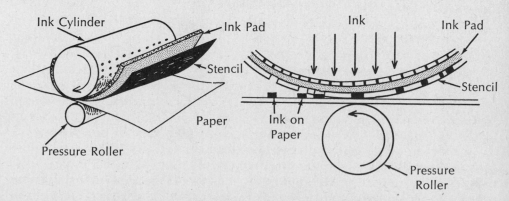

FIGURE 7-4   The Mimeograph (Stencil) Process

In order to create a stencil for use in the mimeograph press, a special fiber-based, wax-coated master is necessary. When the master is typed upon or when a stylus is used to create a line upon the master, the wax is forced aside and only the fibers remain. When the master is printed, the ink is able to pass through the minute openings between the fibers thus forming an image on the paper. Mistakes on the master may be corrected by using a fast-drying correcting fluid that is applied with a small brush. Thermal masters are also available which are simple to use and which give excellent results, especially with pictorial or graphic types of originals.

To image a thermal unit, you should place a faxable original on the paper backing sheet so that it faces toward you. The fibrous master sheet is laid over the original, and finally, the translucent receptor sheet is laid over this. The entire assemblage is then passed through a thermal machine at the standard paper setting (about 2 on most models). The heat that is concentrated in the outlines of the original causes the wax in the master sheet to melt and transfer to the receptor sheet. The end result is a stencil which is similar to the typical hand-cut or typewriter-cut variety. However, the number of copies that can be pulled from this master will be considerably less than with the nonthermal variety.

If your school or media center has an electronic scanning unit, you will be able to create beautiful stencils automatically from a suitable original. The original is placed on one of the two adjacent drums; the master unit is placed on the other one. As the drums spin, a scanning unit "reads" the image and translates it into perforations on the master, thus creating a stencil for use on the mimeograph machine.

To operate the mimeograph, stack the paper in the tray and adjust the tension. Be certain that you are using the proper type of paper for your machine; thin paper will not feed properly in the mimeograph, while smooth papers probably will not accept the ink as well as they should. Remove the cover from the ink pad and place the stencil in position, securing first one end and then the other with the locks provided for this purpose. Check the stencil for wrinkles; these should be removed before the press is activated to prevent the permanent wrinkling and folding of the stencil. Set the counter on 0 and turn on the machine; permit the drum to rotate several times before activating the paper feed. Check the sheets as they emerge from the press. If they seem to be satisfactory, continue the run until the counter indicates that you have the desired number of copies. If you should run out of ink (indicated by a faint image), stop the press and add ink according to the directions on the ink container or in the literature that came with the machine. Some machines use a fluid ink and must be primed through the rotation of the ink lever each time ink is added or if the pad becomes depleted of ink. Paste ink machines have no inking lever and require no priming.

When the machine is secured at the end of the run, remove the stencil, cover the pad with the protective cover sheet, and turn the cylinder so that the pad faces up. This will place the filler hole on the bottom. In this position, the ink cannot escape from the drum. However, if the machine is stored with the pad facing down, the ink will ooze out through the pad and the resultant mess can be very unpleasant to clean up.

THE PLANOGRAPHIC (OFFSET) PROCESS

Planographic printing is the process of printing from a flat surface or plane. The modern planographic process is directly related to the ancient art of lithography, which literally means "printing with stone." Essentially, the technique is based upon the well-known principle that water and oil repel one another. If an oily or greasy substance is placed on a suitable surface and the surface is then covered with water it will be seen that the water adheres only to those areas that are not grease-coated. If a second oily material (ink, in the case of planographic printing) is introduced to the wet surface, it in turn will be repelled, except in the areas where the grease is deposited, and there it will adhere.

If oily or greasy pencils, markers, inks, and tusches are used, drawings may be created upon a suitable flat surface which, in turn, may be inked and then printed onto paper. Modern lithography employs metal, plastic, or paper plates instead of stone for the flat surface and photography instead of grease crayons for marking upon the surface of the plate (although greasy and oily markers of various kinds still may be used along with typewriters equipped with special ribbons to make impressions on the surface of paper masters).

The planographic press most often encountered in the schools is the offset press. The offset press derives its name from the method of transferring the ink from the plate to a "blanket roller" and then to the paper rather than directly from the plate to the paper as in most other kinds of printing processes. This offset technique permits the printer to use rough and textured papers with good results because the soft roller will conform to the irregular surface whereas a metal plate would not.

An offset master "reads" correctly, that is, it is not backwards as is the case with other types of masters. Common sense will tell us that without the blanket cylinder, our reproduced or printed copies would come off the press backward, and, therefore, illegible.

Generally, a person must be an expert of sorts in order to use the offset press correctly. Although a teacher may easily create his own master, he will probably prefer to have trained individuals run the copies for him. Schools that offer this type of service will have a staff of "printers" (often students) who are familiar with the press and eager to please.

Creating an offset master for use in the school press is a simple matter if a few basic rules are followed:

1. Be certain that the master is the correct one for your machine. Also decide how many copies you wish to print and then select the appropriate master for the job. Some paper masters will produce no more than about 500 copies, while others are suitable for thousands of copies. Obviously, the short-run masters are less expensive than the long-run variety.

2. Utilize the guide marks on your master correctly in order that the impressions will be positioned on the printing paper where you want them to be.

3. Make certain, if you plan to type, that the typewriter you use is equipped with a reproducing ribbon. In order for a ribbon to function satis-

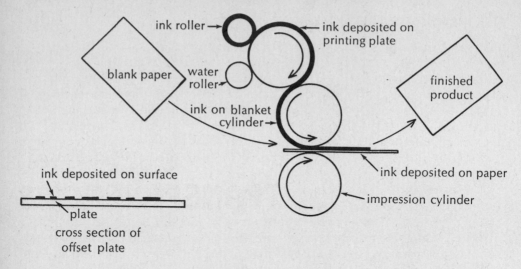

FIGURE 7-5 The Planographic (Offset) Process

factorily on the offset master, it must contain a greasy or oily substance (remember the principle of planographic printing!).

4. When making corrections, do not erase the image too vigorously because this may damage the surface of the plate and render it unsuitable for use.
5. If you plan to create drawings, diagrams, graphs, etc., on the master, render all preliminary work with a nonreproducing pencil. These lines will serve as the basis for the finished illustration which can be drawn with a reproducing pencil or reproducing ballpoint pen. It is also possible to obtain some interesting effects with drawing fluids and crayons made especially for this purpose. Incidentally, the drawing fluid also may be employed in pens of various kinds as well as in lettering devices such as the LeRoy.
6. Masters should be handled with care. Any unwanted oily deposits, such as fingerprints, will reproduce and will cause the finished copies to appear smudged and dirty.

BIBLIOGRAPHY

A. B. Dick Company. **Techniques of Mimeographing.** Chicago, Ill.: A. B. Dick Company, 1966.

———————— . **Techniques of Offset.** Chicago, Ill.: A.B. Dick Company, 1966.

Pett, Dennis W. **Copying and Duplicating Processes.** Bloomington, Ind.: Audio-Visual Center, Indiana University, n.d.

8

OVERHEAD TRANSPARENCIES

INTRODUCTION

Essentially, transparencies function in much the same way as do the mounted pictures, handouts, and so forth. The principal difference between these materials is in the manner of presentation. Transparencies require equipment for projection; other types of still pictures do not. Also, transparencies are enlarged dramatically when they are projected. This is a very real advantage, particularly when all of the members of the class are to share a common experience.

This technique is predominantly teacher-centered, that is, the individual at the projector is the one who controls the learning situation. Of course, a good lesson will include interactions of various kinds; nevertheless, the overhead projection strategy is seldom self-paced, and seldom student-centered. This does not mean that it cannot be very useful; however, its constraints should be recognized.

Transparencies can be strictly verbal in form, or they can be pictorial in the way in which they are rendered. However, the most common type of transparency includes both of these elements, that is, pictures and their descriptive captions. Transparencies that are predominantly verbal are much like other kinds of verbal materials as far as their function is concerned. They are useful mainly in testing situations, in imparting factual information, in problem-solving activities, and so on, but they are not generally effective in the teaching of concrete concepts.

There are situations in which the "verbal" type of transparency can be quite useful in the teaching of concepts, however. When syntax is being stressed, or numerical concepts are being taught, pictorial kinds of embellishments might be superfluous.

Well-designed pictorial types of transparencies—including those with accompanying labels—can be effective if the concept being taught has a visual referent, or if the pictorial material tends to clarify a concept that lacks such a referent.

For example, a transparency might be designed that displays a number of related objects, perhaps shapes. Within this array of shapes are distributed examples of representatives of the concept to be learned, say, parallelograms. An overlay might then be constructed in such a way that it pinpoints the parallelograms when it is placed in position over the basic transparency. This can be done by making colored spots on the overlay that align with the proper shapes thus identifying them as belonging together. Children practice discrimination skills as they attempt to identify the parallelograms in the initial array of shapes. The overlay tends to confirm their selections if they are correct. Handouts might be used that are equivalent to the transparency. The children might color those shapes that are representative of the concept under consideration. Additional exercises might be devised that would encourage the use of generalizing skills in addition to the discrimination skills described above.

TRANSPARENCY DESIGN

One of the primary differences between the printed page, as in a book, for example, and the transparency is that the page is available over an extended period of time to be reviewed, pondered, and examined more or less at the will of the user. The projected transparency, however, is up and gone unless steps, such as providing handouts, are taken to extend the interaction potential.

The following information should help you to design transparencies that are maximally effective during the time that they are on the screen. This information is arranged in several general categories for the sake of organization.

- **Simplicity/Complexity.** Make your transparencies no more complicated than is absolutely necessary. Avoid embellishments such as ornate borders, garish colors, unneeded details and textures, and, in general, elements that do not help to clarify the concept that is being stressed. It isn't necessary to include every bit of information relating to the concept, even if this were possible. Subsequent discussion, reading, and interaction with other media presentations can be used to "flesh out" concepts that are introduced with the transparency.
- **Line quality.** Lines should be clean and bold, but they need not be mechanical (i.e., of uniform width throughout). It is much better to vary the width of the line in logical ways than to have it consistent throughout its length. For example, in an area where a shadow might be located (as under the limb of a tree), the line can be made much heavier than in the area where the light would fall (top of the limb).
- **Data.** Information that is digital in form should be converted to a pictorial form of some kind when this seems feasible. Tables of information are

much more readily comprehended if they are restructured as simple charts or graphs.

Among the most popular types of graphs are the pictograph, the pie or circle graph and the bar graph. Avoid using compound graphs (graphs that have lesser divisions within the major divisions) because they are difficult to interpret.

- **Content.** If too much information is contained on one original, break it down into two, three, or even more transparencies rather than attempting to crowd everything onto a single one. If your visual contains too much information, your audience will eventually lose interest, or, if they maintain interest, proceed on ahead of you thus destroying the correlation between your explanation and the visual on the screen.

  You should avoid covering more than one specific idea on any given transparency. Once again, this can be avoided by creating additional transparencies for additional ideas.

- **Pacing.** A sliding cover on your visual will assist you in controlling the pacing of the presentation (see the plate on mounting transparencies near the end of this chapter for details on creating a "revelation" transparency). Overlays serve the same purpose and can be used when a concept is being built up step-by-step. The film that serves as the basis for the buildup of overlays is called a **basic.** It is attached permanently to the mount while the overlays are hinged and movable.

- **Graphics.** A nice change of pace results from using visuals that incorporate different colors, even though these might be in the form of background only. Black line transparencies on clear grounds are more or less traditional, but they are far from being the most attractive. Generally, dark backgrounds are not as effective as light ones due to the decreased factor of contrast. However, if figures that are light in value are being used then, dark grounds are desirable. Figures that are rendered in light values and colors on clear backgrounds are difficult to see and lose much as they are projected. Make it a habit to think in terms of contrast when creating projected visuals. You can dress up a line visual by adding color to the surface of the film with special markers, pens, and adhesive sheets. An area that needs emphasizing can be made to stand out through selectively adding colors—the bright, warm colors come forward (advancing colors) while the dark ones tend to move away from the viewer (receding colors).

- **Verbal materials.** Words should be structured so that they read in the normal fashion, from left to right. Don't get involved in fancy modifications of this basic rule. Words that are stacked on top of one another, or slant in some manner, are difficult to read and constitute poor design in transparencies.

Each line of words should be separated from the next line by a space that is large enough to accommodate an additional line of words (the letter height can be used as a standard measure). Group related words together in logical blocks; don't scatter them all over the surface area. Strive for unity in your designs; all parts should appear "tied together." It is better to use key words rather than full sentences. The presenter can always clarify the words with a verbal explanation.

A satisfactory way in which to check the visibility of your lettering is to project a sample onto the screen which is then viewed from the back of the room or the furthest viewing distance. Styles such as Gothic are the easiest to read; Roman styles are also satisfactory in most cases. Avoid fancy scripts and texts as a general rule; use novelty styles sparingly.

CHARACTERISTICS OF THE OVERHEAD TRANSPARENCY APPROACH

Motion picture projectors, slide projectors, filmstrip projectors, and overhead projectors are constructed in such a manner that the visual used with them must be transparent. If a page from a magazine is placed on the stage of the overhead projector, the screen will be blacked out since no light will be permitted to pass through the visual. If marks are made on a sheet of film and this film is placed on the stage of the projector, the marks will show on the screen since they block the light while the unmarked areas of the film permit the light to pass through unencumbered.

Transparent or translucent colors, such as dyes, inks, color film, etc., will project in color. Mediums such as tempera and oil paint will not project in color since they are opaque, and do not permit light to pass through them. By using combinations of transparent, translucent and opaque materials, the teacher can create visuals that lend themselves to projection techniques.

Probably the simplest way in which materials for projection can be created is to draw or mark directly onto the surface of sheets of film. The standard slide format is too small for the rendering of any but the very simplest of illustrations. Besides being very small, the super 8 and the 16 mm formats are oriented toward motion and do not lend themselves to direct rendering. This leaves us with the overhead projector format; its large 10" x 10" size is amenable to many treatments.

The large size of the overhead transparency also makes it versatile from the standpoint of utilization. The teacher can draw or write on the film as it is being projected. Overlays can be used to build concepts and "revelation" techniques can be used to stimulate interest.

The overhead projector is normally placed "up front" in the classroom. This permits the teacher to face the class at all times, thus enabling him or her to maintain eye contact, observe the students, and change the pace of the presentation as needed.

One of the interesting features of this approach is that the lights can be left on or the window blinds left undrawn without any substantial loss in the quality of the projected image. If a transition to another type of display, or to a live speaker is desired, the projector is switched off and the projected portion of the presentation is smoothly and effectively terminated. Conversely, moving from the live to the projected presentation is merely a matter of flipping a switch.

Overhead projectors are amazingly simple to operate. Students can be taught how to use them in a short period of time and can then make their own presentations to the class. The machine seldom malfunctions, so students feel confident when using it. Some machines are sufficiently compact and light-weight that even small children can move them about with ease. An important characteristic of overhead projectors is that they are relatively inexpensive to purchase thus making it feasible to equip virtually every classroom with its own machine.

Finally, the potential for in-house production of transparencies is very extensive; so extensive, in fact, that the layman is often confused when it comes to the identification and selection of the various types that are available.

Basically, transparencies can be classified into two groups, those that are hand-made and those that are produced by machines. There is an area in which the two techniques seem to fuse, so the divisions are not quite discrete, but this classification should be adequate.

Handmade transparencies include those made with clear acetate, treated acetate, frosted acetate, and those made by adhering printer's ink from a magazine page to a film (rubber cement lift, self-adhering film lift).

Machine-made transparencies include those made with the spirit duplicator (either handmade or thermal master), the thermal or heat transfer machine, the wet photocopy and the dry photocopy machines. The diazo process often is included under machine-made transparencies; however, it is possible to create the diazo transparency with nothing more than the sun and a bottle containing ammonia fumes. The heat lamination lift includes both handwork and the use of a machine (dry mount press).

HAND-MADE TRANSPARENCIES

Clear acetate. This is the simplest of all transparencies to create from the standpoint of the process involved. It requires no special films, no machines, no special tools, and no special sprays. All that is required is a piece of acetate, mylar, or some other kind of film and something with which to mark on its surface. Cleared x-ray film works fine for this process and is quite inexpensive. A check of your media center probably will reveal a large store of this material.

Although step-by-step instructions on how to create this type of visual are given in Figure 8-1, it might be a good idea to mention a few specific suggestions.

- Handle the plastic sheet only around the edges. Fingerprints on the surface will prevent almost all drawing materials from adhering to it.
- While working on the transparency, keep a clean sheet of paper under your hand at all times. This will prevent smudging and smearing of the image.
- Tape or clip the film securely to the original before you begin to trace; this will prevent the original and the drawing from falling out of register.
- Draw the outlines and details on one side of the film. Do all of the coloring on the opposite side. If you attempt to color over the ink or

1—Select a suitable original and a sheet of clear acetate.

2—Position clear acetate over original, clip or tape in position.

3—Trace on the acetate with one or more of the following materials:

brushes and pens with special acetate inks

fiber-tipped markers

felt markers

grease pencils

transparent film-marking pencils

self-adhering colored film

4—After outline drawing has been completed, the acetate is turned over, and colors are added to the back surface. Self-adhering colored film is pressed into position and trimmed to the proper shape as shown.

5—Grease pencil lines, film-marking pencil lines, typing, and other such nonpermanent images must be protected with a covering of plastic or cellophane.

6—Mount the finished transparency.

FIGURE 8-1 The Clear Acetate Transparency

marker outlines, you will probably smear them or rub them off. Perhaps the most satisfactory way in which to achieve smooth passages of color is to use the self-adhering or pressure-sensitive films that are available for this purpose.

- A protective cover sheet over the transparency will permit you to draw or mark on the surface during a presentation—never mark directly on the original transparency, always use a plastic cover of some kind.
- You can create large letters with a scriber and template; certain kinds of dry-transfer letters work well also. A good electric typewriter is adequate for smaller letters, but don't use lower case letters unless you must—the larger the type, the better.

Treated acetate. This type of material is excellent for the production of transparencies, but it is quite expensive. It consists of a sheet of clear film that is coated with an emulsion-like surface that is compatible with most marking and coloring materials. Treated acetate is used much as the regular clear film is used, that is, it is taped over an original and the original is traced onto the surface of the acetate. The principal difference between the two surfaces is in the kinds of marking devices that are compatible with the two. Just about anything will mark on the treated surface . . . not so for the other one.

Frosted or matte acetate. This material has an etched surface or "tooth" to which most mediums will adhere. Although this film appears gray or trans-luscent, when placed in contact with the original to be traced, it transmits the image quite clearly. Details for creating this type of transparency are covered in Figure 8-2. Many of the special considerations that apply to clear acetate (see above) also apply to this type of material. However, two rather distinct differences should be noted:

- All rendering should be done on the dull side of the film (an exception to this is the pressure-sensitive colored film, which should be applied to the back, or smooth side, of the transparency).
- Matte film must be sprayed with a clear spray such as Krylon in order to make it transparent. To achieve the desired effect, attach the plastic to a piece of cardboard by placing a pin in each of the corners. Shake the can, then with the tip held about six inches from the surface of the transparency move from side to side with a steady movement, overlapping the applications as you go. It may take two or three coatings to completely clear the film— these should be fairly heavy, but not so heavy that the fluid puddles or runs.

Lift transparencies. Teachers often find excellent colored pictures in magazines from which they would like to have transparencies made. Some have simply neglected to follow through with their plans and have forgotten about the transparencies believing that there is no satisfactory way to accomplish the transfer. Others have checked into the possibility of reproducing color on a large film format only to find that the cost for a photographically-prepared visual is prohibitive. Still others have discovered that colored transparencies can

1—Select a suitable original and a sheet of frosted acetate.

2—Position frosted acetate over original, clip or tape in position (rough or dull side up).

3—Trace on the acetate with one or more of the following materials:

plus any of the materials that can be used on clear acetate

pen or brush and ink in black and colors

liquid dyes and water colors

colored pencils soft black pencils

4—All details and colors are applied to the dull or frosted side with the exception of the adhesive-backed colored film—this is applied to the back side.

5—Spray the dull side of the acetate to clear it and to preserve the image. Use clear plastic spray for this.

6—Mount the finished transparency.

FIGURE 8-2 The Frosted Acetate Transparency

be made if special costly equipment is available. One such system involves the use of an electronic scanner which scans the original picture through a set of filters that effect a breakdown of the full color original into its three or four component colors. Each one of the printing plates (one for each color) that results from this is placed in the press, inked, and used to print one color onto the plastic as it passes through. After three or four passes, the successive layers of different colors have combined in such a way as to duplicate the original picture. This is an excellent system, but it is normally not available in the average school or media center. Additionally, such equipment is best used for the production of a large number of visuals rather than for the occasional one or two that might be needed by the teacher.

So, that leaves lifts—they are probably the most satisfactory way for most people to create a full-color overhead transparency from a full-color original.

Lifts are great fun to create and they cost next to nothing. The process might involve the use of plastic that is already sticky (self-adhering lamination film) or plastic that is coated with rubber cement to make it sticky. Certain kinds of sticky clear film can be purchased from variety stores for a modest expenditure. The heavy, self-adhering film is more expensive but may work a little better than the economy material. Rubber cement flowed onto the surface of untreated clear film is probably the most economical, but it requires a bit more skill to obtain a good lift with it.

Excellent lifts can also be made with heat-sensitive lamination film such as Seal-Lamin (see the chapter on picture preservation). However, this process requires the use of a dry-mount press. Because of this, the process has been listed and described in the section on machine-made transparencies.

A picture that is printed on a clay coated paper is essential for the creation of a successful lift transparency. To test for this feature you should dampen your finger and then rub it over a corner of the picture. If a white residue comes off on your finger, the paper is clay coated. The white residue is clay which has been dissolved by the action of the water.

To create a rubber cement lift, you must first etch the surface of the clear film so that it appears frosted (you might use the matte acetate, but it is more expensive than the clear variety). Mix the cement with an equal amount of rubber cement thinner or solvent so that it is of a consistency that permits it to run freely off of the brush. Apply the cement evenly to the etched side of the film and the face of the picture; the strokes on the film and picture should run at right angles to one another. In other words, if the strokes on the film are horizontal, then the strokes on the picture should be vertical; this approach results in a better bond between the two surfaces.

After the cement has dried completely, carefully sandwich the picture and film together. Smooth the sandwich down with the hands and then work down every square inch with a tool such as a comb, large spoon, roller, etc. After the adhering operation has been completed, check the back of the picture for any unwanted rubber cement which will render the paper impervious to water. Remove this cement, otherwise the paper will not release at these points.

It is now time to soak the sandwich in water to dissolve the clay. This releases the paper from the printer's ink which is (hopefully) attached to the acetate. A few drops of detergent in the water will permit it to penetrate a bit faster and will result in more rapid release of the paper from the film. After a short wait, a corner may be tested to see if the paper is ready for removal. Do not force the paper; if it fights back when you try to pull it away from the film, more soaking is needed.

After several minutes, the paper will release and may be disposed of. A thin coating of clay will remain on the acetate and must be removed through careful swabbing with a piece of moist cotton. Be cautious as you wash the film because the image on its surface is very delicate at this point.

When the transparency has dried completely, it must be sprayed to clear it and also to protect its surface. Refer to the matte acetate transparency process for specifics on this step. Obviously, the side to which the picture was adhered is the side that must be sprayed.

The self-adhering or pressure-sensitive film lift is created in much the same manner as the rubber cement variety; however, the film is already prepared and therefore requires no painting on of cement nor etching of plastic.

Release one edge of the backing sheet from the film; position the film over the picture (which should be facing you) and adhere the exposed portion to the picture surface. Now, as you carefully peel the backing sheet away, rub the film down with your fingers—this prevents the formation of bubbles. Proceed to bond the two surfaces together using the approach described in the rubber cement lift process. Or, if a machine such as the Transeal is available, a perfect bond can be obtained with a minimal amount of effort. These machines have adjustable rollers and often are powered by an electric motor. Hand-operated rollers such as those used by the custodian to wring mops also can be adapted to this function. Some media centers possess special laminators that not only contain the rolls of laminating film within them but also laminate both sides of a picture at the same time. Of course, if both sides of a picture are covered with film, the water cannot penetrate the paper to dissolve the clay. Therefore, transparency production cannot be successfully undertaken, or so it would seem. It is possible to split the picture apart by grasping the two sheets of laminating film and pulling them apart to split the picture down the middle. This process will be covered in detail in the section on heat sensitive lamination film lifts.

If machines are not available with which to adhere the film to the picture, find some hard object, such as the back of a comb, and start rubbing. When the bond seems adequate, place the sandwich in the water and proceed as with the rubber cement lift. After the paper has been removed, the film is treated just as the rubber cement lift—it is washed and permitted to dry. If commercial heavy duty self-adhering film is used, spraying will not be sufficient to fix the treated (sticky) surface; it must be covered with a second sheet of film in order that it might be made permanent and nonsticky. If the self-adhering film that can be purchased in rolls from variety stores is used, spraying with clear plastic spray will be sufficient to fix the surface and render it nonadhesive. This type of film is

1—Etch the surface of an acetate sheet with steel wool or a scouring pad.

scouring pad

wooden block

Note: The picture must be printed on clay-coated paper.

2—Apply thinned rubber cement to the picture and the acetate.

3—Adhere picture and acetate together—rub with comb or other hard object.

4—Place sandwich in water containing a small amount of detergent—soak for about 5 minutes average.

5—Carefully peel the paper away from the acetate. The printer's ink will adhere to the plastic.

6—Wash surface gently with wet cotton to remove residual clay.

7—Spray with clear plastic. Mount transparency to complete the process.

FIGURE 8-3 The Rubber Cement Lift Transparency

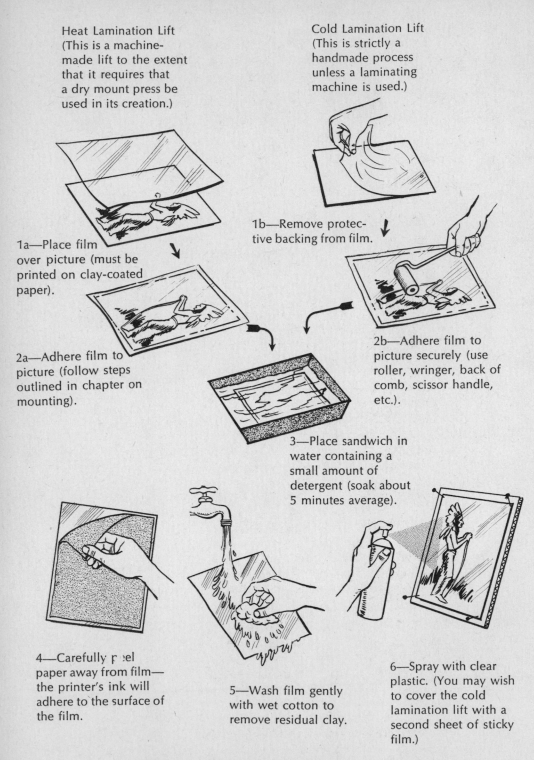

Heat Lamination Lift (This is a machine-made lift to the extent that it requires that a dry mount press be used in its creation.)

Cold Lamination Lift (This is strictly a handmade process unless a laminating machine is used.)

1a—Place film over picture (must be printed on clay-coated paper).

1b—Remove protective backing from film.

2a—Adhere film to picture (follow steps outlined in chapter on mounting).

2b—Adhere film to picture securely (use roller, wringer, back of comb, scissor handle, etc.).

3—Place sandwich in water containing a small amount of detergent (soak about 5 minutes average).

4—Carefully peel paper away from film—the printer's ink will adhere to the surface of the film.

5—Wash film gently with wet cotton to remove residual clay.

6—Spray with clear plastic. (You may wish to cover the cold lamination lift with a second sheet of sticky film.)

FIGURE 8-4 Two Types of Lift Transparencies

less expensive than the heavy duty kind that comes in sheets. It is also somewhat less effective for making lifts. Incidentally, the variety store type of film is normally used for lining drawers or covering walls and is not intended for use in transparency production.

Advantages of Handmade Transparencies

- Handmade transparencies require no special machines for their production.
- This type of transparency is generally quite inexpensive and often employs readily available materials such as cellophane, surplus film, and markers.
- When tracing an original, details may be left out or added, and changes may be easily made.
- Just about anybody can create a simple handmade transparency; it's as easy as tracing.

Disadvantages of Handmade Transparencies

- This type of visual can be quite time-consuming to create.
- Often the quality of the handmade transparency is not on a par with that of the machine-made transparency.
- Handmade transparencies are a "one-of-a-kind" item. There is no potential for reproducing the visual without going through the entire process all over again.
- Handmade transparencies are not the most permanent visuals ever invented. Unless handled with care or sprayed or otherwise protected, they are inclined to smear, crack, smudge, and/or peel.
- Complex handmade transparencies may require considerable skill to complete.

MACHINE-MADE TRANSPARENCIES

Spirit duplicator. Spirit duplicator transparencies may be produced from either the handmade master or the machine-made variety. Both of these techniques require that a machine be used in making the paper copies as well as the transparencies that accompany them; therefore, this process has been listed under machine-made transparencies regardless of how the master has been produced.

The chapter on duplicating processes covers the creation of both types of masters, therefore, it is suggested that you refer to that section for specific directions.

It is best to use a hand-operated duplicator for this process since this machine affords the operator a greater measure of control than does the electric machine; however, either will work.

After the master has been secured in position and several satisfactory paper copies have been produced, it is then a matter of placing the frosted acetate (dull side up) or clear acetate in the paper bin and feeding it through the machine. The resulting visual will have to be cleared if it is frosted; clear film transparencies require no additional treatment. Incidentally, some clear films are more satisfactory for this process than are others; one of the better kinds is cleared x-ray film.

As a final note, some thermal units utilize a thin sheet of plastic instead of paper for the reproducing sheet. When this type of unit is passed through the thermal machine, the carbon transfers onto the plastic and creates an image. The plastic film then becomes the duplicating master as well as the transparency. This process is illustrated, along with the more traditional varieties, in Figure 8-5.

Thermal or heat-transfer. The thermal process permits the spontaneous production of a transparency from most of the varieties of film that are used with it (the "Transparex" is an exception to this general rule). The principle upon which the thermal or heat transfer process works has to do with the retention of heat by the original and the consequent darkening of heat sensitive pigment on the transparency film (a general description of the clear film and tinted film units.) Because the processing of this type of transparency depends upon the capacity of the original to retain heat, it is essential that the original has images that are made up of carbon or a material that reacts to heat in a similar fashion (for example, the silver in a photographic print). Among the originals that are suitable as masters for the thermal process are black pencil drawings (heavy lines), materials printed with black printer's ink (cartoons from the newspaper), illustrations that have been drawn with pen and black ink, electrostatic (Xerox type) copies and black-line photographic prints. This tendency to retain heat and thus to affect the treated film used in the process has been called **faxability.** All originals that are to be used in the thermal process must be faxable; it also helps if they are rendered in line, that is, blacks and whites but no gray or intermediate tones (although many films are currently on the market that will reproduce halftones quite well).

To produce a thermal transparency, a sheet of thermal film is placed over a faxable original. The notch on the film must be placed in the upper righthand corner in order that the emulsion faces in the proper direction. A sheet of clean paper should be positioned under the original, or a silk screen carrier may be used to house the original-film sandwich if such a carrier is available. The paper and the carrier both serve to protect the machine from having an unwanted image burned onto the plastic belt that conducts the sandwich through the machine. The machine is then adjusted to the proper temperature for the film being used; generally, when using a copier such as the 3M "Secretary," the setting of "2" is satisfactory for clear and tinted film, while a cooler setting (higher number) will be needed for the Transparex film. As the film-original sandwich passes through the machine, an infrared lamp is activated which radiates heat through the film and onto the original. The heat is retained by the faxable image whose lines are replicated on the film by the concentrated heat in the image areas.

A second type of machine, such as the Ditto Masterfax, is constructed with a flat glass stage instead of a belt. This machine utilizes a movable infrared lamp

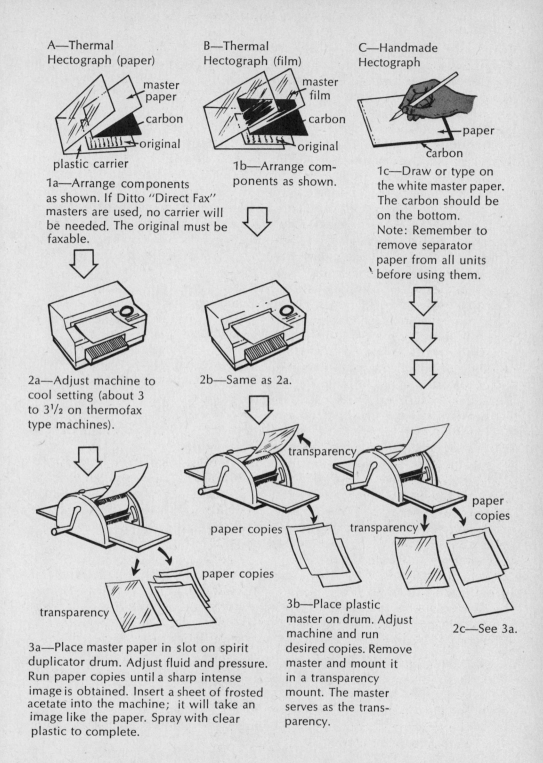

A—Thermal Hectograph (paper)

master paper
carbon
original
plastic carrier

1a—Arrange components as shown. If Ditto "Direct Fax" masters are used, no carrier will be needed. The original must be faxable.

2a—Adjust machine to cool setting (about 3 to 3½ on thermofax type machines).

3a—Place master paper in slot on spirit duplicator drum. Adjust fluid and pressure. Run paper copies until a sharp intense image is obtained. Insert a sheet of frosted acetate into the machine; it will take an image like the paper. Spray with clear plastic to complete.

transparency
paper copies

B—Thermal Hectograph (film)

master film
carbon
original

1b—Arrange components as shown.

2b—Same as 2a.

transparency
paper copies

3b—Place plastic master on drum. Adjust machine and run desired copies. Remove master and mount it in a transparency mount. The master serves as the transparency.

C—Handmade Hectograph

paper
carbon

1c—Draw or type on the white master paper. The carbon should be on the bottom. Note: Remember to remove separator paper from all units before using them.

transparency
paper copies

2c—See 3a.

FIGURE 8-5 Hectograph (Spirit Duplicator) Transparencies

that "scans" the materials on the stage, thereby creating an image. If this machine is used in the production of thermal transparencies, the placement of the "sandwich" is reversed from that for the belt type of machine, that is, the film is placed on the bottom with the sensitive side facing up and the original to be copied is placed face down on this.

The original thermal film was the white image variety. Images were formed through the fusing of the plastic in the areas of concentrated heat; a white or frosted outline was formed on the film which effectively blocked the light during projection thus resulting in a black line image on the screen. Today, a widely varied selection of thermal transparency films is available on the market.

Image tone films on clear or colored backgrounds are used when halftones (pictures from books or magazines that have shading effects) are to be used as masters. If the halftone original is to be reproduced as a colored image, a special film is available that will accomplish this in a number of different hues (each film contains but one color, however).

Then there is the ever popular standard film that produces a black image on a clear or colored background. When the clear ground is used, a variety of coloring mediums can be employed on the surface in much the same fashion as with the untreated films (see the section on handmade transparencies).

Both Arkwright and Bell and Howell produce a film of this variety that is made up of two sheets rather than the usual one sheet. The image activator is incorporated in a second, thin film which is stripped away after processing. Since the background of the resulting transparency contains no chemicals, it will not darken if excessive heat should accidentally build up during projection.

Negative or reverse image films are used to produce a transparency that represents a change of pace from the traditional positive image films. Those lines that are black on the original turn out to be clear on a black ground; also available are negative films that display a red, blue, yellow or green reversal image on the black ground. An interesting version of the negative-type film is the two-color negative. These films are available with a background of one color—say, red—and an image of a second color—perhaps yellow. Incidentally, color can be added to the clear line variety with markers or colored adhesive sheets for a multicolored effect.

The original white line variety (projects black) is still produced by several manufacturers as an economy-type film. These films are no longer limited to the clear background only—a wide selection of colored grounds is available.

Certain problems may be encountered when using the thermal process. Following is a short list of these, along with suggestions for correcting them.

- The transparency has a dark background that is not found in the original. This problem is the result of a machine setting that is too hot; turn the setting to a cooler temperature and try again.
- The lines in the transparency are broken and some of them are missing. The machine setting is not hot enough; turn it to a hotter temperature and run another film.

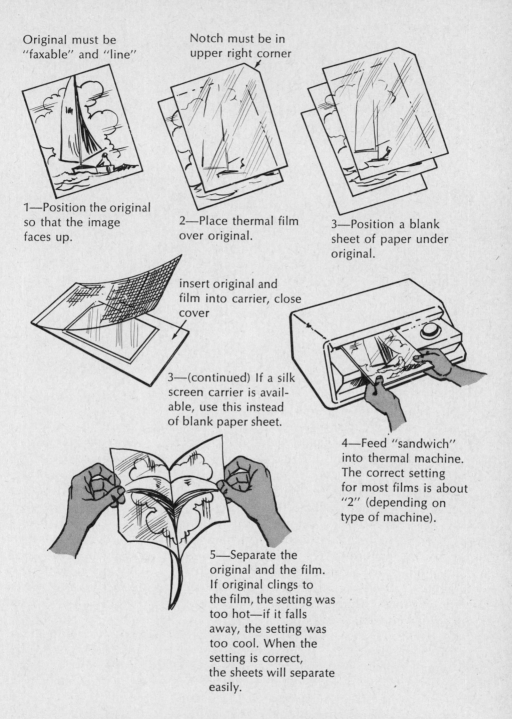

Original must be "faxable" and "line"

Notch must be in upper right corner

1—Position the original so that the image faces up.

2—Place thermal film over original.

3—Position a blank sheet of paper under original.

insert original and film into carrier, close cover

3—(continued) If a silk screen carrier is available, use this instead of blank paper sheet.

4—Feed "sandwich" into thermal machine. The correct setting for most films is about "2" (depending on type of machine).

5—Separate the original and the film. If original clings to the film, the setting was too hot—if it falls away, the setting was too cool. When the setting is correct, the sheets will separate easily.

FIGURE 8-6   The Thermal or Heat-Transfer Transparency

- Certain parts of the original do not register on the film at all. These areas probably are not faxable. Many kinds of black markers do not contain metallic ingredients and therefore will not "burn an image."
- The transparency turns out blotchy, with large areas of black and with details obscured and blended together. You probably tried to process a halftone original on the line film; this will not work. You will have to obtain another original or use image tone film.

One of the interesting and useful innovations of the thermal transfer process is the Transparex film. This material comes coated with a heavy emulsion of color. The color is sensitive to the heat produced by the thermal copier but it is not processed out by the heat as is the case with the other types of film described above. When the transparex sheet leaves the thermal machine, it appears very much the same as it did when it entered. However, the emulsion that was in contact with the lines on the original has been "fixed" by the heat that was concentrated in these areas and will remain intact through the developing process. The sensitized film is now placed on a hard surface and is bathed with water while being rubbed gently with a piece of cotton. The moisture will cause the unsensitized areas of color to wash away, leaving only the brilliant colored lines and shapes that replicate the lines and shapes on the original. The dull side of the film is the treated side and is placed in contact with the original. This is also the side that is swabbed with water in the developing step. The machine must be set on a cooler temperature for this film than for the clear or tinted varieties.

Lifts (machine-made). Heat-sensitive film can be used to prepare excellent picture-transfer "lift" transparencies. Two of the most commonly used films are the Seal-Lamin laminating film and the heat-sensitive film that is especially prepared for use with the thermal or heat transfer machine (a product of 3M Company).

The laminating film used in this process is the same material that is described in the chapter on picture mounting. It is applied in exactly the same manner for a lift as it is for a mounted lamination; however, here the similarity ends. After the film has been securely bonded in the dry mounting press to the surface of the picture to be "lifted," it is necessary to place the sandwich of picture and film into a container of water (which may contain a small quantity of detergent). From this point on, the process is exactly the same as the rubber cement lift process described in the section on handmade transparencies, even to spraying with clear plastic spray.

If you should desire to make lift transparencies from pictures that are printed on opposite sides of the same sheet you may use the "picture split" technique. Laminate both sides of the page, check for imperfections and place back in the press if necessary. Trim the edges to expose the paper on all four sides, then insert a razor blade or other sharp blade between the two sheets of lamination at one of the corners—this should separate the two sides just enough to enable you to grasp them between the thumb and forefinger. Carefully begin to pull on the two sheets of film. The pictures printed on the

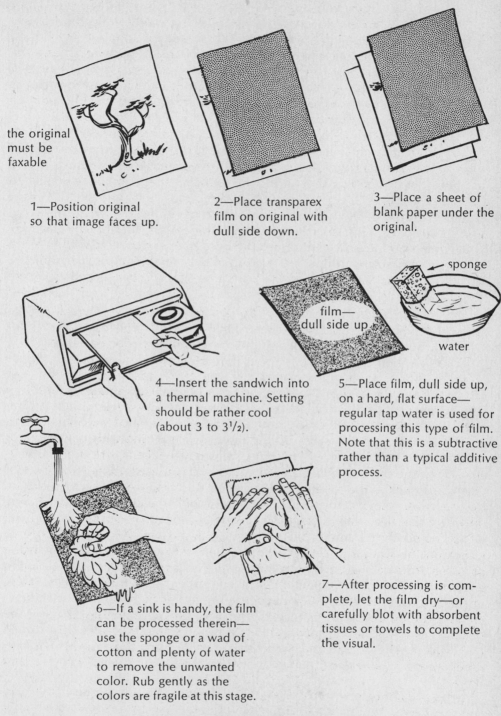

the original must be faxable

1—Position original so that image faces up.

2—Place transparex film on original with dull side down.

3—Place a sheet of blank paper under the original.

sponge

film— dull side up

water

4—Insert the sandwich into a thermal machine. Setting should be rather cool (about 3 to 3½).

5—Place film, dull side up, on a hard, flat surface— regular tap water is used for processing this type of film. Note that this is a subtractive rather than a typical additive process.

6—If a sink is handy, the film can be processed therein— use the sponge or a wad of cotton and plenty of water to remove the unwanted color. Rub gently as the colors are fragile at this stage.

7—After processing is complete, let the film dry—or carefully blot with absorbent tissues or towels to complete the visual.

FIGURE 8-7 The Transparex Transparency

155

two sides of the paper will adhere so tenaciously to the film that the paper actually will be split right down the middle resulting in two laminated pictures that may be soaked for transparencies, or dry mounted for nonprojected visuals.

To produce a thermal transfer lift, a thermal transfer machine instead of a dry mount press is used for the heat source. By using the special heat sensitive laminating film that is manufactured for this purpose and a picture which has been printed on clay-based paper, a secure bond can be obtained between the film and paper. The sandwich is now treated just like any other lift; that is, it is soaked, cleaned, dried, and sprayed to produce a transparency.

When creating this type of transparency, it is necessary to place the machine setting on the hottest temperature (slowest speed) for best results. Also, a special carrier or bonding sheet is provided which should always be employed when laminating.

Another type of laminating machine which can be used to create lifts is the variety that contains the laminating film on continuous rolls within the machine. As the original is introduced into the unit, both sides are covered with film and the correct pressure and heat are applied to the visual. The result is a picture which is laminated on both sides and may be used as it is, or split and mounted, or split and made into transparencies.

Photocopy. Two principal types of photocopy processes are employed for the production of transparencies: the wet photocopy (referred to as the diffusion transfer or reflex process) and the dry photocopy processes.

The wet photocopy transparency utilizes a negative, a positive, and a developing solution. The steps in creating this type of transparency are as follows: first, select an original that displays good contrast, that is, a range of values from very light to very dark in a halftone, or dark lines with light backgrounds for line copy. Place the negative—which must be handled under subdued light because of its sensitivity—on the stage of the photocopy machine with the yellow or sensitive side facing up. Next, position the original, face down, over the negative. Turn the dial to the correct setting (this will vary according to the type of machine as well as the speed of the negative) and activate the lights to expose the negative. Remove the negative, place it with the sensitive (yellow) side down on the clear film. Generally, the film is treated on both sides and will display no notches . . . either side will work with the negative. Separate the two sheets on the front end only and insert them into two separate slots in the mouth of the machine. Separating the sheets enables the developing solution to affect the surface of the film and negative in order that a transfer of the latent image can occur. The sheets are squeezed together by rollers within the machine and they will leave the machine securely bonded together. Observe the negative through the transparent film. As soon as all of the lines have turned dark, pull the sheets apart and discard the negative. Hang the positive up to dry; it will appear clouded and curled at first; however, as it dries it will clear and flatten.

The dry photocopy transparency, like the wet equivalent, uses a negative and a positive. The principal difference between the two processes is in the development step: the dry process utilizes heat as the agent for transferring the

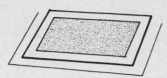

1—Place the negative on the exposure stage with the yellow side facing up.

2—Place the original to be copied over the negative with the image side down.

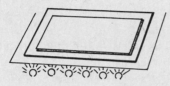

3—Turn the lights on, expose the negative.

4—Separate the negative and the original—set original aside.

5—Place the negative (yellow side down) on a sheet of photocopy film. (Paper copies can also be made.)

6—Insert the negative and film into the developer tank. Sheets must be separated as shown.

7—Permit the sandwich to curl naturally as it leaves the machine.

8—Separate the negative from the film after the transfer has occurred—hang film to dry.

FIGURE 8-8 The Wet Photocopy (Reflex) Process

latent image to the film while the wet process utilizes a developing solution for this.

The dry photocopy process is not so widely used as is the thermal transfer process or the wet photocopy process but it is quite popular in schools where the equipment is handy. Two basic machines are available for creating the dry photocopy transparency. The first variety consists of a light unit (which is placed on top of the original to be copied) and a separate developing unit in which the transfer of the image is effected (an example is the 3M Model 70). The second type of machine is self-contained and looks like a typical wet photocopy machine. It has a light stage on top of the machine upon which the negative sheet and original are placed for initial exposure. In the lower part is a slot which leads to the developing unit and into which the negative and the positive are inserted for processing (an example is the 3M Model 107).

To create a transparency, place a sheet of pink negative film in contact with the original. The negative has a notch in one corner that should be located in the upper right hand position when the sheet is placed over the original. This sandwich is positioned on the machine so that the light will pass **through** the negative during exposure. Next, turn the timer to the correct setting; this will be marked on the machine or it may be determined by experimentation.

During exposure, the pink negative sheet receives a latent image of the original that will later be transferred to the positive film. Now place the negative over the positive film, the notched corners on the two sheets matching. This sandwich is introduced into the developing unit where the transfer of the image to the positive film takes place. In the case of the separate processing unit, the quality of the image may be visually controlled—when the transfer seems acceptable, remove the sandwich from the unit and separate the sheets to complete the visual. Because the self-contained unit has no provision for the visual control of the transfer process, it is essential that an accurate exposure be made in order that a satisfactory transparency will result.

Diazo. The film for the diazo transparency is coated with an emulsion which contains benzine-derived compounds known as **diazonium salts** (thus **diazo**). These salts are not actually dyes in and of themselves, but in an alkaline environment, they react with certain coal tar derivatives called **couplers** to form almost any color in the spectrum.

One of the characteristics of a diazo is that it is very sensitive to ultraviolet light. When a diazo is subjected to an ultraviolet light source (the sun, a lamp, processing machine), it decomposes and becomes a phenol which cannot form a dye. When a diazo is exposed to an alkaline environment (ammonia), it "couples" and forms a bright color. If we control this decomposition-coupling characteristic of the diazo, we can create many kinds of beautiful visuals. The technique is to cover the area of the film that we wish to process with an opaque mask and then to expose the total film to ultraviolet light. The dye in the area of the opaque cover may then be coupled in ammonia and a transparency will result. This process is illustrated by the leaf print. To create a leaf print place a fresh sheet of diazo film on a portable surface such as a sheet of cardboard. The leaves are positioned on the film and a piece of glass is placed on the leaves to keep them from moving. The total sandwich is then carried out of doors and exposed to the sun for about two minutes; it is then carried back indoors and disassembled. When the film is exposed to ammonia fumes, the remaining diazo processes into a color, thus duplicating the shapes of the opaque leaves that were used as the "master."

Intermediate masters are created on translucent or transparent sheets with opaque materials such as india ink, soft pencils, tapes, cut paper, orange carbon paper (used with a typewriter), and paste-up letters. This master is placed face down over the sheet of diazo film; the film should be positioned so that the notched corner is in the upper right-hand position—this causes the emulsion side to face up. This sandwich is backed with a sheet of plain paper such as the separator sheet that comes packed between the films; the complete unit is then exposed to ultraviolet light. The light must pass through the intermediate master before reaching the film; the opaque areas on the master will protect the areas of diazo which will become the image in the processed transparency. The film is now placed in contact with strong ammonia fumes which will cause the image to develop. When the transparency seems satisfactory, it may be removed from the ammonia tank and projected.

Here are some suggestions that will be helpful in processing the diazo transparency:

- Make certain that the materials that are used for the creation of the intermediate master image are as opaque as possible. Any ultraviolet light that leaches through the master will burn out varying amounts of the diazo dye thus causing the image to appear light and weak.
- The paper upon which the master is created must transmit as much light as possible. High quality tracing paper is good for this purpose; shy away from economy brands of tracing paper, typing paper, etc., because these are not sufficiently translucent for good results.
- When typing on an intermediate master, use orange carbon paper on the back side of the master and the typewriter carbon on the front.
- It is possible to underexpose a film (it will have a "background" of color) or to overexpose a film (it will have a light image), but it is not possible to overdevelop the film. There is only so much color in any given film; once this is processed, no more color can result. Diazo is not like photography—photographic films that are overdeveloped turn dark; diazo does not.
- A diazo that appears light or faint after development might be overexposed, but it may also be underdeveloped. Check the ammonia; it may be depleted. If underdevelopment is the problem, simply add more ammonia and insert the film into the tank once more for an additional period of time.
- When rolling the diazo film prior to insertion into the developing tank, be certain that the emulsion side is on the inside of the rolled film. If it faces out, it will contact the inside surface of the tank thereby blocking the passage of the ammonia fumes past its surface and preventing the total processing of the dye. A film thus developed will display a charac-

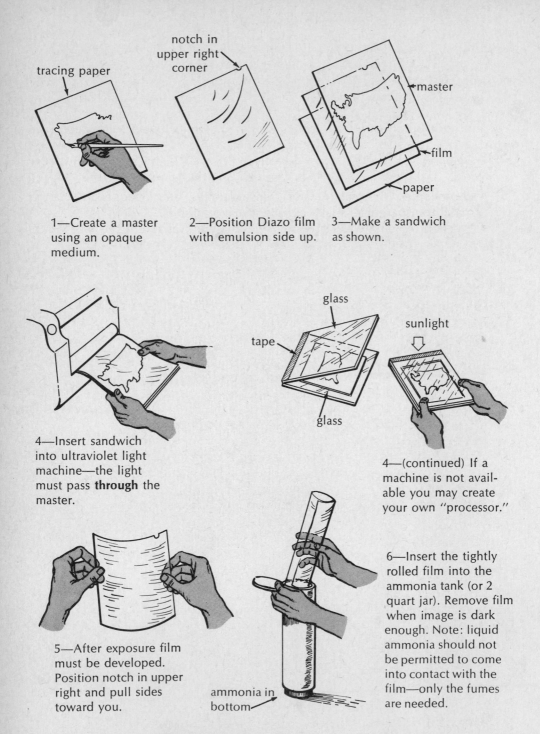

tracing paper

notch in upper right corner

master

film

paper

glass

tape

glass

sunlight

ammonia in bottom

1—Create a master using an opaque medium.

2—Position Diazo film with emulsion side up.

3—Make a sandwich as shown.

4—Insert sandwich into ultraviolet light machine—the light must pass **through** the master.

4—(continued) If a machine is not available you may create your own "processor."

5—After exposure film must be developed. Position notch in upper right and pull sides toward you.

6—Insert the tightly rolled film into the ammonia tank (or 2 quart jar). Remove film when image is dark enough. Note: liquid ammonia should not be permitted to come into contact with the film—only the fumes are needed.

FIGURE 8-9 The Diazo Transparency

teristic white or light line right down the middle of the transparency which gradually blends into the darker colors of the more completely developed dye along the edges of the film. To correct this problem, merely reroll the film in the proper manner and place it back in the tank for an additional period of time.

- Keep ammonia away from the packages of unexposed and undeveloped film. It will find its way into the packages and process the dyes.
- Diazo films left lying near windows will be exposed and will be useless for transparency production.
- Photocopies, thermal transfer transparencies, and opaque-line hand-made transparencies make excellent diazo masters.
- Excellent commercially prepared masters are available. Use these when you can, for they will save you the trouble of making your own.

Color key. The 3M Company has developed a color proofing system for photo engravers, printers, and others in the graphic arts field that lends itself to the production of overhead transparencies. The colored films used in this process are of thin, tough mylar which is coated with a sensitive emulsion. A solution is needed to process the film which may be either negative acting or positive acting. The negative acting is the most common since it enables printers and plate makers to make positive color separations from their photographic negatives.

The procedure for creating a transparency with this material is as follows: First, place a sheet of Color Key film coated side down (dull side) on a sheet of black backing paper. Next, place the photographic negative, or a diazo intermediate master, face down on the film. Expose this sandwich to ultraviolet light; the exposure must be a relatively long one (only experimentation will enable you to determine the correct exposure time). The film must now be placed on a nonabsorbing surface with the emulsion side facing up. The developing solution is poured over the film and is swabbed gently over the surface with a special pad or a wad of cotton; this will remove the areas of unwanted pigment. Finish the transparency by washing it under water and permitting it to dry.

By using several films of different colors in combination, it is possible to achieve virtually any effect that you might desire.

Electrostatic (Xerox type) transparencies. These films are available in variations that are designed for use in the different xerographic copier models. It is necessary, before acquiring the film, to determine which model of copier that you will be using and then to match the film type to the machine. The clear variety is the most common film in use; however, various colored films are also available. The film goes through the same process as the paper, being fed through the machine and out into the tray automatically. (For details on operating the electrostatic copier, see the chapter on duplication.)

Polarizing materials. Although this is not a discrete transparency process in and of itself, it enables the visual designer to add an exciting touch to most of the transparencies mentioned above. Various interesting effects such as motion of varying direction and speed can be achieved by using special polarized adhesive materials on your transparencies. A polarizing analyzer, which is a motorized disc, is placed under the head of the projector so that the light passing through the transparency also passes through the disc.

When the interaction between the moving polarized surface and the stationary one occurs, movement takes place in the transparency. Many kinds of movement can be employed; for example, tapes and sheets are available in linear motion very fast; linear motion fast, sharp; linear motion fast, smooth; linear motion medium; linear motion slow, and so forth. The material is quite expensive and should be used for special effects only.

If prepared polarizing adhesive sheets are not used, other unusual effects can be achieved by placing a material such as cellophane on a polarizing filter which is positioned on the stage of the projector—the results are simple color and motion effects. This latter approach is more of a "light show technique" than a method of embellishing learning materials.

Advantages of Machine-Made Transparencies

- Machine-made transparencies can be made rapidly.
- The quality of this type of transparency is generally better than that of handmade varieties.
- Multiple copies can be produced from a given intermediate master or other type of original.
- Machine-made transparencies require little skill for their production since no handwork is involved (an exception is the diazo process if original intermediates are produced).
- A great array of different kinds of transparency films is available which ranges from halftone-reproducing to brilliantly colored line films.

Disadvantages of Machine-Made Transparencies

- Expensive machines are needed.
- Some machine processed films are quite expensive.
- It is often difficult to modify originals to be copied (although excellent transparencies may be produced from pictures and printed materials that have been cut apart and reassembled into a new composition—this is called a "paste-up". See chapter on Illustration.)
- Some machines and processes are complex and require a background of training and familiarity before they can be successfully utilized.

SOME SUPPLEMENTARY TECHNIQUES FOR USING THE OVERHEAD PROJECTOR

Plastic instruments such as protractors, rulers, etc., may be placed on the stage of the overhead and projected.

Petri dishes may be filled about one-fourth full with food coloring or liquid watercolor or transparent colored inks. These dishes may be superimposed over

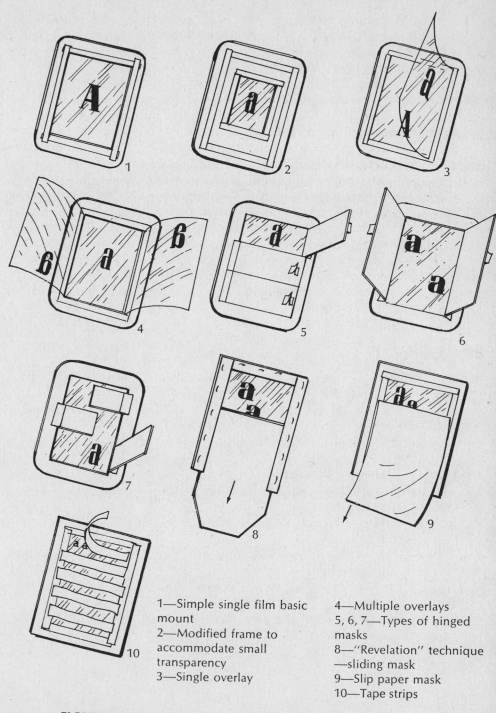

1—Simple single film basic mount
2—Modified frame to accommodate small transparency
3—Single overlay
4—Multiple overlays
5, 6, 7—Types of hinged masks
8—"Revelation" technique —sliding mask
9—Slip paper mask
10—Tape strips

FIGURE 8-10 Some Methods of Mounting Transparencies

one another to demonstrate the principles of color mixing. When a dish with yellow in it is placed over a dish containing blue, the result is green, and so on. It is also possible actually to mix the colors in an additional dish using a dropper to transport the colors to the mixing dish.

A piece of opaque paper placed over a transparency and gradually moved down the surface to expose one item or line at a time creates interest and anticipation on the part of the pupils (revelation technique).

Anything opaque may be placed on the stage of the projector for the creation of a silhouette image on the screen. Leaves, insects, and other natural objects project detailed silhouettes. Live insects may be permitted to scamper across the projector stage as a method of demonstrating insect locomotion.

Writing and marking on transparencies while projecting them is an effective way of directing attention to important aspects of a presentation.

With a bit of imagination, the teacher can adapt an endless variety of techniques to the overhead projector approach. Companies that produce transparency materials provide literature which describes unique applications— this is typically free, or quite inexpensive, and is commonly well-designed and colorful. You may want to check the section on materials and equipment sources toward the end of this book for the addresses of transparency manufacturers.

BIBLIOGRAPHY

Bathurst, Leonard H., Jr., and Klein, Bruce. **A Visual Communication System.** Dubuque, Iowa: Wm. C. Brown Book Co., 1966.

Brown, James W., Lewis, Richard B., and Harcleroad, Fred F. **AV Instruction-Technology Media and Methods.** 5th ed. New York: McGraw-Hill Book Co., 1977.

Coffman, Joe W. **Technology of the Diazotype Processes.** Holyoke, Mass.: Tecnifax Corporation, 1957.

A Guide to More Effective Meetings. St. Paul, Minn.: Visual Products Div., 3M Co., n.d.

A Guide to Overhead Projection and Transparency Making. Holyoke, Mass.: Education Division, Scott Paper Company, 1971.

Kemp, Jerrold E. **Planning and Producing Audiovisual Materials.** New York: Thomas Y. Crowell Co., Inc., 1975.

Minor, Ed, and Frye, Harvey R. **Techniques for Producing Visual Instructional Media.** New York: McGraw-Hill Book Co., Inc., 1970.

Schultz, Morton J. **The Teacher and Overhead Projection.** Englewood Cliffs, N.J.: Prentice-Hall, Inc. 1965.

Smith, Richard E. **The Overhead System: Production, Implementation, and Utilization.** Austin: University of Texas, n.d.

9

DISPLAY AND DEMONSTRATION BOARDS

INTRODUCTION

This chapter is devoted to such devices as the chalkboard, flannel or felt board, magnetic board, bulletin board, and hook and loop boards. Essentially, none of these display devices can be considered complete without its various attendant materials—felt board figures, chalkboard patterns, bulletin board pictures, and so forth. Consequently, attention will also be given to the creation of such materials.

All of the devices listed above require that several skills be employed in their construction. For example, a bulletin board may utilize still pictures that have been mounted, large handmade letters for the main heading, mechanical or dry transfer letters for the captions, and an enlargement for the central motif. Also important is the manner in which the total display is arranged. This involves a knowledge of composition. Obviously, this kind of teaching device is more complex than is a simple set of still pictures that is held up or passed around for the class to see. We are dealing with a "message" now rather than with a simple component of the message.

When properly utilized, display and demonstration boards can, in many cases, do a fairly good job of teaching a concept to the students. To a large extent their effectiveness depends on how skillfully they have been conceived and constructed as well as on how complex or how simple the concept that is being emphasized happens to be. Basic numerical concepts can be taught quite nicely with a felt board and the appropriate figures—and with active teacher-student interaction, of course. On the other hand, it would be difficult to teach the concept of cubes and prisms with a flat felt board. In this instance, three-dimensional constructions would be better for the initial experiences at least.

Bulletin boards can display sequential kinds of things in much the same manner that flip charts, a slide series, and overlay transparencies can. One of the interesting features of the flip chart and overlay, however, is the built-in capability for holding attention. A student's curiosity is aroused as he or she anticipates the turning of the page and the revelation of the content of the next page or overlay.

The chalkboard is always handy and available. If a teacher should suddenly have an inspiring idea that lends itself to visualization, he or she can pick up a piece of chalk and within seconds can illustrate the concept that is being taught. Pounce patterns, templates, and other tools for use on the chalkboard are of special value in making this device useful and practical.

The kind of display device that is selected for use depends on a number of considerations, foremost of which is the type of concept that is to be learned—that is, if the teaching of concepts is the principle reason for using this kind of display. Additionally, the student group that is involved will have an effect on selection. For example, if the group consists of primary children, the colorful, simple shapes that are used with the felt board make this device especially useful. Again, space availability is an important consideration that should precede the selection of a display strategy. If you lack sufficient space for the construction of a bulletin board, perhaps a peg board could be used.

Consider also the kinds of materials that are available. It will be futile to plan for the use of magnetic chalkboards if you are unable to acquire the materials and funds with which to construct them. Perhaps an alternative could be a homemade flannel board.

One of the major advantages of the display device is its self-paced character. Students are able to interact with the information being displayed at any time and for any length of time. Many traditional kinds of projected materials lack this self-paced feature and are, therefore, much less accessible to the student who desires a greater degree of interaction with the materials. As traditionally employed, the overhead projector transparency, 16 mm films, and slide-tape programs lack the desirable self-paced feature. Many slide programs (especially those that have the verbal portion built into the slide format), super 8 loops, and filmstrips incorporate self-pacing.

You should make every effort to involve your students in the creation of your teaching displays. Elicit student input when the initial design is being conceived. Encourage them to construct the letters that will be used for the "headlines" or the captions. Teach children to dry mount and to enlarge with the opaque projector, among other things. And permit them to have a hand in the construction of the actual display, even though some of the pictures and lines of letters might come out slightly lopsided or off-center. You will find that the strategy of involving your students in the conception and construction of your teaching materials will pay off handsomely in the increased interest that will be displayed in their content.

Students should also be encouraged to use the demonstration board whenever appropriate. Instead of submitting papers and themes, they might present the information to the class via such devices as the hook-and-loop board, chalkboard, or felt board.

THE CHALKBOARD

Chalkboards are to be found in practically every classroom in the nation and probably constitute the most widely used of all media with the exception of books. In the worlds of business and industry, this device is an indispensable tool for the development and communication of ideas.

Because of the availability and versatility of chalkboards, and because few individuals take full advantage of their potential, it seems appropriate that some coverage should be given to such considerations as the construction of boards and their attendant tools as well as to the care and maintenance of chalkboard surfaces.

Creating a Chalkboard

The base material should be some kind of sturdy, hard material to which paint will adhere readily. One of the more popular materials for this purpose is masonite; however, such surfaces as plywood, cardboard, and even the plaster wall of a room can be used. If the paint is applied to a metal surface, a magnetic board results (you will find a description of this type of device on page 000).

Cut the board to the desired size, sand the edges as well as the surface if it seems rough. Lengths of one-inch lumber can be glued around the edge of the back side of the board if additional support is desired. If the proper equipment is available, a grooved frame can be constructed into which the board is fitted. This approach results in a neat, professional looking product.

Next, cover the surface with a primer of some kind. This fills the pores and seals the surface so that subsequent coats of chalkboard paint will be smooth and permanent. Sand the primer coat lightly after it has dried. An additional coat might be necessary to produce the desired effect; this, too, should be sanded.

The paint, which is variously referred to as "chalkboard finish," "liquid slating," "chalkboard paint," and so on, should be thoroughly mixed before being applied. If spray paint is used, the can should be agitated according to instructions. Paint in pint and quart cans should be stirred until the heavy pigment is evenly distributed throughout the mixture. The **slating,** or heavy pigment, does not remain in suspension for very long but has a tendency to collect in the bottom of the can where it solidifies to a certain extent. You may have to pour the liquid contents into a second container in order to more easily break up the heavy pigment. The liquid can then be returned to the original can to be mixed with the slating to form a smooth paint.

Apply the paint as evenly as possible with a clean brush or a roller. In spite of every precaution, you will generally discover that the surface exhibits a slight texture after the paint has dried. A light sanding with fine sandpaper or steel wool should correct this problem. Normally, a primed surface will require a single coating of paint. However, second coats are recommended for a more substantial finish.

Your completed board should be primed by rubbing chalk into the surface either by using a stick of chalk which is held on its side or an eraser that is loaded with chalk dust. This preparation will make erasing easier and will prevent the formation of "ghosts" (images that remain after erasure).

Marking on the Chalkboard

Use only those chalks that are specifically designed for chalkboard use (art chalks and pastels leave permanent images). Although they appear less intense in color than the art varieties when examined in the hand, chalkboard chalks appear quite brilliant when applied to contrasting surfaces.

If you desire permanent lines on your board, these can be drawn with permanent markers. Lines (for lettering, music, etc.) that are drawn in water soluble markers can be removed with a damp sponge when desired. By soaking chalk in a solution of three parts water and one part sugar, it is possible to create a "permanent" medium that will not erase as will regular chalk. However, when removal is necessary, a damp cloth or sponge can be used for this purpose.

When lettering on the board, use a simple, single-stroke Gothic letter or an uncomplicated cursive style. An arbitrary height for lettering is about 3 inches, but this may be varied on the basis of the size of the room and also the size of the audience and their distance from the board.

Creating Tools for Use on the Chalkboard

Templates. These can be cut from cardboard, plywood, or masonite. Enlarge the design to the desired size using one of the processes which are described in the chapter on illustration. Cut the design out using sharp knives for cardboard, saber or coping saws for other materials. Sand the edges where appropriate. You may wish to attach a drawer pull or an empty thread spool to make the template easier to handle. A coat or two of paint makes a more attractive device, but this isn't really essential. By gluing a layer of styrofoam or foam rubber to the base of the template, a nice surface is formed that will prevent slippage as well as noise when the device is placed against the board.

To use a template, merely place it in the proper position and trace around the periphery with chalk. Add details as needed.

Pounce patterns. The pounce pattern is created when holes are punched around the basic lines of a picture or drawing. An eraser loaded with chalk dust is then "pounced" over the picture which is maintained against the chalkboard. The dust is transferred to the board through the perforations and a light dot pattern results. These tiny dots are then joined together by hand to create a replication of the original picture. Basically, the steps are as follows:

(a) If your picture is large enough, you will not need to reproduce it, but if it is smaller than you desire, you may use any of the techniques for enlarging described in the chapter on illustration to "blow it up" to the proper size. Do this on heavy paper such as oak tag or index stock.

(b) Place your drawing over a piece of cardboard box or other such material and punch a series of holes around the lines that you want transferred. Make holes with a probing needle, a pin, or a "pounce wheel" such as dressmakers use for tracing around patterns.

(c) If you desire a very substantial pattern, you may wish to shellac it. Or you may find that spraying it with plastic spray is easier.

(d) Place the pattern against the surface of the chalkboard and have a student hold it there (or you can tape it in position).

(e) Use a chalkboard eraser which is loaded with chalk dust to transfer the image. Merely "pounce" the eraser around the lines of perforations and the dust will penetrate to create a dotted image.

(f) Remove the pattern and connect the small dots . . . your drawing is now complete.

Incidentally, a simple way in which to place designs on the chalkboard is to use the projected approach. Any image that can be projected onto a screen may also be projected onto a chalkboard and traced. A 16 mm projector that has a still-frame feature may be used to accomplish this. Slide projectors, film strip projectors, and overhead projectors all may be used. The most common device, however, is the opaque projector, since it permits the utilization of the common opaque still picture for this purpose (see the chapter on illustration for instructions pertaining to this technique).

You may also wish to purchase or construct such devices as compasses, protractors, line-templates, multiple-chalk holders (used to draw several parallel lines simultaneously), and others.

Caring for the Chalkboard

Using the proper chalk is an important factor in the care of chalkboards. However, in spite of taking this precaution, deposits will build up in the tiny recesses on the surface. At this point, a good washing with clean water is recommended. If ghost images persist, it may be necessary to use a powdered household cleaner (not a solvent or liquid cleaner) to remove them. You should test the board surface by rubbing some of the cleaner over an obscure corner to determine whether or not the surface is sufficiently permanent to withstand such treatment. If none of the pigment is removed when the cleaner is wiped off with a damp cloth, you can safely proceed to clean the total surface. In extreme cases, it may be necessary to repaint the board. Where wall-mounted boards are involved, it is recommended that this be done by professionals.

Magnetic Chalkboards

The chalkboard in your classroom might also be a magnetic board since many of the newer ones are either painted with a magnetic paint or have a metal base to

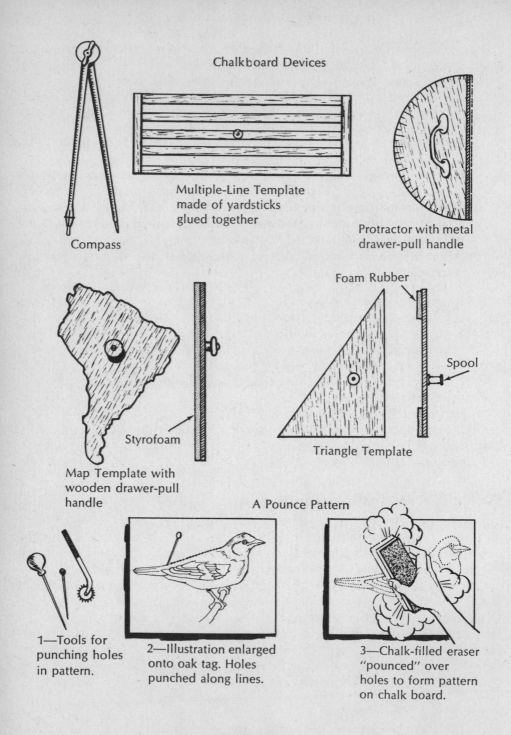

Chalkboard Devices

Compass

Multiple-Line Template
made of yardsticks
glued together

Protractor with metal
drawer-pull handle

Map Template with
wooden drawer-pull
handle

Styrofoam

Foam Rubber

Spool

Triangle Template

A Pounce Pattern

1—Tools for
punching holes
in pattern.

2—Illustration enlarged
onto oak tag. Holes
punched along lines.

3—Chalk-filled eraser
"pounced" over
holes to form pattern
on chalk board.

FIGURE 9-1

which the standard liquid slating is bonded. If you need a small, portable magnetic board, you might purchase one from a vendor. However, you might also wish to make your own. A homemade one can be constructed by following these steps:

1. Acquire a piece of galvanized sheet metal from a heating shop or hardware store. An oil drip pan such as those used in garages works very well.
2. Glue the metal to a piece of masonite or plywood using contact cement. If you use the oil drip pan, this isn't necessary.
3. Wash the metal with vinegar and then spray it thoroughly with water (this may be done before step two if desired). This prepares the surface to accept the chalkboard paint.
4. Spray, brush or roll chalkboard paint onto the surface; this may require the application of several coats of paint.
5. You may wish to bind the raw edges of the board with Mystik tape for a neater effect.
6. Go over the board with the side of a piece of chalk . . . this primes the board. The chalk should then be erased.
7. The magnetic board is now finished, but you will want to create magnetic figures for use on it. This is easily accomplished. You may use virtually any flat visual on the magnetic board by adhering one of the small magnetic strips which are available from many supply houses to the back of it. These magnetic strips are rubber-like and can be cut with scissors. One brand of magnetic material has an adhesive along one side so that it can be readily adhered to the back of the visual. Plastic three-dimensional objects also can be used on the board if they do not weigh too much.

FLANNEL BOARDS

Flannel or felt boards are simple to construct and easy to use. They can be large in size and permanently attached to a wall, or, more typically, they can be portable. The most common materials from which figures for use on the board are made seem to be felt and paper backed with felt. However, other materials that are satisfactory for this purpose are sandpaper, textured pastel paper, pellon, flocked paper, wool yarn, string, cotton, flannel, burlap, styrofoam, foam rubber, cloth and paper which have been sprayed with pattern spray, and so forth.

To construct a flannel board, you will need some kind of sturdy backing material. A section of a large cardboard furniture crate can be used, but materials such as masonite, plywood, or cellotex work better.

Cut a piece of felt or flannel so that it is several inches larger than the backing board. Smooth this on a flat surface. Place the board in position over

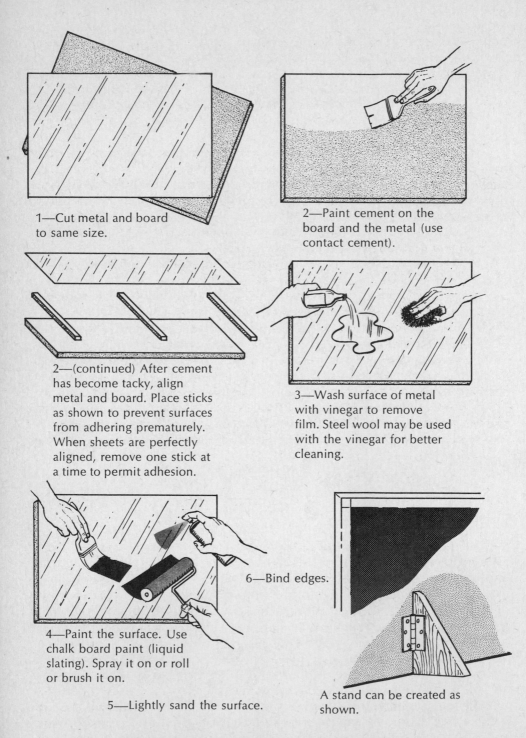

1—Cut metal and board to same size.

2—Paint cement on the board and the metal (use contact cement).

2—(continued) After cement has become tacky, align metal and board. Place sticks as shown to prevent surfaces from adhering prematurely. When sheets are perfectly aligned, remove one stick at a time to permit adhesion.

3—Wash surface of metal with vinegar to remove film. Steel wool may be used with the vinegar for better cleaning.

4—Paint the surface. Use chalk board paint (liquid slating). Spray it on or roll or brush it on.

5—Lightly sand the surface.

6—Bind edges.

A stand can be created as shown.

FIGURE 9-2 Creating a Magnetic Chalkboard

the felt in such a way that the material extends equally beyond the edges of the board. Run a bead of Elmer's or some equivalent glue on the back side toward the outer edge of the board; then fold the cloth over and smooth it down so that the glue penetrates the surface fibers. Tape the cloth in position, or use tacks for this purpose. Staples work well on surfaces such as wood or cellotex. If you should have difficulty folding the corners so that they lie flat, you may wish to remove a section as shown in the diagram so that much of the bulk is done away with.

The felt or flannel might also be dry mounted to the surface of the backing board. Although this approach is more expensive than the method described above, it results in a smooth, permanent product. You should cut the cloth and dry mount tissue to the exact size of the board. The tissue is positioned on the board and tacked in place with an iron. Next, place the cloth over the tissue and align it with the edges of the board. Go over the surface with a household iron, or place the assembled materials in a dry mount press. If certain areas fail to adhere, heat these with the iron, then rub them down by hand while they are hot. To complete the project, fold strips of plastic tape over the edges in the manner of the passe partout technique. This will prevent the cloth from releasing along the edge and will give a finished appearance to the board.

The figures for use on the board might be cut from brightly colored sections of felt which are left unembellished. If details are desired, however, these can be added with such mediums as opaque fabric paints or markers. Paper and Pellon can be marked upon with virtually any type of medium, however, water-based paints might cause some wrinkling and distortion to occur. Paper illustrations should be backed with a section of felt, flannel, sandpaper, or even abrasive metal screen so that they will adhere to the surface of the board. Don't overlook the possibility of acquiring commercially prepared materials which are widely available from such outlets as school supply houses.

BULLETIN BOARDS

Bulletin boards can be planned ahead of time by creating a sketch, or "rough," that displays the basic proportions, arrangement, and colors of the finished product. The actual materials can then be arranged on the floor or on a table using the sketch as a guide.

Most bulletin boards are permanently installed in the classroom, but you can make your own portable one by covering a cork board or piece of cellotex with some kind of fabric. You might leave the materials uncovered for that matter, but the surface will soon become unsightly as pins and tacks penetrate and scar it.

For the bulletin board figures, you may use pictures from magazines, books, calendars, etc.; mounting materials such as posterboard, railroad board, and construction paper; lettering such as ceramic letters, precut cardboard, paper, and plastic letters. You may also wish to create your own lettering using cutouts.

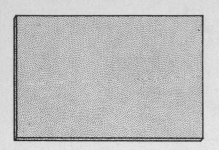

1—Cut the backing board to size.

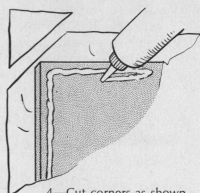

2—Trim felt larger than board.

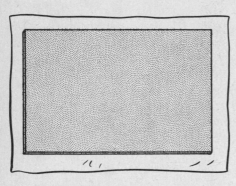

3—Smooth felt, place board over felt.

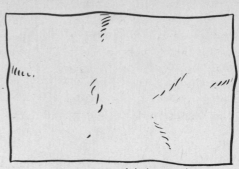

4—Cut corners as shown. Apply casein glue around edge (do not apply to front side).

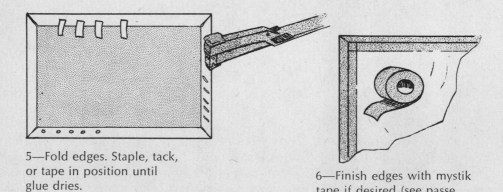

5—Fold edges. Staple, tack, or tape in position until glue dries.

6—Finish edges with mystik tape if desired (see passe partout mounting).

FIGURE 9-3 Creating A Felt (Flannel) Board

Speedball and felt pen captions are useful, and novelty letters can be created from materials such as yarn, string, wallpaper, sponge, Styrofoam, and so forth. Real objects can be displayed on the bulletin board and so can sculptured objects made from papier-mache, cut and folded paper, plastic, wood, etc. Paper plates may be used as the backing for mounted visuals, and soda straws and pipe cleaners lend themselves to various kinds of construction. Silhouettes

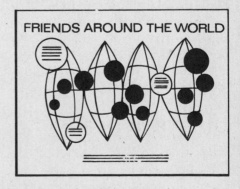

FIGURE 9-4 Examples of Student-Designed Bulletin Boards

cut from different kinds of materials will add interest to a display, and yarns, rope, etc., will serve nicely to "tie" things together or unify them.

Composition is a very important consideration where bulletin boards are concerned. If you will refer to the chapter on composition, you will find numerous suggestions that can be applied directly to the construction of such visuals. Suggestions that relate to appropriate lettering styles and techniques are to be found in the chapter on lettering. If you wish to mount pictures for use on the board, the chapter on picture preservation will give you numerous pointers on how this might be accomplished.

HOOK AND LOOP BOARDS

The unique hook and loop system is made up of a surface sheet that consists of thousands of tiny "loops" of nylon (usually) and a second type of material—the "hook" part—that is made up of stiff curved or hooked fibers. This material is much like that which is used in place of zippers and buttons on clothing but comes in wide rolls rather than in narrow strips.

To create a hook and loop board, you will need a sheet of sturdy material such as masonite or plywood. To this, staple or glue the loop material. You may wish to make a simple stand for the back, or a hanger can be added which will enable you to hang the board on the wall. Secure small sections of the hook material to the backs of objects which are to be displayed. Use a strong glue, such as Franklin's or Elmer's, or, better still, staple the sections in place.

Attaching the object to the board is simply a matter of pressing it against the surface. The hooks will engage the loops so tenaciously that it will take some effort to separate the two surfaces. Heavy objects such as three-dimensional realia are held securely in place with this system. You may, of course, purchase ready-made boards that are both attractive and serviceable. These come in a variety of sizes and colors. Numbers, letters, and other kinds of figures are manufactured expressly for use with the hook and loop board, or you can prepare handmade or ready-made letters and other items for use by attaching the hook material to the back.

A strip board is made by stapling or gluing the looped portion of the commercial strip material called Velcro to a board. The second strip (the hooked part) is trimmed into segments and attached to the objects to be displayed. This material can be purchased in any store that sells sewing equipment or cloth yardage.

OTHER TYPES OF BOARDS

Special boards can be purchased that have an enameled surface upon which various markers can be used. Some companies produce markers that dry instantly to a chalk-like finish that can be erased with a felt eraser. Water soluble markers can also be used on enameled finishes, but these must be removed with a damp cloth.

You can create your own special demonstration boards in a number of ways. For example, a sheet of enamelled metal from an old refrigerator will serve nicely as a writing surface. Grease pencils, certain kinds of transparency pencils, and markers are all suitable for rendering and writing on this type of "board." Various prefinished wall panels have a surface that is virtually impervious to every kind of stain. If light-colored, unpatterned panels are obtained, these can serve nicely for such techniques as those mentioned above.

By covering a surface with a clear plastic sheet, another kind of "demonstration board" can be created. Lines might be drawn on the base material which can serve as guides for lettering or writing and remain intact as the marks are removed from the plastic thus making the unit reusable. Or, a map or diagram might be substituted for the guide lines; the plastic cover makes it possible for the students to add all kinds of embellishments without doing damage to the basic illustration.

Peg board sheets, which are actually masonite or tempered boards that have perforations at intervals, can be purchased at practically all lumber yards for a reasonable cost. Special wire hooks are placed in the holes, and materials of various kinds are hung from these.

Numerous additional kinds of demonstration and display boards can be devised by the innovative teacher.

DISPLAY STANDS

When easels are not available, supporting various kinds of display materials can become awkward and even embarrassing. Sometimes, chairs are put into service or chalk trays are utilized, but most of these stop-gap measures tend to lessen the flexibility that the presenter has in utilizing his visual materials. For example, a flip chart which is placed in the chalk tray cannot be "flipped" because there is no way for the pages to be moved up and over unless the chart is physically pulled forward away from the board as each page is turned.

You can produce your own display stands with a few inexpensive materials and a small investment in time. Figure 9-5 shows three ways in which stands can be made. However, with a little imagination, you should be able to invent stands that will serve for any special support problem. The first stand might be attached to a chart or a felt board (in this case, it should be made of something more sturdy than cardboard). The second can be made to any scale and is useful as a support for almost any kind of flat visual. Number three is excellent where two different kinds of surfaces are to be used. For example, you might wish to make one of the surfaces a felt board and the other one a chalk board.

Materials such as corrugated cardboard, plywood, masonite, poster board, and bristol board work well for stands. You can use book mending tape or even masking tape for the lighter, smaller stands; hinges are sometimes necessary where larger, heavier stands are being used. A coating of spray paint will add a finishing touch to the product and will make it more serviceable as well as more attractive.

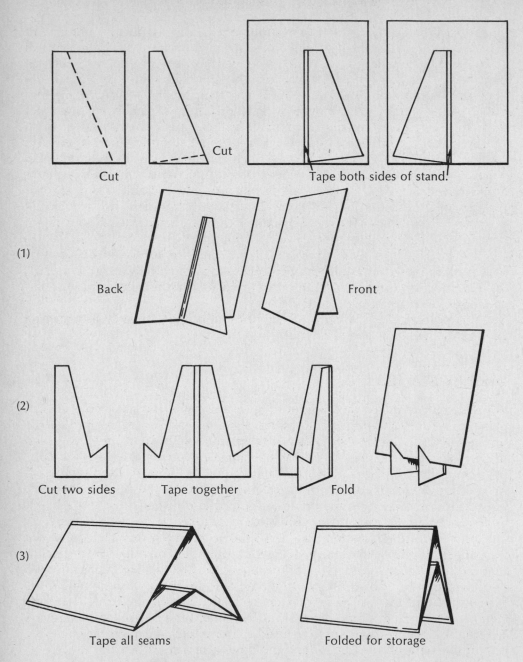

(1)

Cut

Cut

Tape both sides of stand.

Back

Front

(2)

Cut two sides

Tape together

Fold

(3)

Tape all seams

Folded for storage

FIGURE 9-5 Three Types of Display Stands

BIBLIOGRAPHY

Brown, James W., Lewis, Richard B., and Harcleroad, Fred F. **AV Instruction—Technology, Media and Methods.** New York: McGraw- Hill Book Co., 1977.

Calder, Clarence R., Jr., and Antan, Eleanor M. **Technique and Activities to Stimulate Verbal Learning.** New York: Macmillan Company, 1970.

Kemp, Jerrold E. **Planning and Producing Audiovisual Materials.** 2nd ed. Scranton, Pa.: Chandler Publishing Co., 1968.

Kosky, Thomas Arthur. **Baited Bulletin Boards.** Palo Alto, Calif.: Fearon Publishers, Inc., 1954.

Kosky, Thomas Arthur. **How to Make and Use Flannel Boards.** Palo Alto, Calif.: Fearon Publishers, Inc., 1961.

Lockridge, J. Preston. **Better Bulletin Board Displays.** Austin: University of Texas, n.d.

Randall, Reino W., and Haines, Edward C. **Bulletin Boards and Displays.** Worcester, Mass.: Davis Publishing Co., 1961.

Weseloh, Anne Douglas. **E-Z Bulletin Boards.** Palo Alto, Calif.: Fearon Publishers, Inc., 1959.

Wittich, Walter A., and Schuller, Charles F. **Instructional Technology, Its Nature and Use.** 5th ed. New York: Harper & Row, 1973.

10

THREE-DIMENSIONAL TEACHING DEVICES

INTRODUCTION

Whereas many of the materials that are used in education appeal either to the sense of sight or of hearing or both, three-dimensional materials display an additional quality that appeals to the sense of touch—that is, a tactual quality. These materials project a visual image, of course; they are also subject to verbal descriptions. But their most important characteristic is their form or three-dimensionality.

Many three-dimensional materials are made with the explicit idea that they are to be handled by the students. This additional dimension often can be useful in assisting students to formulate more legitimate concepts about things—a particular concern where younger children are involved. A considerable portion of children's knowledge of their world enters their perceptual systems through tactual sensing mechanisms. They handle objects incessantly; they turn them over and over, inspecting every detail; they determine the nature of the substance from which the object is made and make assessments as to how the materials react to various treatments such as hitting, pressing, squeezing, and bouncing. This kind of experience can be very valuable for young children who are in the process of building a storehouse of concepts and need every bit of sensory evidence relating to the environment that they can get.

For older children, the experience of actually creating three-dimensional objects that will later be used in a display can be very exciting. This activity gives the child the opportunity not only of being creative, but also of learning about the physical qualities of such raw materials as clay, papier-mâché, and plaster.

In junior and senior high school, the basic concepts of clay and papier-mâché are fairly well formed so that the experience becomes primarily a creative one.

If three-dimensional materials are used strictly in a display sense—that is, without student involvement in their production—then their value may be related primarily to their similarity to the real objects that they represent. Even simple models have form—a quality possessed by just about everything that we encounter in nature.

For older students, the three-dimensional display can aid in the development of concepts related to form; however, evidence indicates that a realistically rendered flat picture or a photograph can do a good job of simulating this quality, and at considerably less cost.

The array of three-dimensional objects ranges all the way from an abstract piece of paper sculpture to the actual object in its natural environment. Some of the more commonly used types of 3-D materials are the diorama, the puppet, the mask, papier-mâché objects, models, paper sculpture, and mounted objects and specimens.

DIORAMAS

A **diorama** is a miniature scene in 3-D treatment that is meant to replicate reality. Dioramas are to be found in virtually all museums where they make up a large portion of the things to be seen there. They frequently include mounted birds, mammals and fishes which are naturally posed in realistic settings. Often, such displays are miniature only to the extent that they are limited in the manner in which they portray the environment; the creatures depicted are generally full-sized—even to the elephants. The skill and imagination of the experts on a modern museum staff can bring the sensation of stark reality into the lives of people who might otherwise never experience the particular scenes being displayed.

Most, if not all, school displays are miniaturized. They seldom include actual objects, such as mounted animals, because of the problems that are involved in acquiring and utilizing such objects. Small reproductions of people, buildings, animals, trees, and so forth, are constructed and painted in natural colors. These are then positioned in a setting that accurately captures the essence of the situation being portrayed. At times, commercially available objects such as plastic cars and miniature figures are included in a diorama where they seem appropriate—and using these ready-made items often saves considerable time and effort.

Some school districts possess portable dioramas that depict such scenes as an Indian village, or dinosaurs eating and fighting. These dioramas are checked out to the teachers in much the same way that films, filmstrips, and transparencies are. Teachers then utilize them to enhance their teaching units.

As a rule, most dioramas are "home-grown," that is, they are produced through a team effort in the classroom. Dioramas normally consist of four principal parts: (1) the case or stage, (2) the painted background, (3) the three-dimensional middle and foreground, and (4) the figures, constructions, and modelled objects that are placed within the case.

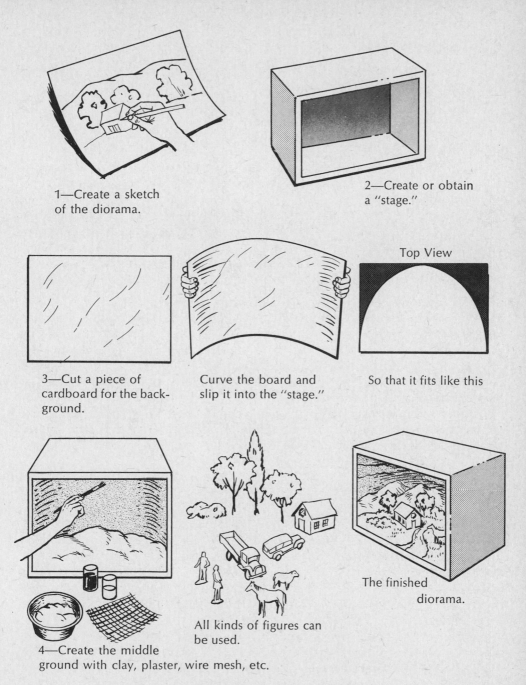

1—Create a sketch of the diorama.

2—Create or obtain a "stage."

3—Cut a piece of cardboard for the background.

Curve the board and slip it into the "stage."

Top View

So that it fits like this

4—Create the middle ground with clay, plaster, wire mesh, etc.

All kinds of figures can be used.

The finished diorama.

5—Paint the foreground and middle ground.

FIGURE 10-1 Creating a Diorama

To construct a diorama, the following steps are suggested:

1. Start with a full-sized sketch of the diorama. This might be rendered on a large sheet of butcher paper.
2. Secure the materials that will be needed and proceed to construct the stage. The stage might be nothing more than a cardboard box with the front cut out, or it might be a more elaborate case built of plywood and then painted.
3. Next, a piece of illustration board is curved around inside of the case so that it forms a background area upon which the distant elements will be painted.
4. Now, create the middle and foreground by using chicken wire covered with plaster of paris, or use burlap dipped in the plaster. If the ground is to be flat, sand or flocking can be glued to the bottom of the case. Clay might be used to model hills, valleys and other details.
5. The background and the foreground are now painted at the same time.

It is necessary to proceed in this fashion in order that all parts of the diorama will be blended together. As the paint dries, it is possible to sprinkle sand, flocking, sawdust, etc., into it for textured effects. Place the figures in position and glue them securely so that they will not fall out of position when the diorama is moved. These figures may consist of houses and buildings constructed of cardboard or small boxes and berry containers. Figures of people and animals may be modeled from clay or they may be purchased from toy stores and hobby shops. Toy cars and trucks fit well into dioramas; actual plants can be dried and used for vegetation. A tree can be created by using the small, end twigs from an actual tree to which bits of green sponge are glued.

PUPPETS

A puppet is an inanimate collection of various materials that suddenly assumes lifelike qualities when activated by someone. A puppet can become the medium through which children express themselves, often in a role-playing fashion. Puppets can assist the child in assuming the role of the character that he is portraying. Because the puppet operator is generally not seen, the anonymity that results can lead to a freer expression and a less inhibited activity on the part of the child.

Older students enjoy using puppets also. For example, an interesting use to which they can be put is related to the learning of classics and poetry. **The Rime of the Ancient Mariner** becomes more exciting if the students are encouraged to construct the various elements of the story in puppet form. The albatross, the sailors, the ship, and the backgrounds all combine with the spoken lines and appropriate musical accompaniment to create a unique experience. Interestingly, the students seem to learn the lines more readily and to remember then more accurately than if they are required to do this via the traditional rote method.

Puppetry seems to be a worldwide phenomenon and there is scarcely a civilization in which these objects of expression have not played an important role. Ancient and primitive cultures used them in rituals and rites of various kinds. Modern sophisticated people enjoy watching puppet shows as a form of entertainment.

Four principal kinds of puppets are in common usage today—these are the string puppets (marionettes), the hand puppets, the rod puppets, and the shadow puppets.

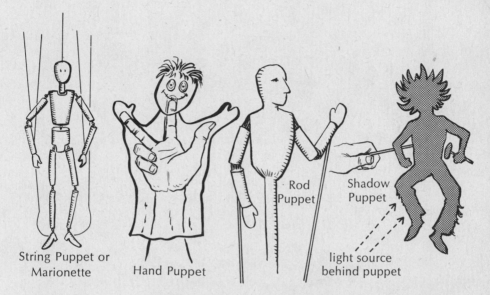

String Puppet or Marionette

Hand Puppet

Rod Puppet

Shadow Puppet

light source behind puppet

FIGURE 10-2 Types of Puppets

Marionettes. These are generally constructed of wood with articulating joints that replicate those of human beings. The joints may be fashioned by carving the wood and then joining the parts together with wire to form a kind of hinge; or small screw eyes might be used for a joint which is more flexible. Heads are easily constructed from papier-mâché, plastic wood or balsa wood. Paints such as poster paints, oil paints, or enamel paints are all suitable for finishing the exposed parts of the marionette. If poster paints are used, however, they should be shellacked or varnished in order that they might be made waterproof.

Attaching the strings in the proper way is a tricky business. It is necessary to form a wooden "control" of slats of wood to which is attached the string (carpet thread). The control can be a simple one with a string to the head and additional strings to the arms and legs, or it can be quite complex and include strings to the legs, shoulders, arms, head and hips. The amount and kind of movement desired will dictate the way that the marionette will be strung.

Hand puppets. This type of puppet is made to slip over the hand like a glove. Indeed, this is the way that a hand puppet is created, that is, the

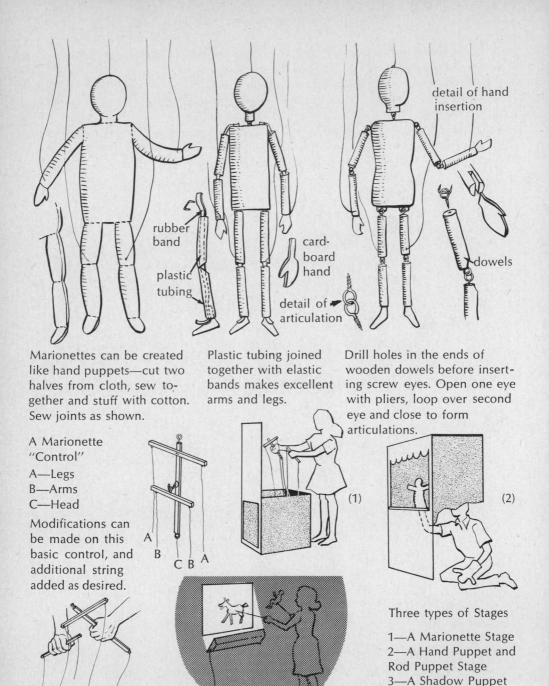

rubber band

plastic tubing

cardboard hand

detail of articulation

detail of hand insertion

dowels

Marionettes can be created like hand puppets—cut two halves from cloth, sew together and stuff with cotton. Sew joints as shown.

Plastic tubing joined together with elastic bands makes excellent arms and legs.

Drill holes in the ends of wooden dowels before inserting screw eyes. Open one eye with pliers, loop over second eye and close to form articulations.

A Marionette "Control"
A—Legs
B—Arms
C—Head

Modifications can be made on this basic control, and additional string added as desired.

A

B

C B A

(1)

(2)

Using the Control

(3)

Three types of Stages

1—A Marionette Stage
2—A Hand Puppet and Rod Puppet Stage
3—A Shadow Puppet Stage—note that the back view is shown.

FIGURE 10-3 Marionettes and Stages

186

operator's hand is traced on a piece of material and this becomes the body of the puppet as well as a "glove" for the operator. A cardboard tube into which the fingers will fit serves as the neck for the hand puppet. Onto this can be built a head with a Styrofoam ball, plastic wood, papier-mâché, or paper sculpture using construction paper. Another method of building puppet heads is to mould the head in clay and then to cover it with layers of paper dipped in paste. After the paper has dried, it can be cut up the middle and the clay removed. The two halves are then glued back together and painted to form a very effective head. All kinds of embellishments can be added to the bodies as well as to the heads of the puppets.

Rod Puppets. Rod puppets are constructed around a central supporting rod. They are held upright by the puppeteer and their lower parts—along with the operator—are concealed by a screen. The arms are jointed as in the marionette, but instead of being controlled by strings, they are controlled from below by stiff wires. The rod puppet generally is constructed without legs or with legs that do not articulate, but the upper parts, including the head, are most often carefully and completely constructed. Heads can be carved from wood or made of paper-mache or plastic wood.

Simpler rod puppets may be silhouettes of animals and people or detailed two-dimensional cutout pictures mounted on a stick. This type of rod puppet is very effective in the elementary and primary grades.

Although this kind of puppet is often more or less two-dimensional in nature, its effectiveness is dependent to a large extent on its movement through space. It seems logical, therefore, to classify it under the general heading of three-dimensional materials.

Shadow Puppets. Shadow puppets are two-dimensional in nature. They are normally controlled by rods that are much thinner than the typical ones that are used to support the rod puppet. It is necessary to have a translucent screen (rear-view screen) and a light source in order that this type of puppet might be effectively used. The screen can be tightly stretched cloth, or it might be a piece of frosted acetate or even tracing paper. If a commercial rear-view screen is available, this will work very well. The screen should be relatively large and should be covered on the sides and bottom with opaque material so that the operator can function without being seen from the audience and so that the ambient light will be screened from the audience—they should be in complete darkness for the best effect.

The most satisfactory illumination consists of a strip of lights along the bottom of the stage opening, or fluorescent lights mounted in the same position. Incidentally, an interesting alternative to the backlighted stage is the overhead projector. Students can position small puppets on the projector and can act out a story as the figures are projected onto the screen in a greatly enlarged format.

Shadow puppets may be constructed of heavy art paper or cardboard. Puppets may be colored and have wax ironed into them to make them trans-

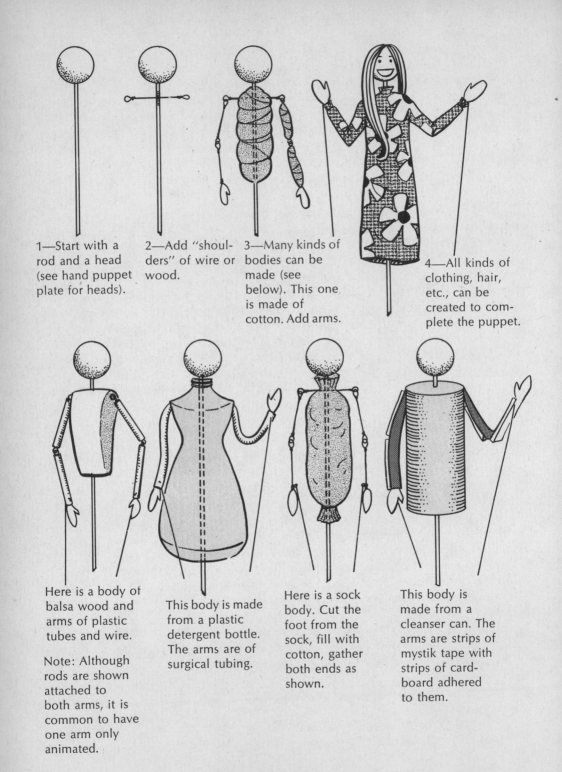

1—Start with a rod and a head (see hand puppet plate for heads).

2—Add "shoulders" of wire or wood.

3—Many kinds of bodies can be made (see below). This one is made of cotton. Add arms.

4—All kinds of clothing, hair, etc., can be created to complete the puppet.

Here is a body of balsa wood and arms of plastic tubes and wire.

Note: Although rods are shown attached to both arms, it is common to have one arm only animated.

This body is made from a plastic detergent bottle. The arms are of surgical tubing.

Here is a sock body. Cut the foot from the sock, fill with cotton, gather both ends as shown.

This body is made from a cleanser can. The arms are strips of mystik tape with strips of cardboard adhered to them.

FIGURE 10-4 Rod Puppets

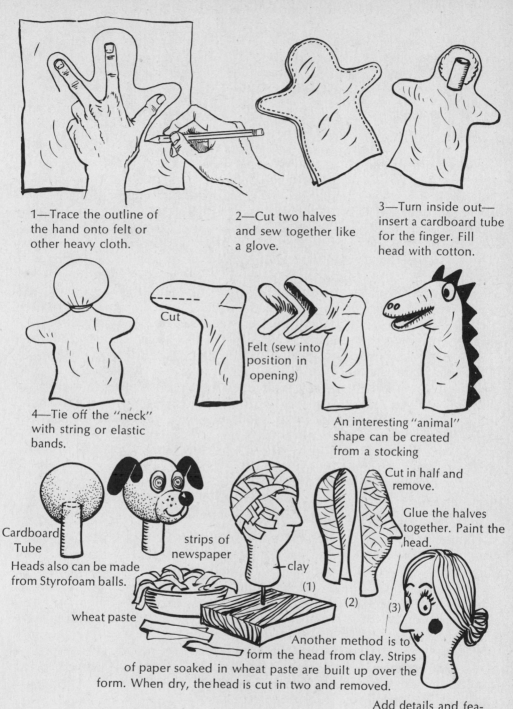

1—Trace the outline of the hand onto felt or other heavy cloth.

2—Cut two halves and sew together like a glove.

3—Turn inside out— insert a cardboard tube for the finger. Fill head with cotton.

4—Tie off the "neck" with string or elastic bands.

Cut

Felt (sew into position in opening)

An interesting "animal" shape can be created from a stocking

Cardboard Tube

Heads also can be made from Styrofoam balls.

strips of newspaper

clay

(1)

(2)

(3)

Cut in half and remove.

Glue the halves together. Paint the head.

wheat paste

Another method is to form the head from clay. Strips of paper soaked in wheat paste are built up over the form. When dry, the head is cut in two and removed.

Add details and features. Shellac or varnish to complete.

FIGURE 10-5 Hand Puppets

lucent; they then project in color on the screen. The puppets can be jointed, say in the middle, and additional rods used to create a certain amount of movement. Plastic can be used for the puppets and colored tissue may be adhered to the plastic to create a colored image on the screen.

MASKS

Masks were common in many primitive societies and played an important role in their religious rituals. Most ancient cultures also created and used masks. A study of the northwest Indian tribes would not be complete without some consideration of the masks and totem poles of these people. African tribes used some of the most imaginative of all masks, and don't overlook the masks that were constructed and worn by the Chinese and ancient Greeks.

In developing concepts about the religions, social customs, arts and crafts, and folklore of other cultures, you will find the mask in all its fascinating versions to be a useful stimulus. Have the students create their own masks and then have a "show and tell" session during which the meaning and use of each mask is explained. With younger children, plays can be acted out. Masks, like puppets, make the actor somewhat anonymous. This quality can be worthwhile if it assists a self-conscious child to express himself more freely.

Older students enjoy creating the mask as an art project. Often they enjoy outdoing one another in the color and detail that they build in to their works of art. This is a good exercise in design. It also stimulates the imagination and encourages research. Additionally, this kind of activity is excellent for developing skills in the manipulation of various kinds of materials.

Many kinds of masks can be constructed, but some of the materials and techniques that are necessary for the more elaborate varieties are not available in the average classroom. The following varieties can be simply made with available raw materials or with materials that can be purchased for a few cents. For something stimulating and different, try one of these:

Paper bag masks. One of the simplest masks to create is the paper bag variety. All that you need to make one of these is a paper bag that will fit over the head, some scissors and paint, and a good imagination. The first step is to place the bag over the head; the eye positions are then marked by locating the eyes with the fingers and then pinching the paper bag at this point. The bag is then removed from the head and the features are drawn in. Unless you are attempting to depict an actual mask from a certain culture, or a specific animal or character that requires a certain precision in rendering, you should let your creative bent run wild at this point. You may want to try simple expressions, or exaggeration, or even a caricature. The eyes are now cut out with scissors and the mask is returned to the head in order to make certain that the holes are where they should be and that vision is not impaired. After checking the eyes, flatten the paper bag out on the table and proceed to paint it. The most satisfactory paint is probably an opaque variety such as tempera or poster paint; however, wax crayons can be used, and so can transparent water colors in a pinch. Do not use pastels or chalks on masks; the dry pigment will not only transfer off onto clothing, but onto faces and hands as well. After the paint has dried, certain kinds of embellishments such as yarn for hair, buttons for teeth, paper for noses, and fur for eyebrows can be added for interest.

Balloon masks. Another interesting type of mask is the balloon mask. A balloon is inflated and then strips of newspaper which have been soaked in wheat paste are applied to the surface of the balloon. After sufficient paper has been added to the balloon so that a strong, self-supporting coat has been formed, it is permitted to dry until hard. The balloon is then deflated and removed from inside the mask. You should now make a detailed drawing of the various parts of the face on the surface of the paper sphere. Opaque paints such as tempera or poster colors are next used to complete the mask. Often, embellishments such as those used on the paper bag mask are employed in order to create the desired effect.

Construction paper masks. This type of mask can readily be made from common colored construction paper. By making a simple pattern and using this for the basic mask, it is possible to successfully create a generalized form that will fit just about any child's face. Through the imaginative use of color, details, etc., each basic mask partakes of the personality of its maker, and no two finished masks will look alike.

To create the basic pattern, measure one of the children's heads and mark these dimensions on a piece of heavy paper such as oak tag. Next, determine the position of the eyes—they will be just about in the middle of the head—and mark this dimension on the paper. Do the same thing with the mouth and nose. This pattern may now be cut out and can be used by students to establish their initial sketch that will serve as the basis for the finished mask.

Papier-mâché masks. One of the most popular ways to make a mask is to start out with a clay "armature" which is carefully modeled to the exact shape and with the precise detail that the creator desires. After the clay form has been shaped, it is coated with Vaseline, and strips of newspaper which have been soaked in wheat paste are placed over this form. It takes up to six layers of this material to create a mask of satisfactory thickness. Some of the layers might be of paper sack for strength, and it would be desirable to make the last layer of paper toweling so that a smooth, clear, surface might be available for painting. After the layers of paper have dried, the mask is removed from its armature and sanded lightly. It is then painted with poster paint and shellacked or varnished. Hair, earrings, different kinds of eyes, teeth, etc., may all be added at this time to complete the mask.

PAPIER-MÂCHÉ OBJECTS

Newspaper is a useful construction material when torn into thin strips and soaked in wheat paste. Although this material is not a true papier-mâché, it is generally referred to as this. A base or armature is ordinarily formed in order that the limp material might be supported until it is dry and firm. Armatures

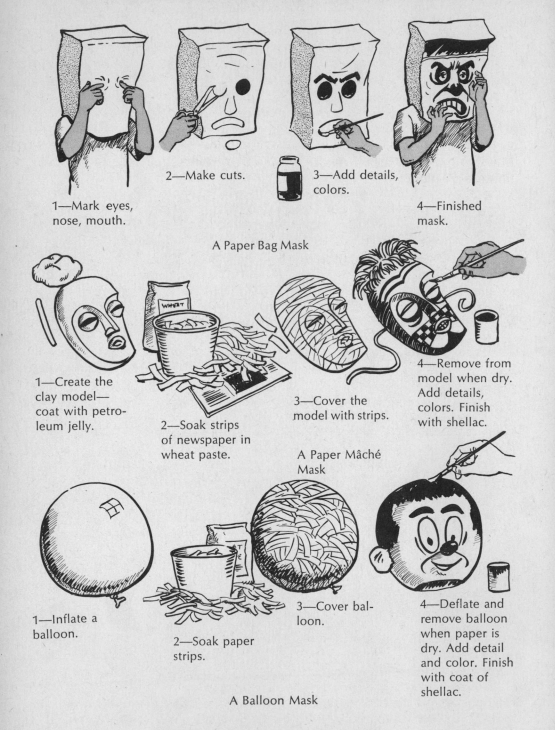

1—Mark eyes, nose, mouth.

2—Make cuts.

3—Add details, colors.

4—Finished mask.

A Paper Bag Mask

1—Create the clay model—coat with petroleum jelly.

2—Soak strips of newspaper in wheat paste.

3—Cover the model with strips.

4—Remove from model when dry. Add details, colors. Finish with shellac.

A Paper Mâché Mask

1—Inflate a balloon.

2—Soak paper strips.

3—Cover balloon.

4—Deflate and remove balloon when paper is dry. Add detail and color. Finish with coat of shellac.

A Balloon Mask

FIGURE 10-6 Three Types of Masks

can be made from aluminum clothesline wire, wire clother hangers, strips of wood, rolled and tied newspaper, cans, boxes, and other objects that are used singly or tied or taped together. After the basic shape has been created with the armature, the strips of paste-soaked paper are added. The form is built up with strips, larger pieces, and crumpled wads of paper until its appearance is satisfactory, then a final coating of strips of paper toweling soaked in paste is added to complete the form. Finally, the object is painted with opaque paints and varnished or shellacked for permanence and luster. Often yarn, buttons, corks, feathers, and other such items can be added to enhance the appearance of the finished creation.

MODELS

Models are replicas of real objects. They may be larger than the thing that they replicate—as with an amoeba or a grasshopper— or smaller than the real thing (as the earth). Generally speaking, models do not actually "work," that is, they may be exact replicas of the thing they represent, but they do not involve as part of their function the operation of the item. Models can be made to show interior views of objects, and they can be simplified to any extent desired in order that the basic concept represented by the model may be communicated most adequately. Models may also use a kind of color coding which enables the student to pick out certain essential features of the object.

Many of the elements of the diorama could accurately be classified as models; however, it is the integration of the models along with the other elements of the diorama display that makes this type of visual unique.

Models are typically constructed from premade kits of various kinds. The variety of such kits available today is sufficient to satisfy almost any need a teacher might have in this area; therefore, models are seldom made "from scratch" these days. One of the most useful materials in the construction of the homemade model is balsa wood. This ultra-soft material can be acquired from any model or hobby shop and from a considerable number of lumber yards. You can cut it with a razor blade or a sharp knife, and you can shape it with a piece of rough sandpaper or an electric disc sander. Model airplane cement is excellent for joining the various parts of the model together; however, the kind that is made exclusively for use on plastic is not satisfactory for balsa wood. Colors can be added to your model by using a model paint such as the lacquer varieties that come in bottles as well as spray cans. Water paints can also be used but they have a tendency to dry flat and dull and may need a finishing coat of lacquer, varnish, or shellac.

Models are excellent for teaching concepts about things that are three-dimensional and concrete in nature. Although it would be impossible to bring a clipper ship into the classroom, and it would be difficult to take the class to the clipper ship (field trip), an accurate model of such a ship could be displayed with ease on the corner table. When models are used in conjunction with other kinds of media, it is possible to develop rather accurate concepts of many kinds.

1—Armatures can be made of aluminum clothesline wire

or newspaper rolls which are taped or tied in position.

2—Wheat paste should be of a creamy consistency. Use newspaper strips for all but last coat.

3—Cover armature with wads of newspaper for rough form.

4—Refine form with strips of paper.

5—After form is complete, cover with one last coat of paper toweling soaked in paste.

6—Paint with poster paints. Add embellishments such as felt shapes, buttons, feathers, etc. Finish with coat of shellac.

FIGURE 10-7 Papier-Mâché Objects

PAPER SCULPTURE

Paper-sculptured objects can be used for many things including bulletin board displays, poster embellishments, dioramas, etc. These objects can be readily created by the students after a modest amount of practice in cutting and folding heavy construction paper. There are a few basic techniques that must be mastered before the art of paper sculpture can become a tool of expression for the student. It is essential that one know how to properly "score" paper. This calls for the cutting of the paper surface so that the cut penetrates halfway through the paper (no more than this). Scoring permits the paper to be folded along the scored line in virtually any configuration desired, including curved and shaped lines. Another important basic technique is that of "curling." If a piece of paper is pulled across the sharp edge of a table, the paper will curl. Smaller strips of paper can be curled by using a ruler or the blade of a pair of scissors. "Perforating" is a technique involving the cutting into the surface of the paper to create different kinds of textures and designs. An example of perforating is the cutting through the surface of a fish form with small semicircles to create a scaly appearance.

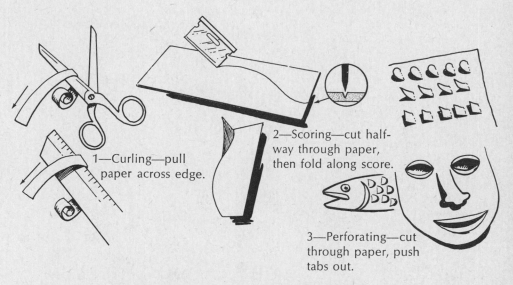

1—Curling—pull paper across edge.

2—Scoring—cut halfway through paper, then fold along score.

3—Perforating—cut through paper, push tabs out.

FIGURE 10-8 Basic Paper Sculpture Techniques

Paper-sculptured figures are best constructed with a glue such as Elmer's glue; rubber cement is not strong enough to cause the different parts of an object to adhere together for any length of time. While the glue is drying, the parts can be held together with masking tape, paper clips or rubber bands.

An easy way to create a piece of paper sculpture is to find a picture in a book or magazine and trace it onto tracing paper. Separate the head, limbs, body, tail (if an animal), ears (if an animal), etc., so that instead of a unified figure, the separate parts are now represented on construction or heavy watercolor paper. Cut the parts out and score them in places that seem logical to you.

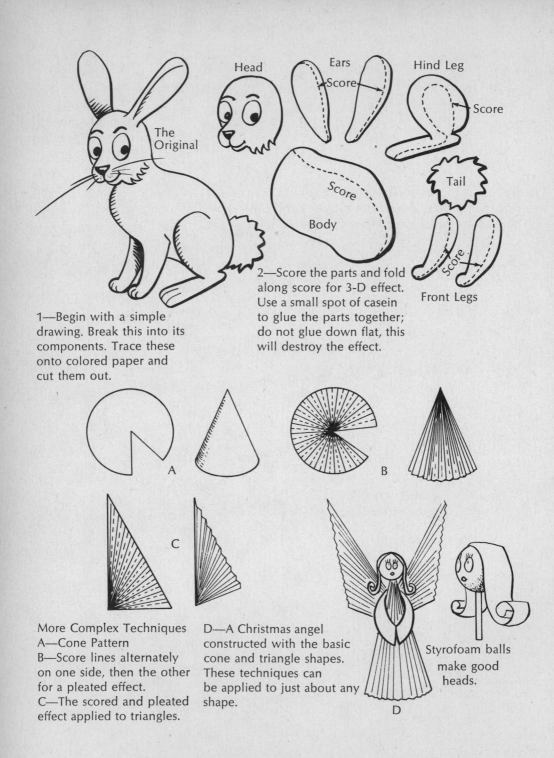

The Original

Head

Ears
Score

Hind Leg
Score

Tail

Body
Score

Front Legs
Score

1—Begin with a simple drawing. Break this into its components. Trace these onto colored paper and cut them out.

2—Score the parts and fold along score for 3-D effect. Use a small spot of casein to glue the parts together; do not glue down flat, this will destroy the effect.

A

B

C

D

More Complex Techniques
A—Cone Pattern
B—Score lines alternately on one side, then the other for a pleated effect.
C—The scored and pleated effect applied to triangles.

D—A Christmas angel constructed with the basic cone and triangle shapes. These techniques can be applied to just about any shape.

Styrofoam balls make good heads.

FIGURE 10-9   Paper Sculpture

By folding along these scored lines a three-dimensional effect can be obtained. Now glue these parts together to once again unite them into a unified form. This object may then be completed by adding details with pencils, ink, crayons, etc.

MOUNTED OBJECTS AND SPECIMENS

When the real thing is available, it is often desirable to use it if it is not so complicated that it becomes confusing for the student. At times, real objects can be too complex for effective cognition on the part of the student. When this occurs, models, along with pictures and other kinds of media, might be desirable as an initial experience for the student.

Some examples of specimens and objects are insects, leaves, mounted birds and mammals, Indian arrowheads, a lamp bulb, bottles, pioneer guns, silk from Japan, dividers, compasses, instruments from an airplane, eating utensils, etc. Specimens and objects might be mounted where practical—this may be desirable for biological specimens. However, certain kinds of objects and specimens are most effective when the students are permitted to handle them. Through such first-hand experiences, accurate concepts are formed. Such items as tools, stones, etc., can be handled without too much chance that they will be damaged. Make sure, however, that the students are not permitted to handle objects that may endanger them. A bolo knife from the Philippines may be an object that cannot be damaged by the children, but what it might do to the child must be a prime consideration also.

There are a number of ways that biological specimens can be preserved. Perhaps the easiest way to preserve leaves, grasses, etc., is to laminate them with Seal-Lamin (use a dry mount press set on about 300°). The passe partout mounting technique is an effective way to mount specimens such as moths and butterflies. A cotton layer is placed in the bottom of the shallow box which can be ready-made or made of cardboard or balsa wood strips. Glass is placed over the box and is taped into place with wide strips of Mystik bookbinding tape. Moth crystals should be placed in the box prior to sealing it so that insects do not destroy the specimen. It is also possible to preserve specimens such as lizards, snakes and amphibians in alcohol in stoppered bottles.

An effective method of mounting specimens is to embed them in plastic. It is necessary to have a special liquid plastic which is made specifically for casting plus a catalyst which is used to make the plastic change from its liquid state to a solid one. Use a suitable container for a mold, or make one from pieces of glass or metal. Coat the inside of this with a mold release compound then mix a sufficient amount of plastic and the proper amount of catalyst to fill the mold about one-third full. If any air bubbles form, these should be worked out with a needle or pin. After the plastic has become firm enough, the specimen should be carefully positioned and adjusted to the desired final configuration. Mix another quantity of plastic and pour this into the mold—the thickness of this layer should be just sufficient to barely cover the specimen. Now pour the final layer; permit the mount to dry for several hours. To speed the curing process,

Preserving a Specimen
in Plastic

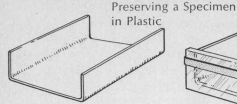

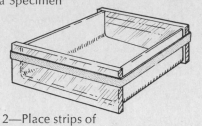

1—Create the mold base from a strip of metal from a tin can or other source.

2—Place strips of glass over open ends and secure with rubber band. Coat inside with mold release.

3—Mix the catalyst and plastic in a disposable cup.

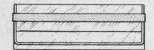

4—Fill the mold about 1/3 full of plastic; allow to become stiff enough to support the specimen.

5—Position specimen; cover with plastic. Permit to harden, then add last layer. Curing can be accelerated by heating the coating with an electric light bulb.

6—Remove casting from mold and sand with sandpaper.

FIGURE 10-10 Preserving a Specimen in Plastic

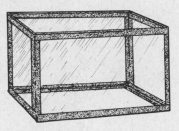

Sheets of single-strength window glass can be taped together with mystik tape to create a terrarium.

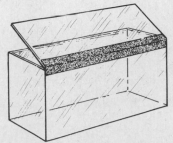

Plastic sheets can be adhered together by applying acetone to the surfaces to be joined. Strips of tape will support the plastic sheets until the bond has cured.

A lid can be added if desired.

FIGURE 10-11 Making a Terrarium

you may wish to place the mold in an oven at a temperature of about 130° to 150° for several hours; or, you can rig a light bulb in a box so that it will do a similar job. After the mold has been removed from the plastic cast, it is necessary to polish its surfaces. Begin this process with sandpaper and end with silver polish or some other such fine abrasive.

An interesting side note: These plastic-mounted specimens can be projected with the overhead projector. Many of them will project in color—their wings being just transparent enough to permit the light to pass through them. There are many other ways in which specimens can be preserved, and a number of very good books are available that describe these in considerable detail. In particular, you will want to research the biology section in the book store and the card catalog in the library for specific directions dealing with various kinds of specimens.

Finally, live specimens can be displayed in containers and cages of all kinds. A simple, home-built terrarium that is suitable for lizards, insects, snakes, and other kinds of specimens is made from sheets of glass or plastic. Use tape to bind the glass and acetone to fuse the plastic. Such displays can afford students with fascinating, first-hand experiences with real, live creatures.

BIBLIOGRAPHY

Baranski, Mathew. **Mask Making.** Worcester, Mass.: Davis Publications, 1954.

Binyon, Helen, **Puppetry Today.** New York: Watson-Guptil Publications, Inc., 1966.

Brown, James W., Lewis, Richard B., and Harcleroad, Fred F. **AV Instruction: Media and Methods.** New York: McGraw-Hill Book Co., 1969.

Fabri, Ralph. **Sculpture in Paper.** New York: Watson-Guptill Publications, 1966.

Jackson, Sheila. **Simple Puppetry.** London: Studio Vista, 1969.

Johnston, Mary Grace. **Paper Shapes and Sculpture for School Use.** Worcester, Mass.: Davis Publications, 1958.

Morland, John E. **Preparation of Inexpensive Teaching Materials.** San Francisco: Chandler Publishing Co., 1963.

Wolchonok, Louis, **The Art of Three-Dimensional Design.** New York: Dover Publications, Inc., 1959.

PHOTOGRAPHY

INTRODUCTION

Photography, in its varied forms, is one of the most satisfactory graphic methods for capturing and recording "reality." Although skilled artists sometimes create paintings of a magnitude and power that are "bigger than life," very few people have either the skills or the time to invest in such activities. The same thing can be said of the top-flight photographer. It takes a combination of talent, training, and dedication to become a professional in this field, just as it does in the field of painting.

There is a decided difference between photography and painting, however. Whereas it is difficult if not impossible for a novice to pick up a brush and render a representational picture accurately, anyone can pick up a simple camera and snap a picture. Of course, there's a good possibiltiy that the picture will not be of professional quality, but it will be recognizable and, in all probability, will delight the person who made it.

So, here is a technique that will permit you, and your students, to create highly useful visuals from all kinds of original materials—and all this with a modest initial investment of time and money.

Still photographs, such as slides and prints, are useful when concepts that are related to the visual characteristics of things are being stressed. If movement is a factor, motion pictures are ordinarily superior to stills, particularly when students are given the opportunity of seeing the film more than once.

Photography is versatile. It lends itself either directly or indirectly to visualization techniques in virtually any subject matter area. Stories, both written and spoken, can be based on the photographs that the students themselves have created. It is considerably more interesting for the student to develop his own theme for a story than it is for the teacher simply to assign one to him.

Unexpected designs appear at every turn to the student who is consciously looking for them. Weathered wood, a rusty machine, a strange rock, or frosty patterns on a window all assume a new identity when photographed from odd angles or through close-up lenses. It's exciting and educational for the class to try to identify the original subject matter of such slides—and it leads to increased perceptual awareness as well.

Science is made to order for the photographic appraoch. How about collecting insects with a camera instead of with a bottle? If your Super 8 motion picture camera has a zoom lens, you and your students will be able to create some very exciting and intimate studies of the insects, birds, mammals, and plants that you encounter on field trips. A bird feeder placed outside the school window will attract many visitors to within close-up range, especially in the wintertime.

Although this medium is virtually without peer when it comes to the portrayal of the appearance of things, it should not be relegated solely to this function. Both still and motion pictures have a tremendous potential for recording dramatic events and emotional situations which go well beyond strict visual portrayal. When appropriate photographic essays and motion pictures are used as part of a simulation activity or in conjunction with role playing, concepts that emphasize affective behaviors can be developed.

One of the most common ways in which slides and filmstrips (and to a certain extent, photographic prints) are used is in the self-instructional sequenced package. Students are able to learn all kinds of skills and information from interactions with carefully prepared programs that are based on the still picture format. Generally, the visual portion of the program is accompanied by a verbal portion that might be printed (as in a workbook) or taped (typically on a cassette). Interaction sheets of various kinds, tests, and response devices as well as actual materials and equipment are normally included with the program in order that the student might become actively involved in the learning experience.

Single concept motion picture films are used when motion is an important consideration. These are often packaged in cassettes and used with projectors that either play the film continuously as a loop, or rewind it automatically for additional replays as desired. When housed in a carrel along with supplemental materials, these single concept films are extremely effective for individual or small group instruction.

Simple still cameras that utilize roll film in cassettes, 35 mm slide cameras, and super 8 motion picture cameras all are useful for these kinds of activities. If nonprojected pictures are preferred to the projected type, film can be used that will produce negatives from which contact prints and enlargements can be created in the dark room.

This chapter will stress the three types of cameras just mentioned. However, it might be a good idea to describe certain other varieties of cameras in order that the best fit between the camera type and the photographic problem might be obtained.

TYPES OF STILL CAMERAS

There are four basic types of still cameras that are commonly in use today. These are the viewfinder camera, the single lens reflex camera, the twin lens reflex camera, and the view camera. You will notice that the main criterion for separating these into four categories is the viewing principle involved.

The **viewfinder camera** has a separate viewing device and a separate lens for taking the picture. The viewing device in this instance is somewhat like a window through which the photographer aims prior to taking the picture. Some viewfinder cameras have the lens coupled with the viewfinder in such a way that the lens and the finder work together. When the image looks sharp, the lens is properly adjusted to that particular range. Such cameras are often referred to as **range-finder** cameras.

A VIEWFINDER CAMERA
Courtesy Eastman Kodak Company

Viewfinder cameras are simple, lightweight, inexpensive and easy to use. When utilized for close-up picture taking, they do, however, exhibit a problem that has to do with the placement of the picture on the film. This problem is referred to as the **parallax problem.** It is best illustrated by the portrait with the top of the head missing. What actually happens in this situation is that the photographer aims through the viewfinder and sees one image while the light from the subject passes through the lens of the camera to give a slightly different image. Because the viewfinder is located slightly above the taking lens, the image that the photographer sees will be of an area that is slightly higher up on the subject than the actual area that is captured by the film. The tendency to shoot an image that differs slightly from that seen causes the viewfinder camera to be less desirable than the single lens reflex camera for copy work.

The single lens reflex camera (SLR) solves the problem of parallax while introducing certain other problems. Although extremely popular and versatile, these cameras are rather heavy and somewhat noisy. Efforts are being made by manufacturers to reduce the weight and bulk of the SLR, both of which have increased as the cameras have become more complex and more automatic. The noise factor derives from the manner in which an SLR operates. Essentially, a mirror hangs down in front of the film plane in a position that permits the light entering the lens to be reflected up to the viewfinder. When the shutter release is pressed, this mirror must retract out of the way so that the light entering through the lens can impinge on the film to create a latent image. The movement of the mirror is the direct cause of most of the noise that is heard when an SLR is in operation. Once again, this problem is being studied by the manufacturers and it appears that a silent SLR is a possibility for sometime in the future.

SINGLE LENS REFLEX CAMERA
Courtesy Honeywell, Inc.

The advantages of this type of camera greatly outweigh the disadvantages. Copying on the copy stand is a simple process when an SLR is used because the image that is seen on the viewing screen is essentially what the film will record. Also, lenses of all varieties are easily interchanged by simply seating them in the lens mount and giving them a twist so there is no need to use supplementary lenses over normal lenses. This is made possible because the shutter is built into the body of the camera in most instances and not into the lens as with most other types of cameras. With few exceptions, leaf shutters that are positioned within the lens system make it impossible to remove lenses.

The **twin lens reflex camera** (TLR) has a separate viewing lens and a picture-taking lens. These are coupled together in such a manner that when the picture on the viewing screen appears sharp and in focus, the picture-taking lens is in the proper position to record an equivalent image. Once again, however, the problem of parallax must be considered. Because the two lenses are separate, the image seen on the screen is in a slightly different position from that which impinges upon the film (mainly at close ranges), so the problems which were described for the viewfinder camera apply here also. One nice thing about the twin lens is the beautiful, sharp image that appears on the viewing screen. Because a separate lens system is provided for the viewing mechanism and because the screen itself is so large, the image that appears is much higher in quality than that which results when the SLR or viewfinder cameras are used. One exception to this statement must be noted—the new generation of large format SLRs (such as 2¼ x 2¼) vie with the TLR for image quality. In most cases, however, these cameras are considerably more expensive than are the twin lens varieties.

TWIN LENS REFLEX CAMERA
Courtesy Bell and Howell-Mamiya

Finally, the **view camera** should be mentioned. Often, students and others who see a view camera for the first time are heard to say, "Oh, an old-fashioned camera." The view does look old-fashioned. It consists of a rail upon which two adjustable supports are located that are connected to a bellows and a viewing screen-film holder housing. To focus the camera, one or both of the focus knobs is released and the bellows is racked back and forth until a sharp image appears on the screen. Focusing is accomplished with the aperture wide open and with no film in the camera. One of the obvious disadvantages of such a camera is its mammoth size. It isn't the type that one would take on a fishing trip or to a football game. Additionally, such a camera uses sheets of film rather than rolls, so this, too, becomes cumbersome. But if you desire a large, sharp negative, along with the potential for unlimited image modification, then this is the camera for you.

Incidentially, the reference to image modification relates to the fact that several adjustments are provided on a view camera which, if properly used, enable the photographer to alter the image on the viewing screen in a variety of ways (i.e., he or she might correct for the apparent tilt that is seen in tall structures such as towers and skyscrapers). One last bit of information concerning view cameras should be mentioned. So much has been made of the parallax problem that we should not leave the view camera without emphasizing the fact that there is absolutely no such problem with this camera. Not only does the photographer look through the taking lens, but he or she looks right through the camera body as well.

Now, with this background, let us proceed to an in-depth look at one of the most basic kinds of viewfinder cameras. We might call it the **simple** camera.

4 X 5 VIEW CAMERA

Among the simple cameras that are available are the Argus, Rollei, Kodak Instamatic, and Minolta. The term "simple" is used to describe this type of camera not because it is simple in concept but because it is uncomplicated as far as operation is concerned. There is no winding of film, no focusing (in most models), no adjustment of settings, and no reading of light values—all this is built in. Just about anyone can successfully operate a simple camera after a brief explanation, and the results will be amazingly good.

To make loading easy, preloaded cartridges of film are used. These can be placed in the camera in one position only, so there is no danger of improper loading. No threading and no rewinding is necessary since the film is sealed in the cartridge until it is removed by the processor for developing. Most cameras

A 110 CARTRIDGE CAMERA
Courtesy of Eastman Kodak Co.

of this type have preset lenses, that is, lenses that are set for standard conditions and distances. Of course, this can be a limitation when certain unique problems arise; however, for most school situations, this camera will be adequate for the tasks that it is expected to perform.

Some units use a self-contained four-sided flash cube that requires no batteries. The cube rotates a quarter of a turn each time the film is advanced so that four exposures result from a single cube. Others, such as the Rollei A-26, employ an electronic flash for low-light photography.

Although some models of simple cameras will give clear images of objects that are as close as two feet, they are not suitable for close-up work that involves lesser distances than this. Kodak produces a compact copy stand that can be coupled with the instamatic camera and used when close-up pictures are desired; this system is virtually foolproof. The copy stand with its camera (called a "Visualmaker" by Kodak) is placed over the picture or objects to be photographed, a flash cube is inserted, and the shutter release is depressed to expose the film and create the picture. The Visualmaker stand has a built-in supplementary lens that is prefocused to give a consistently sharp picture. It also has a diffuser that controls the amount of light that illuminates the original so that exposures are always correct.

Colored slides, colored prints, and black and white prints can be created with this type of camera. The 126 film format—a 2" x 2" mount with a square image—is the common slide size obtained; however, some other simple cameras offer the 110 and 35 mm slide and negative formats as well.

KODAK EKTAGRAPHIC VISUALMAKER
Courtesy Eastman Kodak Company

35 MM CAMERAS

Probably the most popular 35 mm camera for general production work is the single lens reflex (SLR) variety. As mentioned earlier, the term **single lens reflex** refers to the construction of the viewfinding apparatus which is based on a system of optics that enables the operator to view the subject through the same lens that takes the picture of the subject. There is no problem of the camera shooting a slightly different image than the one seen through the viewfinder when the single lens reflex system is used.

The 35 mm slide has a ratio of 2 to 3; it is not square as is the 126 variety mentioned above. If you intend to copy from books, magazines, or pictures, you should attempt to match the format of the picture with that of the film. A square picture will have part of its content "cropped" or excluded from the slide because it will not fit the rectangular 35 mm format. One way that oddsized pictures can be made to fit the 2 to 3 configuration is to mount them on colored cards using one of the processes described in the chapter on mounting. If a portion of the card shows on either side of the picture, it will appear as if this was planned, and it will be perfectly acceptable.

The successful operation of the 35 mm camera requires that some familiarity with the parts and their functions be acquired. The camera that is illustrated is the Pentax, a popular brand that is commonly encountered in the production facilities of media centers, schools, and commercial processors. Your camera may not look exactly like the Pentax, but it will have the same parts, even though they might be located in slightly different places and may appear slightly different in shape and structure from the ones illustrated. Remember that every camera must have a body, or light-tight box, upon which is located a viewer or rangefinder along with a lens and lens opening (aperture) and a shutter to control the entry of light into the body. Within the camera is a support of some kind to hold the film.

Parts of the Camera (Refer to Figure 11-2)

a. The **film advance lever** moves the exposed film out of the film plane and advances a new frame into position. It also cocks the camera so that another picture can be taken.
b. The **frame counter** shows how many frames have been exposed.
c. The **shutter release** is pressed to activate the shutter, thus exposing the film.
d. The **focus ring** enables the photographer to adjust the lens until an image of maximum sharpness is obtained. This is accomplished by rotating the ring while viewing the subject through the viewfinder. The aperture (f-stop) should be wide open during this process.
e. The **f-stop ring** is rotated to open or close the aperture (hole through which the light passes when entering the camera). The f-numbers are commonly listed in a series such as 1.4, 2, 2.8, 4, 5.6, 8, 11, 16—the larger the number, the smaller the opening. Also, each succeeding number admits half as much light as the preceding one. For example, if the f-stop

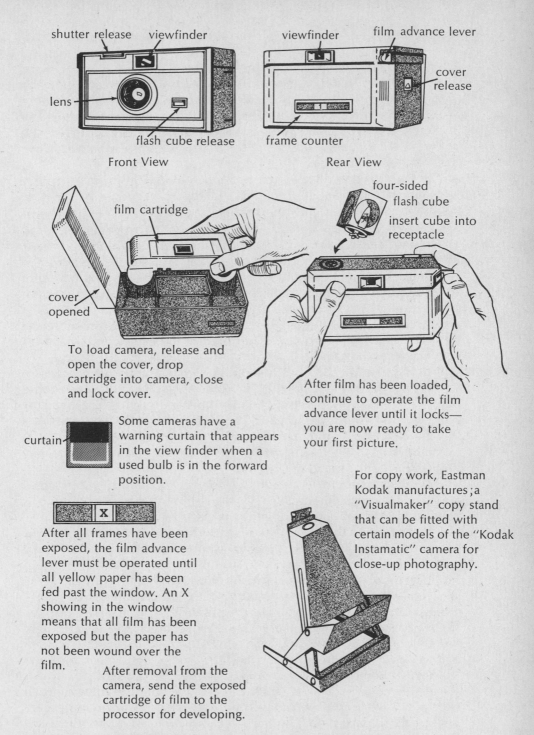

shutter release viewfinder

lens

flash cube release

Front View

viewfinder film advance lever

cover release

frame counter

Rear View

film cartridge

cover opened

To load camera, release and open the cover, drop cartridge into camera, close and lock cover.

curtain

Some cameras have a warning curtain that appears in the view finder when a used bulb is in the forward position.

X

After all frames have been exposed, the film advance lever must be operated until all yellow paper has been fed past the window. An X showing in the window means that all film has been exposed but the paper has not been wound over the film.

After removal from the camera, send the exposed cartridge of film to the processor for developing.

four-sided flash cube

insert cube into receptacle

After film has been loaded, continue to operate the film advance lever until it locks— you are now ready to take your first picture.

For copy work, Eastman Kodak manufactures;a "Visualmaker" copy stand that can be fitted with certain models of the "Kodak Instamatic" camera for close-up photography.

FIGURE 11-1 Operating a Simple Camera

setting is adjusted from f5.6 to f8, half as much light will be permitted to pass into the camera. The reverse is also true; if the setting is changed from f8 to f5.6, the amount of light is doubled.

f. The **light meter button** is pressed in order to obtain a reading on the light entering the camera. A needle within the camera will be seen to move as the meter is activated. The correct combination of f-stops and shutter speeds is obtained by adjusting one or the other or both of these settings until the meter needle is located exactly at the midpoint of the scale within the camera.

Some cameras utilize a light meter system that has a scale of numbers rather than the + and - scale of the Pentax. In order to obtain the proper setting with this system, it is necessary to adjust the f-stop ring to correspond to the number indicated by the meter needle.

g. The **rewind crank** is used to rewind the film back into the cassette after all of the frames have been exposed. When rewinding the film, it is necessary to press the rewind button (generally located on the bottom of the camera) before the crank is turned. It is important that this button be depressed because damage to the camera or the film might result if it is not. Depressing the button places the take-up spool in a free-wheeling state and enables the film to be returned to the light-tight cassette for removal from the camera.

h. The **film speed (or ASA) dial** is coupled with a small window through which the ASA may be observed. This device permits the camera to be adjusted to the specific type of film that is being used. The film speed (or ASA) is a film's sensitivity to light. The higher the ASA rating, the more sensitive the film is to light, or the "faster" it is. The ASA rating may be obtained from the literature that is packed with each roll of film and may range from a slow speed of 6 up into the hundreds.

To adjust the ASA setting on the camera, rotate the housing upon which the film speed window is located until the proper number is centered in the window . . . that's all there is to it.

i. The **shutter speed dial** and the f-stop (aperture) work together as a pair of interrelated adjustments. Generally, shutter speeds will be indicated with numbers such as 1, 2, 4, 8, 15, 30, 60, 125, 250, 500 and 1000. These numbers represent fractions of seconds or 1 sec., 1/2 sec., 1/8 sec., 1/15 sec., 1/30 sec., and so on. As with the f-stops, each succeeding number admits half as much light as the preceding one. For example, if the shutter speed is adjusted from 1/15 sec. to 1/30 sec., half as much light will be permitted to pass into the camera (because the shutter is open half as long). The reverse is also true.

Consequently, if it is determined (by reading our light meter) that the setting of 5.6 at 1/30 sec. will admit just the right amount of light to expose the film correctly, and we desire a **faster** speed, we must compensate for a faster shutter setting by opening the f-stop wider (making the aperture larger). Changing the shutter speed from 1/30 to 1/60 will

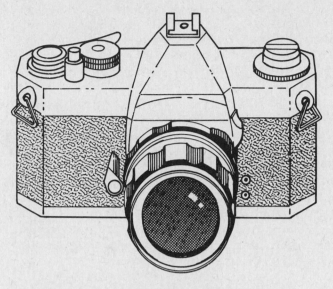

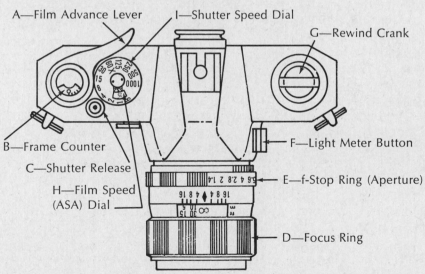

A—Film Advance Lever   I—Shutter Speed Dial

G—Rewind Crank

B—Frame Counter

C—Shutter Release

H—Film Speed
(ASA) Dial

F—Light Meter Button

E—f-Stop Ring (Aperture)

D—Focus Ring

FIGURE 11-2   35 mm Single Lens Reflex Camera

cut the amount of light that enters the camera in half; to compensate, it is necessary to open the f-stop one setting from 5.6 to 4 to double the amount of light coming through the aperture and thereby bring the light intensity back into the proper balance.

Because of the wide diversity among the various kinds of 35mm SLR cameras, it is difficult, if not impossible to present a coverage that will adequately deal with all models. The description of the various components which is given above is, of necessity, rather general in nature and relates to a basic camera with manual adjustments. The later generations of cameras incorporate a number of features and options that were not commonly available a few years ago. For example, automatic exposure control is a handy, virtually foolproof option that is built into many of the 35mm SLRs currently on the market. There are two basic kinds of automatic exposure control systems, both of which are referred to as "preferred" systems. Neither of these systems can be said to be truly "automatic" in the accepted sense; it is necessary for the operator to preset either the shutter speed or the aperture. One or the other is "preferred," hence the name for this type of system. If your camera is a shutter-preferred type, then the shutter speed must be set according to the requirements of the situation. If, on the other hand, your camera happens to be the aperture-preferred variety, then the aperture (f-stop) must be adjusted to the prescribed setting. In both cases, the other setting will be adjusted automatically (f-stop of shutter speed). Such cameras feature a manual override in case the photographer prefers to adjust both f-stop and shutter speed himself.

In addition to the automatic exposure control feature mentioned above, modern SLR cameras come with either additional options built-in or have options that can be acquired and fitted to the basic body. An example of this is the motor drive unit—an attachable package that fits on the bottom of the camera thus causing the film to advance and the shutter to cock automatically. Bulk film packs (actually an older concept that has been updated) are available that hold a sufficient amount of film to enable the photographer to take over two hundred pictures on a given roll. Many kinds of interchangeable lenses are also available, including the "normal" lens. Macro lenses permit continuous focusing out to a certain point. Extenders can be slipped between the macro lens and the camera body to extend the focal length of the lens. Zoom lenses of various kinds permit the photographer to move from long, telephoto shots through intermediate shots to close-up shots while remaining in focus at all times. Tilt and shift lenses permit the user of the 35mm camera to adjust for various kinds of distortion problems by moving the lens in different direction. This feature gives to the 35mm some of the versatility that is claimed as the exclusive domain of the view camera.

Let us now move back to the basic, manual camera and proceed through the steps that are involved in making an exposure. Remember, even though your camera is an automatic, you should nevertheless develop the expertise that is required to successfully utilize a manual version. Good photographers know that there will always exist special instances in which the automatic feature is not fully adequate (i.e., when shooting objects that are back-lighted—

this typically results in a false reading and requires a certain amount of interpolation for best results).

Shooting a Picture with the 35 MM Camera

To take a photograph, follow these steps.

1. Open the camera and load it with film (check first to see if it is already loaded; you may do this by cocking the camera and checking the rewind knob to see if it turns). The film will come loaded in a cassette that will have a "leader" extending from the light-tight opening. Hook the leader into a slot in the take-up reel and advance the film by moving the film advance lever forward and pressing the shutter release alternately. When the film is properly engaged, close the camera and lock it.

2. Continue to advance the film until the first frame is in position (as indicated in the frame counter). As you advance the film, you should observe the rewind crank or knob; it should turn counter-clockwise as the film moves onto the take-up spool. If it does not, the film is not advancing and you must open the camera and reset the film leader.

3. Adjust the ASA rating on the film speed dial to correspond to the rating listed in the literature which is packed with the film.

4. Adjust the shutter speed by twisting the dial until the desired speed matches with the dot or arrow on the housing. The speed selected is up to you; however, as a general rule, rapidly moving objects require a fast speed, while slower moving objects require a medium speed, and still objects a slow speed. Or, you may wish to adjust the aperture setting (f-stop) instead of the shutter speed. If this is the case, then the consideration will not be one of speed, as with the shutter adjustment, but one of depth of field as a general rule. You should know that the smaller the opening (f-stop), the greater the depth of field. Conversely, the larger the opening, the shallower the depth of field. The term **depth of field** is used to describe the total expanse of field that is in sharp focus. When you focus on a specific object, there will be a certain area both behind the object and in front of it that will also be in focus (1/3 in front, 2/3 behind)—this is the "depth of field."

5. Focus on your subject while viewing it through the viewfinder. Turn the focus ring back and forth until the subject appears very sharp. It is best to adjust the focus with the aperture wide open (on the lowest f-stop number, that is, 1.4)—on some cameras this feature is automatic. If your camera has a preview lever, adjust it to the automatic position and make it a point to leave it there. With the preview lever or button in this position, the aperture will always be fully open when you are viewing your subject but it will automatically close down to the preset f-stop when the exposure is made.

6. Activate the light meter by pushing the meter button; the needle will move to some position on the scale.

7. If you preset the shutter speed, rotate the f-stop ring until the needle moves to a center position on the scale (if this is the type of scale that

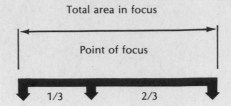

Total area in focus

Point of focus

1/3   2/3

FIGURE 11-3   Depth of Field

your camera has; many different versions are available). If you preset the aperture, move the shutter speed dial until the needle indicates that the proper amount of light is entering the camera (see above). You are now ready to make the first exposure.

8. Proceed to take photographs.
9. After all the film has been exposed, depress the rewind button and, with the rewind crank, rewind the film into the cassette.
10. Remove the cassette for processing of the film.

Following is a checklist of steps involved in using the 35mm camera:

[ ] Load the camera
[ ] Advance the film to exposure 1
[ ] Adjust the ASA
[ ] Set the shutter speed or f-stop
[ ] Focus on the subject
[ ] Read the light meter
[ ] Adjust the f-stop (aperture) or shutter speed
[ ] Expose the film
[ ] Rewind the film

FILMSTRIP CAMERAS

Filmstrip cameras are very much like the 35mm camera that has been described in detail above. The filmstrip camera differs in the size of the picture it takes and in the proportions of the picture. It employs the standard 35mm film, but it utilizes a format that is one-half of the standard full-frame 35mm slide. The proportion of the filmstrip frame is different from the full-frame slide, having a ratio of 3 to 4 rather than 2 to 3.

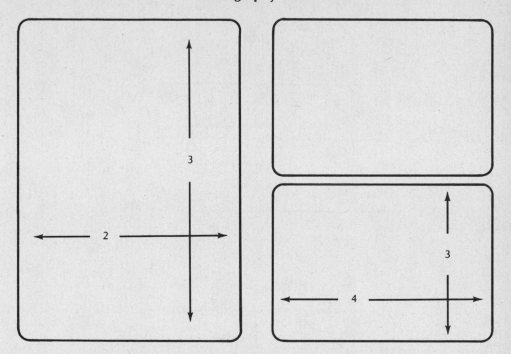

The half-frame (filmstrip) frame is 1/2 the size of the full frame (or slide).
Note the different proportions.

FIGURE 11-4 Proportions of the 35 mm Slide and Filmstrip Frame

Filmstrip cameras will take 72 frames on a standard 36-exposure roll of film, but the frames will be only one-half as large as the slides taken with the full-frame camera. Filmstrips are never cut; the frames are left attached to one another in a continuous sequence that never becomes disrupted. Of course, one of the disadvantages of the filmstrip is that it cannot be edited or changed once it has been completed . . . something that can be accomplished easily with the slide series.

The fact that the filmstrip frames remain in the sequence and position in which they were shot without providing any potential for altering them means that there is no second chance when producing this type of visual unless, of course, you would care to reshoot the total strip. Therefore you must be certain that you do it right the first time through. One way that this can be accomplished is through the use of a system that prevents either a missed frame or a frame that is photographed more than once. Some individuals stack the visuals on one side of the copy stand, place them on the stand and shoot them, then move them to a stack on the other side of the stand. You should be able to devise a system that will work for you. Incidentally, be certain that the top of your visual faces in the opposite direction from the movement of the film as it is advanced (see diagram), otherwise some of the frames may be upsidedown, or the total strip might turn out to be backwards.

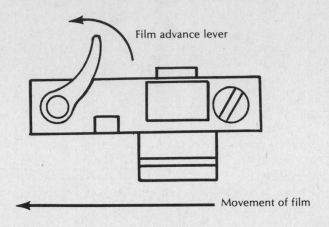

Film advance lever

Movement of film

Top of picture

FIGURE 11-5 Camera and Picture Position for Filmstrip Production

Due in part to the increased use of self-instructional packages, the filmstrip has enjoyed a considerable resurgence in popularity in recent years. Although an excellent selection of commercial strips is available, teachers frequently find it desirable to produce their own for one reason or another. The Pen FT single lens reflex has been the standard half-frame unit for the local production of filmstrips for a number of years, although the Petri, the Pen EE, and other similar units have been widely used. These cameras were rigged on various kinds of copying stands and used with different lenses, bellows, tubes, etc., according to the availability of such equipment and the ingenuity of the photographer.

Because of the demand for specialized filmstrip equipment, several companies have produced modestly-priced units of considerable sophistication and versatility. The Filmaker kit by Radmir, Inc., consists of several units that make possible the production of strips from a mix of slides, existing filmstrip frames, and "live" materials. The Filmaker pulser puts synchronizing pulses on cassette or reel tapes if automatic advancing of the strip is desired.

Standard produces an excellent filmstrip maker which is built around the Gatling 72 half-frame camera. This camera has an automatic light meter and a power film advance. Once again, a pulsing unit is available.

Standard and DuKane both produce cassette filmstrip projectors that will accommodate the sound strips that are produced with the above equipment. Of course, if the automatic advance feature is not desired, then any filmstrip projector can be used and the frames advanced manually.

COPYING WITH SLIDE AND FILMSTRIP CAMERAS

A substantial portion of the photographic work that is undertaken in the creation of teaching materials occurs right inside the media center or the classroom rather than out in the field. Pictures, drawings, photographs, and actual objects are positioned on a copy stand, illuminated with lights and photographed to make slides or filmstrips. This kind of work requires certain skills and certain kinds of equipment that differ somewhat from those which are used for general purposes.

Various kinds of copy stands are available from photo supply stores. Or, you may wish to build your own. Eastman Kodak provides the plans for a sturdy, wooden stand which can be constructed inexpensively and easily by anyone with a basic knowledge of carpentry. A copy stand should permit a wide range of vertical adjustments for the camera because of the need to accommodate many different sizes of art work.

After the camera has been secured to the stand, it must be focused on the art to be copied. Frequently, you will discover that this is not possible with the normal lens as installed on your camera. Alterations must be made in order to extend the focal length. One way in which the focal length can be multiplied is with an extension tube set. Extension tubes are tubes of various lengths that fit between the camera and the lens. These are perhaps the least expensive of any of the devices which are available for the purpose of adapting a camera for close-up photography.

Then there is the macro lens. A macro permits continuous focusing through an extended range, so it isn't necessary to add or subtract elements as with the extension tube system. For extreme close-up work, you might wish to employ a bellows attachment of some kind. These are similar to the extension tube system in that they are used between the camera and the normal lens, thus making it unnecessary to purchase an additional lens at considerable expense.

The information on close-up accessories given above is only applicable if a camera with a removable lens is being used. It does not apply if your camera is one of the viewfinder varieties that lacks this feature. In a case such as this, you will find it necessary to acquire close-up lenses that screw on over the normal lens thus making it possible to focus on small objects or pictures that otherwise would be beyond the capability of the normal lens. If you should use this approach, however, remember that the parallax problem should be resolved before you begin to take pictures. Handling the problem of parallax involves some a priori preparation that is somewhat time-consuming but, once accomplished, need not be repeated.

Attach the camera to the copy stand; set the shutter on T (time) or B (bulb) so that it will remain open; open the aperture to the widest setting. Next, open the back of the camera and place a small piece of opal or frosted glass or matt plastic in the film plane (the position that the film occupies when the camera is loaded). Now, turn out the overhead lights while illuminating the area upon which you will be focusing; position the picture to be copied. Adjust the camera until the image fills the frosted glass and is in sharp focus, then, mark the position that the four corners of the picture (the original being copied) occupy on the base of the copy stand. You may wish to tape a sheet of cardboard to the base before proceeding with the marking step. Measure the distance from the base of the stand to the lens of the camera, and indicate this on the stand, or in a tablet, along with an identifying mark for the lines just scribed on the base of the stand. This will give you two figures with which to work—the distance figure and the letter or number that identifies the particular configuration on the base of the stand that correlates with it. You should also indicate which, if any, close-up lenses were employed.

You can now proceed to derive any number of combinations by using the system just described with different sizes of pictures. In each instance, the distance from camera to stand base will change as the size of the visual changes. Eventually, you will have a series of lines on the stand that will correspond to a variety of picture sizes. Positioning the material to be copied in the frame of the proper size and adjusting the camera to the proper height will enable you to create excellent photographs that are free from parallax error.

Let's consider lighting. It is possible to use many light sources for photographing various kinds of subject matter. Flood lights are good for controlled photography such as that involving the use of a copy stand and flat pictures. Daylight is a fine light source when using the copy stand, if no shadows are cast by windows, curtains, trees, etc. Daylight, of course, is also used for outdoor photography of various kinds. Light from overhead lights, table lamps, windows, display cabinets, and so on is often the only available light and must be used. Colored photographs taken under available light may display strange color effects due to the unknown qualities of the light. Typically, slides taken indoors under available light will exhibit a greenish cast that will cause them to look quite different from the original subjects as far as color quality is concerned.

Strobe and flash light sources give much better color control than is generally obtainable under available light conditions. However, light from electronic sources such as these may "fall off" rapidly causing background objects to be darker than foreground objects. Flood lights are excellent for use with the copy stand; they are also very versatile when shooting posed subjects in the lab.

It is essential that the color film be matched to the light source as closely as possible. Daylight film should be used with blue flashbulbs and cubes, natural light and daylight strobes. "B" films (tungsten) work best with lamps that are marked "3200°" (the light temperature for which the film is adjusted). Black and white film will work well with any light, as long as it is bright enough, because color is not a factor with this kind of film.

A satisfactory method for arranging the lighting is to use two lights which are placed on either side of the copy stand and angled down toward the material to be copied at a slant of about 45°. If reflections are evident as you look through the viewer, you should manipulate the lamps until an even illumination is obtained. Reflections are particularly problematical when a sheet of glass is placed over the visual to hold it flat (unless special nonglare photographic glass is used). Professional photographers often resolve the problem of glare by employing special polarized filters on the camera along with a set of polarized lights for illumination. Incidentally, many of the reflections that you might pick up on your film often originate with the camera itself. Chrome and silver cameras are beautiful to look at, but they have a nasty habit of reflecting light from their shiny surfaces. A simple strategy for overcoming this problem is to fit a baffle made of matt black paper or card with a hole in the center over the lens barrel. If the hole is cut so that it is slightly smaller than the diameter of the barrel, the baffle will fit snugly in place when in use but can be readily removed when it is not needed.

You are now ready to load the camera with the proper type of film and to make the necessary camera adjustments; then you can proceed with the copy work.

FILMS AND FILM PROCESSING

Various types of films are available that are designed to meet a variety of needs and conditions, but only a small selection of these is commonly employed in the production of teaching materials.

A high contrast black and white line film such as Kodalith is useful for creating titles as well as slides and prints from line originals. This type of film has a slow filmspeed and must be exposed for a longer period of time than is the case with other faster films. Consequently, it is suitable for use only with cameras that are held stationary and with subjects that lack movement. Kodalith can be obtained in 35mm, 4x5, and 8x10 sizes, among others. This is an ortho-chromatic film which can be processed under a red light source (the term "orthochromatic" is used to identify films that lack sensitivity to the red band of the spectrum).

Various types of colored slide films are available that are balanced for different light sources. Matching the film with the kind of light that is being utilized produces color effects of maximum fidelity. Among the films that are meant to be used with daylight are Kodachrome 25, Kodachrome 64, and high speed Ektachrome. Kodachrome II Professional is listed as a "Type A" film—such films are meant to be used with photolamps rated at 3400 K. High speed Ektachrome "Type B" film is a popular variety for use on the copy stand. It is used with a tungsten light source of 3200 K. Of course, it is perfectly feasible to use one type of film for all kinds of light situations. However, this approach will necessitate the use of an appropriate selection of filters for best results.

A wide selection of black and white films is also available. Kodak Plus X is a negative film that is available in the 35mm format; it is a general-purpose panchromatic film of medium speed which is an ideal all-around choice for most work. Incidentally, the term "panchromatic" is used to describe films that are, for all practical purposes, sensitive to the full range of the visible spectrum—these must be processed in total darkness.

Another good black and white film is Kodak Panatomic-X. It has a slow speed of 32 which limits its versatility somewhat, a limitation that is more than offset by the high quality of the negatives that are produced. Use it if you plan to make prints with a high degree of enlargement. For a faster film, try Kodak Tri-X, which has a speed of 400—a good choice for subjects that are moving rapidly or for subjects in low-light situations.

Once your films have been exposed, you will want to process them. This may be accomplished in the school darkroom or in any room that can be modified to exclude all light. Processing is quite simple and represents a creative and exciting extension of the traditional use of the camera. Color processing takes considerable time, but it is not as difficult as many people imagine it to be. Color processing kits may be purchased from the local photo supply store for a reasonable price. Generally, it is more economical in the long run to send the colored film to a commercial processor for development and mounting unless the objective is to give students the experience of actually running through the sequence. You might also wish to process your own film if time happens to be a factor, although in some locales it is possible to get one-day service with such films as Ektachrome. One last reason for engaging in such processing might be the factor of control—not quality control, for commercial processors are normally very careful about this, but the control of the development process that enables you to do things with the film that are out of the ordinary and not possible unless changes and alterations in times and temperatures, among other things, are made.

Black and white films are easily processed by the teacher and/or students. Black and white film, unlike colored film, produces a negative rather than a positive upon processing (although special direct-positive reversal processing will result in black and white positives). This means that the film must be printed onto other film or print paper in order to obtain positives, or it must be used as a negative frame.

Continuous tone black and white film (such as Plus X) may be processed following the directions shown on the continuous tone film processing plate. The negatives that result must then be contact printed or enlarged to create photographic prints. The correct times and temperatures for various kinds of film and chemicals are indicated in the literature which is packed with the chemicals.

Line film (such as Kodalith) may be processed according to the directions shown on the line film processing plate. Line film has a slow ASA (about 6) and is generally used to photograph flat pictures and diagrams. This film will not photograph grays (continuous tones) as gray, but sees everything as either black or white. It photographs dark grays as black and light grays as white. This film gives a striking black and white negative which may be stained with water colors, dyes, or food coloring for an attractive effect and used just as it is without reprinting it as a positive. Line film is particularly effective for class use because

Processing Continuous Tone Film

1—Remove the exposed film from the cassette and load it onto a processing reel. This must be done in total darkness.

2—Place reel in tank, position lid. Light can now be turned on. Pour developer into tank (refer to data sheet packed with film for details).

3—Agitate film (refer to data sheet packed with film for details).

4—After film has been developed for specified length of time (see data sheet for details) pour developer into another container—fill tank with stop bath—rinse film for 30 sec.

5—Pour stop bath into another container—fill tank with fixer—fix for 5-10 min. Pour stop bath back into its container.

6—Wash the film in running water for about 20 min. Hang up to dry. After drying, the negatives can be printed onto film to form slides or onto paper to form prints.

Printing from Negatives

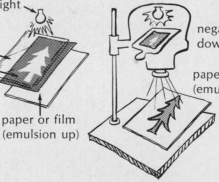

A sheet of glass will hold the negative in position

negative (emulsion down)

Contact printing is accomplished by placing the negative against the film or paper in such a manner that the exposing light will pass through the negative. If a contact printer is available, this will simplify the process.

light

paper or film (emulsion up)

negative (emulsion down)

paper or film (emulsion up)

Enlarging is accomplished with a photographic enlarger and enlarging paper or film.

Processing the positive is much the same as processing the nega- tive: develop, rinse, fix, and wash. Refer to data sheet packed with films and papers for correct chemicals, temperatures, and times.

FIGURE 11-6 Processing Continuous Tone Film

of the fact that it is not essential to go to the time and trouble to make a positive print or frame from the negative as is the case with continuous tone film. It is also low in cost, easy to process (you may do it under red lights), and slow in processing; even elementary students can work with line film successfully. This type of film is particularly good for creating titles.

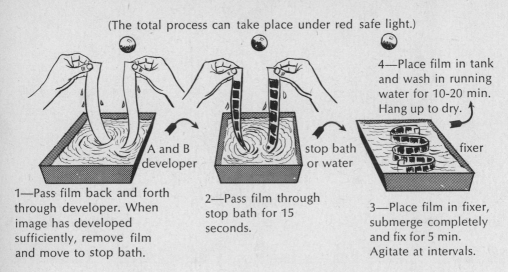

(The total process can take place under red safe light.)

A and B developer

stop bath or water

fixer

4—Place film in tank and wash in running water for 10-20 min. Hang up to dry.

1—Pass film back and forth through developer. When image has developed sufficiently, remove film and move to stop bath.

2—Pass film through stop bath for 15 seconds.

3—Place film in fixer, submerge completely and fix for 5 min. Agitate at intervals.

FIGURE 11-7 Processing Line Film Using the Tray Method

INSTANT CAMERAS

It seems inappropriate to leave the subject of still cameras without making reference to the instant cameras that are so popular these days. The grandfather of them all was the original Polaroid Land model that first made its appearance over a generation ago. A wide variety of improved models have been introduced over the years including the MP-4 system which enables the photographer to do everything from microphotography to large-format copy work with one camera.

Recently, Eastman Kodak introduced the EK4 and the EK6 instant models and will make the folding model EK8 available in the near future. The EK4 utilizes a hand crank to feed the film through the camera, while the EK6 is automatic in this respect. Both cameras have electronically controlled apertures and shutter speeds and are therefore fully automatic. A red low-light signal is triggered in the viewfinder when the light level is too low for exposure. At this point, the operator resorts to the flip-flash, which is a bank of flash cubes that makes it unnecessary to handle the cubes individually.

Focus is made possible through the use of a unique circle distance finder. It is merely necessary to frame the subject inside of the circle to insure that the image will be sharp.

INSTANT CAMERAS
Courtesy Eastman Kodak Co.

The instant print film used with the Kodak model is packaged in a ten-picture pack that is inserted into the camera as a unit. The resultant image is about 2½ x 3½ inches in size.

The educational potential for the instant camera is considerable. Over the years, this approach has made the recording of visual images both simple and immediate and has made it possible for the picture to become an integral part of the magic happening while it is taking place by cutting out the extended lag time that used to take place between the time the exposure was made and the vendor returned the processed prints.

The continuing improvements in instant films and cameras will make it possible for the teacher to be ever more creative and innovative in the classroom.

PHOTOGRAPHIC COMPOSITION

The suggestions that were outlined in the chapter on composition apply to all forms of graphic design including photography. You may want to review this section in order to determine ways in which you can make your pictures more effective and attractive. Generally, the informally balanced design will be more pleasant than one that is stiff and formal. Have your subjects looking into the picture rather than out of it; the viewer's eyes will then move into the picture more readily, and the message will be communicated more effectively. Remember to emphasize the important part of the scene through the use of placement, size, color, etc. Look for unity in your designs; this is the characteristic that makes them "hold together" and gives them a feeling of oneness.

PRODUCING SUPER 8 MOTION PICTURES

Although the super 8 camera is a popular item around the house, it finds its best application in the production of educational films in the school. Because of the careful planning and programming that precede the production of most school films, their quality and content will generally be considerably more professional than will that of the typical home movie. This seems to be the key to successful motion picture production—planning, and plenty of it. Before you begin the shooting sequence, sit down and carefully determine precisely what it is that you want to accomplish. A good idea at this point is to write some objectives. You may find that a slide series, or some transparencies, can do the job as well as or better than can the motion picture; so, use the medium that will most effectively achieve the desired results.

After you have decided that the motion picture is the best alternative, jot down your ideas in some kind of sequential order. You may prefer to create a "storyboard" that consists of small cards upon which you will indicate the scene to be photographed, the camera position (long shot, close-up, medium shot), and the verbal accompaniment or script. These cards can then be sequenced by tacking them to the bulletin board or by laying them out on the table. Read through the cards; do they make sense? How about the transitions? These should be smooth and logical. The storyboard approach should be used whenever a sequenced visual presentation is planned. For additional information on creating and utilizing the storyboard, refer to the section on this subject on page 000.

One important last suggestion before you pick up the camera and squeeze the trigger: keep your productions modest and simple; don't attempt to produce an epic. Leave this to Hollywood; they're better equipped than you are. A good rule is to restrict the subject matter to one concept, and one concept only. If additional material is to be stressed, think in terms of a series of single concept films that go together to make a set. These films will be useful when shown as "singles" or when combined in a lengthier session.

Parts of the Camera (Refer to Fig. 11-8)

a. The **audio-gain switch** automatically adjusts the sound level during recording.
b. The **auto-manual selector** permits the lens opening to be set manually or to be controlled electronically.
c. The **earphone monitor** makes it possible, when the earphones are plugged in, to hear the sound as it is being recorded.
d. The **fade control** either causes the image to gradually appear out of the darkness (fade-in), or causes the image to gradually turn completely dark (fade-out).
e. The **filter switch** adjusts to the type of film (indoor or outdoor) being used.
f. The **focusing ring** is manipulated to bring the subject into sharp focus.
g. The **microphone outlet** is where the microphone is plugged in when sound movies are to be produced.

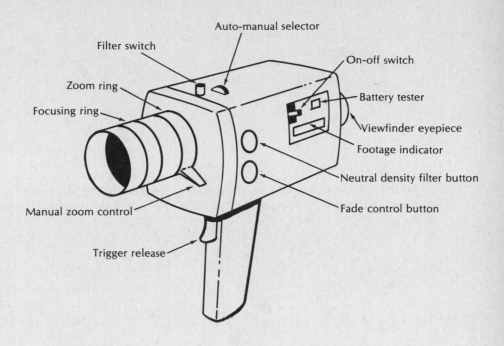

Auto-manual selector

Filter switch

On-off switch

Zoom ring

Battery tester

Focusing ring

Viewfinder eyepiece

Footage indicator

Manual zoom control

Neutral density filter button

Fade control button

Trigger release

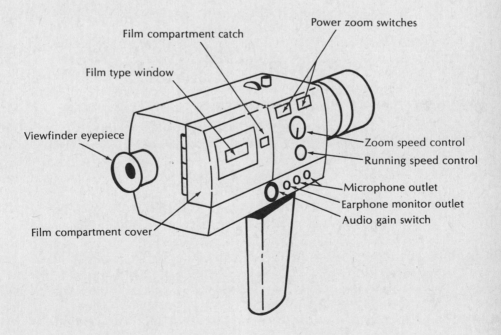

Film compartment catch

Power zoom switches

Film type window

Viewfinder eyepiece

Zoom speed control

Running speed control

Microphone outlet

Earphone monitor outlet

Audio gain switch

Film compartment cover

FIGURE 11-8   A Generalized Super 8 Motion Picture Camera

h. The **neutral density filter** prevents overexposure from too much light.
i. The **running speed control** permits effects such as slow and fast motion, as well as normal speed effects.
j. The **zoom speed control** permits adjustment of the speed at which the movement from wide angle to telephoto occurs.
k. The **zoom switches (power)** control the in-out movement of the lens. One is a wide-angle switch; the other is a telephoto switch.
l. The **zoom control (manual)** permits the photographer to control the wide-angle and telephoto effects manually.

FILMOSONIC SUPER 8 CAMERA
Courtesy Bell and Howell

Shooting a Movie with the Super 8

After all of the preliminary steps have been taken and you are ready to begin the actual shooting, you should follow these steps:

1. Open the film compartment and load the camera with a fresh cartridge of film. Determine what your light source will be. If you will be working out of doors, make certain that the camera is adjusted to sunlight. If you will be indoors, set the light adjustment for artificial light. Some cameras have a miniature sun and a tiny light bulb printed on either side of the filter switch; others use different identifying marks or symbols.
2. Turn the on-off switch to the "on" position; set the film speed selector to "18".
3. If your camera has a manual override, check this setting to make sure that it is in the automatic mode. The manual override is a feature that permits the photographer to uncouple the automatic aperture control from the light-sensing mechanism within the camera. Cameras that have built-in light meters will have self-adjusting apertures that make it unnecessary to adjust the f-stop on the camera manually. However, there are situations when you may desire to employ a manual control (for example, in fade-in and fade-out sequences). When this is the case, such a feature can be useful.

4. When viewing through the viewfinder, a scale of f-stops will be visible. On either end of the scale, a red area indicates too much or too little light for proper exposure. If the needle is observed to be i either red area, you should not attempt to photograph the scene. However, if the needle indicates overexposure, it is possible to cut the amount of light entering the camera by moving the neutral density filter (generally identified with an "ND" designation) into the lens system. When the ND filter is in position, you will notice that the light meter needle will move back out of the red area and into the "shooting range." Make certain that you retract the ND filter when it is no longer needed, that is, when the light is diminished or less intense, or when a slower film is being used.

    To focus, zoom the lens to the telephoto position, then align the infinity symbol with the mark on the lens barrel. Look through the viewfinder at a distant object. If the image is not sharp, adjust the focus until a satisfactory image is obtained. Fine focus is obtained through the manual adjustment of a knob or ring.

5. With the camera turned on, and the aperture control in the "auto" mode, you are now ready to focus on the subject.

6. You are now ready to photograph the subject. To use the zoom lens, you may zoom in or out (from wide angle to telephoto) until the image size is satisfactory, then begin the shooting sequence. Or, you may wish to use the zoom feature during the act of filming. In this instance, interesting effects can be obtained that often add to the quality of the presentation. One word of caution: do not overdo the use of the zoom feature when creating a film. The end effect can be somewhat like taking a roller coaster ride with images racing toward and away from you in a manner that is quite unpleasant. Zooming should be a steady, slow process which is free of jerky movements. All that you have to do now is expose the film. With the trigger unlocked, slowly squeeze until the camera begins to operate, then maintain a steady, level support as the film is exposed. Use a tripod, particularly in the telephoto mode, whenever feasible.

7. After the desired footage has been shot, secure the camera by turning the power switch to the "off" position.

8. After the film has been completely exposed, the cassette is removed and sent to the processor for development.

Many special effects are possible with the super 8 camera. Depending on the model you are using, you will be able to accomplish several, or even all, of the following techniques:

Zoom effects. Zoom effects are the result of moving the lens from telephoto to wide angle and vice versa while shooting is in progress.

Fadings. The effect of fading-in or fading-out is used to represent a change in time or location. Moving the aperture control from a larger to a smaller opening will give a fade-out, while the reverse movement will result in a fade-in.

The time-lapse technique. The time-lapse technique is used to record an extremely slow action, such as a flower bud opening into a flower. By exposing individual frames one at a time and then running the film at normal speeds when it is being viewed, an action that may have taken hours appears to occur in a matter of minutes. Some cameras have an attachment that permits time-lapse techniques to be accomplished automatically.

Slow motion. The slow-motion technique is the opposite of the time-lapse technique described above. When a motion takes place too rapidly for adequate study, it may be desirable to capture it in slow motion. If the camera is adjusted to photograph more frames than are needed for normal projection, the action will appear to be slowed down when the film is projected at the normal rate. Most super 8 cameras have the slow motion feature (36 frames per second), but few of them include the time-lapse feature. An examination of your camera will tell you whether or not these techniques will be possible with your equipment.

Animation. If the camera that you are using has a single-frame feature, you will be able to create some interesting animation effects that can include cartoons and other artistic creations. Movement in an animation sequence is accomplished by photographing a series of visuals one at a time (single framing). The visuals display slight modifications from frame to frame in the sequence. If a cartoon character is to raise his arm, the arm in each succeeding picture will be slightly higher than in the preceding one. When all of the frames are completed and are projected at a normal speed, the illusion is one of continuous movement. Animation can be accomplished with actual objects, such as a dry mount press or a set of cardboard letters. By positioning a picture in the press a stage at a time and then photographing it at each stage, it will appear to move into the press all by itself with no observable help from any outside source.

An interesting titling effect can be created by building the title one letter at a time and one frame at a time. The title seems to pop up out of nowhere in an exciting, animated manner. You will be able to invent any number of additional ways in which animated effects can be created that will add spice to your super 8 motion pictures.

Titling. The most common method of making titles involves the use of letters that are placed on or adhered to some kind of background (see chapter on lettering techniques). These cards are then exposed for several seconds on the motion picture film. Other approaches include placing the letters on a piece of glass which is then supported over a background material to give a three-dimensional look to the title. Then there is the animated title described in the section on animation. This effect can be achieved only if you have access to a camera that will single-frame. Another technique that incorporates motion involves photographing the title as it is being written or printed on a chalkboard or card.

Taking pictures under subdued light conditions. Many super 8 cameras can be used with "fast" color film (ASA 160) to create good motion pictures under low-light conditions. Available light conditions indoors are normally not suitable for making motion pictures; some supplementary light source is needed. It may not be practical to illuminate activities such as basketball games, assemblies, and plays to the extent that the standard cameras and films can be used. This is when the combination of fast camera and film comes into play.

In order for equipment to be compatible with the 160 film it must have a lens system, or shutter system, or both, that permits more light to enter than is typically the case. A check with your photographic vendor will give you the information that you need about low-light photography techniques and equipment.

Sound. Modern sound cameras have the built-in capability of recording the visual and the audio simultaneously thus making sound movies simple and practical to produce. A microphone, which is attached directly to the camera by a long cord, can be positioned in such a way as to pick up the desired audio while at the same time being unobtrusive. Some microphones have a remote on/off switch which enables the individual to control the operation of the camera from the point at which the microphone is located. This means that the filming of a presentation is possible without the assistance of outside personnel—a single person can act as camera and sound man as well as actor and narrator.

Cameras are normally equipped with an automatic gain control which serves to pick up the dominant sound—which should be the desired narration or other effect—while at the same time suppressing the background noises. This is useful when recording "on the spot." However, there may be times when synchronized filming and recording either is not desired or is impractical for one reason or another. If such is the case, then it is a simple matter to leave the sound track blank (don't activate the sound system when filming) to be filled in at a later time.

You should know that the specific picture frame and the sound that accompanies it are separated from one another by a gap of eighteen frames. This results, of course, from the fact that the film gate and the sound drum are physically separated on the projector. As a picture is being projected onto the screen, the attendant sound is being sensed by the sound drum "downstream" from the frame. This lag must be considered when filming because editing will be next to impossible otherwise. In other words, if the sound starts at the exact beginning of a particular visual sequence, no latitude for cutting and splicing is built in—a cut at the beginning or end of a visual sequence will result in the sound track being cut apart also. You should allow the camera to operate at least two seconds before beginning to record sound. Additionally, you should follow this rule at the start and finish of any particular segment that might eventually be edited out for resequencing.

THE STORYBOARD

Because your slide, filmstrip and motion picture presentations are basically visual in nature, it will be useful to orient yourself to thinking in visual terms while planning the presentation. An aid to visual thinking is the storyboard. It forces you to relegate the verbal material to a secondary role, which is as it should be in the case of the photographic presentation. If you have ever tried to describe a visual phenomenon to someone else (and who hasn't), you know how difficult it is to successfully communicate the precise impression that you wish to with words alone. So, a storyboard becomes a method by which you can reveal your ideas to others in a visual mode even before you go to the time and expense of encoding them in some permanent form such as a slide or print. By examining your storyboard, others can give you important suggestions as to how improvements can be made in sequence, continuity, etc. If you "can't draw a straight line," just use stick figures, or rough approximations of what the finished visual will look like. You can always look for an example of the thing you want and then photograph it. Or, you may have students who are good artists. Then, too, you might pose "models" and photograph them. Or, find pictures in books and magazines that can be photographed on the 35mm format.

A typical storyboard frame consists of the following parts:

Sequence. The particular sequence within the total presentation should be identified. For example, a filmstrip on outdoor cooking might have several sequences including one on the dutch oven, one on cooking with foil, etc.

Frame. The frame within the total strip. Example, frame #1, #2, etc.

An example of a completed storyboard frame

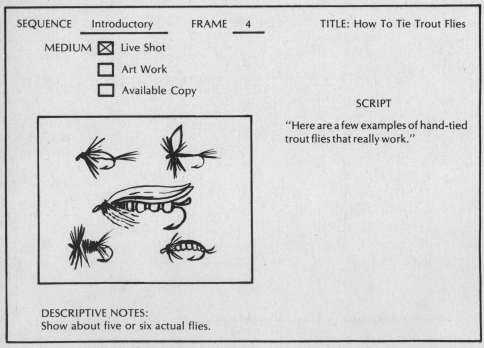

FIGURE 11-9   An Example of a Completed Storyboard Frame

Title. The title of the strip or slide series, such as "Outdoor Cookery."

Medium. The medium is divided into (a) live shot, or a slide of something or someone "out in the real world"; (b) art work that you or your students will have to draw; (c) available copy, such as a picture in a book or magazine, etc.

Descriptive notes. A space below the rectangular area which is provided for the sketch is set aside for such descriptive notes as might be deemed useful. A typical descriptive note might be "drop out white title from colored slide of campfire."

Script. The script is the verbal portion of the frame. Remember, this is a visual presentation. If you have a lengthy narration in this space, you may wish to divide it into two, or even more segments that might stretch over an equivalent number of additional visual frames. You may have problems in devising visuals for each segment of wording; however, consider the possibility of using several views of a given visual item. Or try shots from different distances. For example, a lengthy introduction to out-door cookery might be stretched over a half dozen slides that illustrate pans on a campfire. These slides could be taken from a distance, to show the campsite surrounding the fireplace; from a middle range to concentrate on the fire and pans; from a close-up position to emphasize the interesting features of the old smoke-blackened camp utensils; and then you might look right down into the pans to show the trout sizzling in the bacon grease.

SCRIPTS

Scripts should be created in such a manner that anyone can use them. They should normally be made up of three columns. The first column lists the frame number; the second has a sketch of the slide; the third column contains the script. The script should be short enough that its attendant slide will not remain on the screen for too long a period (fifteen seconds is optimal for most slides). Including a rendering of the slide (can be a simple line drawing) will insure that the synchronization between the visual screen image and the text can be maintained. Pausing at the end of each verbal segment for about two seconds and underlining or capitalizing the last word in the segment will alert the operator to the fact that it is time to change the slide. See Figure 11-10.

EDITING

An essential last step in the production of photographic visuals is that of editing. As far as the slide or still picture sequence is concerned, this can be as simple as laying the pictures out on a table (for the nonprojected prints) or on a slide sorter (for the transparent slides) for examination and reorganization. But the motion picture film is a different matter. It is more complicated and time-

3-D TEACHING MATERIALS

FRAME	VISUAL	SCRIPT
1	3-D Teaching Materials	Three-dimensional materials are all around us. They constitute examples of form, and they display the quality of actual depth. They often furnish tactual experiences where these are desired.
2	Puppets	There are many kinds of three-dimensional materials. First, let's consider puppets.
3		These collections of buttons, rags and thread assume life-like characteristics when an active child manipulates them. One variety is the hand or glove puppet. This one was made from an old sock.
4		Here's another sock puppet. The foot becomes the dog's head.

FIGURE 11-10   Three-Dimensional Teaching Materials

consuming to edit this type of material because it must be cut and spliced rather than simply moved around.

With a little practice, you will become very adept at editing. Initially, you will probably be quite hesitant about cutting the film into pieces, and particularly about discarding any portion of it. However, be brutal where this is concerned and think only of the ultimate quality of the finished product.

Many types of editors and splicers are on the market which range from extremely simple, inexpensive pocket models to professional versions that can be relatively expensive. All will do a satisfactory job, although the better ones are probably easier on the operator because they take less effort to use and are more efficient as far as time is concerned. Check with your local camera vendor for this type of equipment—if you desire good motion pictures, it is indispensable.

BIBLIOGRAPHY

Bell and Howell. **Operator's Manual, Focus-Matic Super 8 Model 672/XL.** Chicago: Bell and Howell Consumer Products, n.d.

The Camera. New York: Time-Life Books, 1970.

Eastman Kodak Company. **Better Movies in Minutes.** Rochester, N.Y.: Eastman Motion Picture and Education Markets Division, 1974.

——————— . **Movies with a Purpose.** Rochester, N.Y.: Eastman Kodak Motion Picture and Education Markets Division, 1969.

——————— . **Planning and Producing Slide Programs.** Rochester, N.Y.: Eastman Motion Picture and Education Markets Division, 1975.

Frye, R. A. **Photographic Tools for Teachers.** Mapleville, R.I.: Roadrunner Press, 1976.

Holmes, Frank. **Facts You Should Know About Filmstrips.** San Fernando, Calif.: Frank Holmes Laboratories, 1965.

Honeywell Pentax Operating Manual. Littleton, Colo.: Honeywell, n.d.

Kemp, Jerrold E. **Planning and Producing Audiovisual Materials.** New York: Thomas Y. Crowell Company, Inc., 1975.

Kennedy, Keith. **Film Making in Creative Teaching.** New York: Watson-Guptill Publications, 1972.

Resch, George T. **Super 8 Filmmaking.** New York: Franklin Watts, Inc., 1975.

Wittich, Walter A., Schuller, Charles F., Hessler, David W., and Smith, Jay C. **Student Production Guide to Accompany Instructional Technology.** 5th ed., New York: Harper & Row, 1975.

12

AUDIO TECHNIQUES

INTRODUCTION

Recordings can be used alone or in conjunction with presentations that include other kinds of media. Both approaches will be considered in this chapter, as will such other concerns as equipment operation, kinds of materials, and production techniques.

Audio recording equipment of various kinds is not only common in the classroom, but in the home as well. Because of this wide range of availability and the relatively low cost of equipment and tapes, the audio approach to teaching and learning is both popular and effective.

APPLICATIONS

A wide selection of tape recordings is commercially available that will meet many needs. Also, the simplicity of in-house recording makes it possible to produce tapes that are tailored to specific purposes.

Whether you elect to use a commercial recording or to create one of your own, the potential for various kinds of uses is virtually limitless. Here are just a few of the ways in which recordings and recorders can be useful in the classroom:

- Tapes are virtually indispensable when individualized approaches to learning are being employed. When the sound-slide or sound-filmstrip package is being used, signals on the tape let the student know when to advance to the next frame. If the package consists of a flip chart-sound combination, the signal alerts the student to turn the page.

- Instructions relating to processes can be recorded onto tape for play back as the individual works through the sequential steps. For example, although the mixing of pigments is a highly visual activity, verbal directions can lead the young artist through the steps of combining colors to create new ones.
- Students who have been absent can catch up with the rest of the class if they have access to recordings of your presentations. Just think of the time and effort that this saves you as a teacher!
- When students don earphones, they effectively cut out the extraneous classroom noise and are able to concentrate much more adequately on what they are attempting to learn.
- Creative activities might include the recording of unusual sounds that are synthesized in a number of ways. An interesting experiment involves attempting to develop sounds that represent different feelings or moods.
- A voice that is recorded and then played back can be evaluated as to quality, inflection, and so forth. Individuals benefit from this activity since it gives them the opportunity to correct or improve problems that might be identified.
- Interviews with famous people, professionals, or others who may not have the time to visit the school can be recorded onto tape for playback at a later time.
- Poetry, music, dramas, all can be recorded and preserved.
- Recordings are invaluable aids in learning a foreign language.
- Instead of using the traditional paper-and-pencil method of responding, students can do their lessons on tape and submit these instead of themes and other written materials.
- Students might make a sound trip by recording sounds as they are encountered during a walk around the school grounds or neighborhood. It is an interesting exercise to see if others can retrace the trip on the basis of sounds only.
- In some schools, students are encouraged to take recorders and tapes home with them. This extends the classroom environment into the home and involves parents more directly in the teaching-learning process.

THE PRINCIPLES OF TAPE RECORDING

Audio tape consists of a thin strip of mylar or acetate that has a binder which is impregnated with iron oxide particles on one side.

As the tape moves past an electromagnet, these minute particles are rearranged into a different pattern. This rearrangement occurs as a result of the electronic conversion of sound waves into magnetic impulses. Since the initial signals are weak, amplification is required to make the conversion more efficient.

Once the sound has been encoded onto the tape in the form of a pattern, it can be decoded and converted from magnetic signals to sound waves to complete the cycle.

The electromagnetic units that are responsible for the conversion of the sound to the stored signal and back again are called **heads.** There are three functions that the heads serve—recording, playing and erasing. Although some recorders have a separate head for each function, most recorders combine operations so that only heads are needed.

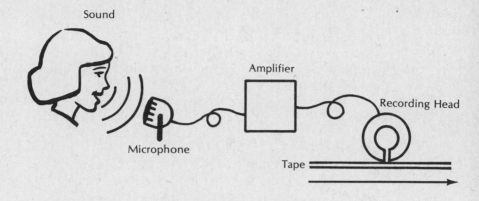

Recording Sequence

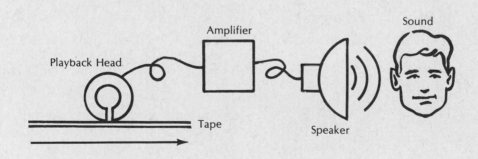

Playback Sequence

FIGURE 12-1 The Basic Principle of Tape Recording

TRACK PATTERNS AND TAPE SPEEDS

The term **track pattern** is used to describe the configuration of the sound pattern on the tape.

A track that is played singly is termed **monaural.** When two tracks are played simultaneously, this is **stereo** configuration. Although one and two tracks are played for monaural and stereo respectively, most monaural recordings are made on what is termed the **half track** format; most stereo recording is done on the **quarter track** format. This is easy to understand when you consider the fact that tapes are normally played on one side, then turned over and played on the opposite side. This means that when a half track monaural tape is played, only one of the two tracks is read as it passes by the play head; then, upon being reversed, the other track—now in playing position—is read. Since the stereo mode requires that two tracks play simultaneously, a quarter track format is needed in order that the cassette or reel can be turned over and played back through the machine.

The track arrangement described above makes it possible to place twice as much material on a tape as would be the case if a single track, for monaural, or double track, for stereo, were used.

The quarter track cassette pattern differs from that of the reel-to-reel quarter track pattern in that the two adjacent tracks, rather than alternate tracks, pass by the play heads simultaneously. This makes it possible for a given recorder to play either a monaural or a stereo tape. Although cassette recorders play at the one speed of 1⅞ inches per second (ips), reel-to-reel recorders have a range of 1⅞, 3¾, and 7½ ips.

As a general rule, the fast speed of 7½ ips is used for the recording of music, or when optimum fidelity is desired. The speed of 3¾ ips is a good average

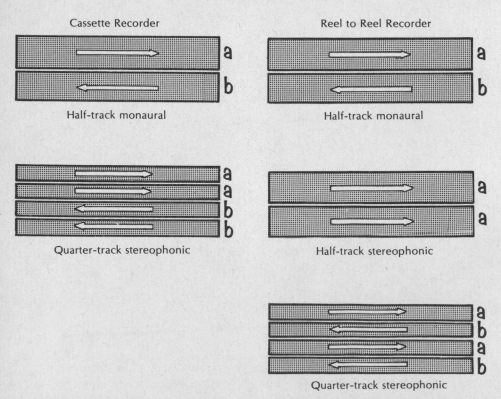

FIGURE 12-2   Different Track Patterns

setting for most work, while the slow speed of 1⅞ ips permits the recording of considerably more information on a given segment of tape. It should be noted, however, that improvements in the slower machines have greatly increased the potential for quality sound reproduction.

OPERATING THE TAPE RECORDER

Recorders differ considerably between models and brands. However, the information given here is compatible with most of the equipment that is to be found in the average school or media center. The best way to approach the problem of operating a recorder for the first time is to begin by identifying the various parts on the machine. Next, procure a tape or cassette and proceed with the loading and operating sequences. Recorders are rugged and there is little likelihood that you will do any damage even if you should make a mistake or two.

CASSETTE TAPE RECORDER
Courtesy Bell and Howell

The Cassette Recorder. Cassette recorders differ widely in their appearance, but underneath the cosmetics, they are all pretty much alike. All will have a cassette compartment and a device that opens this so that the cassette can be inserted or removed. A record button is provided on the models that include the record mode (some models are used for playback only). A rewind control, fast-forward control, stop button, and play button are also included. A volume control permits the sound level to be varied; many machines contain an automatic sound level device for the control of sound inputs. Various jacks for headphones, speakers, and microphones will be found in different locations on the recorder case. Cassette recorders often have a power cord for AC current operation in addition to self-contained batteries.

1. Insert the cassette by opening the cassette compartment (1). This is accomplished by pressing the "eject" button (2) on some machines, while others have this feature coupled with the "stop" button. The cassette should be placed in the compartment so that the tape side faces

out. Cassettes have a side marked "A" and one marked "B"; when recording, the "A" side is used first, then the "B" side.

2. After closing the lid, press the "rewind" button (3) or the "fast-forward" button (4) to move the tape to the proper position. If the tape is already rewound on the take-up reel, you can omit this step.

3. Press the "play" button (5) and adjust the "volume control" (6).

4. After the tape has finished playing, press the "stop" button (7). To play the opposite side of the tape, eject the cassette, turn it over, place it back into the machine, and repeat the above steps.

5. To record, plug the microphone into the "mic" jack (8).If your machine has a built-in microphone, omit this step.

6. If the microphone has a remote control switch (9), turn this to the "on" position. Most machines will have an automatic sound level control that will adjust the volume of the incoming sound automatically so you will not need to be concerned about this.

7. Depress the "play" (5) and the "record" (10) buttons simultaneously to place the machine in the record mode.

8. Press the "stop" button (7) after the recording session has been completed. To record on the second side of the tape, turn the cassette over and repeat the above steps.

The Reel-to-Reel Recorder. Each brand of reel-to-reel recorder will differ in outward appearance from every other brand, yet they will all be the same as far as basic construction and functions are concerned. All recorders will have the following components: an on-off switch and a volume control; play, fast forward, stop, rewind, and record controls; various jacks for microphones, external speakers, etc.; volume-level indicator, and tone control.

To operate the reel-to-reel tape recorder, follow these steps (you may have to adjust them slightly to fit your specific type of machine):

1. Plug the power cord into an outlet.

2. Place an empty take-up reel on the take-up spindle (1) (the spindle that spins in the "play" mode). Place the feed reel that contains the tape on the feed spindle (2).

3. Thread the tape through the tape slot (3) and attach the loose end to the take-up reel. Turn the "on-off" control (4) to the "on" position.

4. Press the "play" button (5), turn up the "volume" control (6).

5. After the tape has finished playing, press the "stop" control (7).

6. Press the "rewind" button (8) to return the tape to the feed reel.

7. To record, place a fresh tape (or a used tape that you wish to re-record) on the feed spindle. Thread as described above; turn the control to the "on" position.

8. Plug the microphone into the "mic" jack (9).

9. Activate the "record" controls (10). Your machine will have some kind of safety combination that will prevent the accidental recording on a tape that is being played. Generally, this consists of a double control combination such as a record button that must be depressed at the same time as the play button.

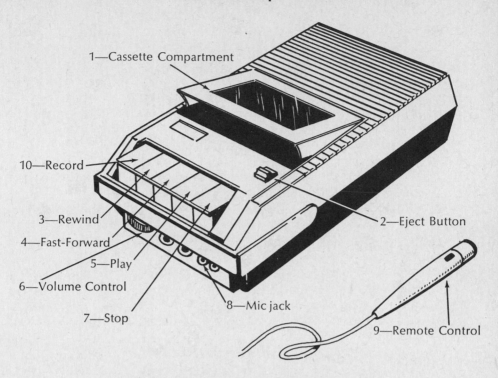

1—Cassette Compartment

10—Record

3—Rewind

4—Fast-Forward

5—Play

6—Volume Control

7—Stop

8—Mic jack

2—Eject Button

9—Remote Control

FIGURE 12-3 The Cassette Tape Recorder

WOLLENSAK RECORDER

Courtesy Minnesota Mining and Manufacturing

10. Record into the microphone; observe the movement of the needle on the record-level indicator; adjust the sound input until the needle moves into the red area only during the loudest sounds. Some varieties of recorders have types of level indicators other than the needle variety described above. Examine your machine to determine precisely what type of indicator it has and how this device functions.

11. Rewind the tape and replay it following the steps outlined for this process.

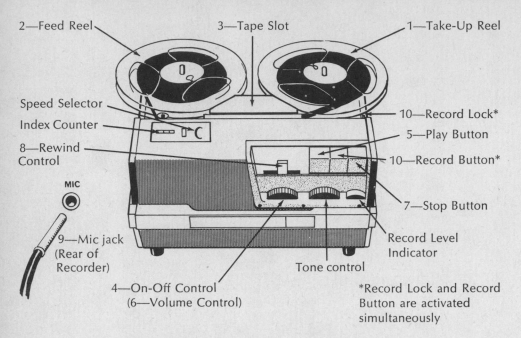

2—Feed Reel   3—Tape Slot   1—Take-Up Reel

Speed Selector
Index Counter   10—Record Lock*
   5—Play Button
8—Rewind
Control   10—Record Button*

MIC

   7—Stop Button

9—Mic jack
(Rear of   Record Level
Recorder)   Indicator

   Tone control

4—On-Off Control   *Record Lock and Record
(6—Volume Control)   Button are activated
   simultaneously

FIGURE 12-4   Reel-to-Reel Tape Recorder

CASSETTES

A cassette consists of a plastic housing within which a pair of reels is positioned between a pair of shields. Idler rollers direct the tape past the recorder head while a pressure pad maintains the tape against the head at the proper pressure.

Cassettes operate at 1⅞ ips at playing times of 30, 60, 90 and 120 minutes. A 30 minute tape has 15 minutes of time on each of the two sides; a 60 minute tape has 30 minutes on each side, and so on.

Cassettes have a pair of tabs on the edge that is opposite from the exposed tape. The tabs are broken off and discarded if you wish to preserve the tape and protect it from being erased. Placing a piece of thin tape over the holes will permit the contents to be erased and the cassette reused. Cassettes have an "A" and a "B" (sometimes a "1" and a "2") which identify the two sides. The tabs are located next to the letter of the side which they control. To protect side "A", remove the tab next to this letter; the same for the other side, of course.

DUBBING

Although most recordings are the result of an individual speaking directly into a microphone, there are other techniques that are frequently employed. Most of these involve a process called "dubbing." This is nothing more than a kind of copying in which an original recorded sound track is re-recorded in some manner.

This figure indicates playing time of tape.

Removing this tab will prevent erasure of the "A" side of the tape.

FIGURE 12-5 The Audiocassette

Recorder to recorder. A patch cord (a cord with appropriate fittings on the ends) is connected from the output of the source machine to the input of the recording machine. To copy a tape, place the recorded tape on one recorder and a blank tape on the second recorder. Connect the patch cord to the speaker or headphone output of the source machine and to the auxiliary or tape input of the recording machine. Press the play control on the source machine and the record control on the recording machine.

Record player to tape recorder. Connect one end of the patch cord to the speaker output on the record player. If this feature is lacking, use alligator clips to connect the cord to the speaker terminals. Connect the other end of the cord to the phono input of the tape recorder.

Motion picture projector to tape recorder. If you plan to record the sound track from a film, use a cord to connect the speaker output of the projector to the tape or auxiliary input of the recorder.

Television to tape recorder. Connect the speaker or headphone output of the television set to the tape recorder input jack. The sound portion of a video cassette can also be recorded on an audio tape by using this set-up.

In all of the instances listed above, it is possible to record onto the audio tape by placing the recorder microphone near the sound source. This is a

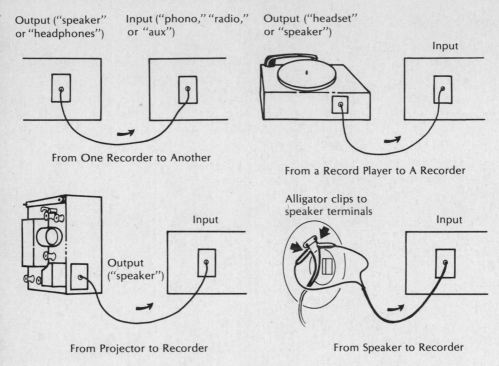

Output ("speaker" or "headphones")   Input ("phono," "radio," or "aux")

From One Recorder to Another

Output ("headset" or "speaker")

Input

From a Record Player to A Recorder

Input

Output ("speaker")

From Projector to Recorder

Alligator clips to speaker terminals

Input

From Speaker to Recorder

FIGURE 12-6 Methods for Recording From Various Sources

decidedly inferior method to those listed because background noises are virtually impossible to eliminate. This is particularly true when the motion picture projector is involved.

MIXING TECHNIQUES

At times, you may wish to add sound effects or a musical accompaniment to a narration in order to make it more interesting or informative. One method often used for this involves mixing during the recording session through the simple process of playing the musical accompaniment as the narration is being read. Both sounds enter a common microphone which is connected to the recording machine. The music or other accompaniment might come from a second recorder or from a record player. Once again, background noises and the loss of sound quality are the byproducts of this approach.

A better method is to use a stereo recorder which permits the individual recording of two congruent sound tracks. These can be edited and corrected separately before being mixed to create the final version. This process is possible only if a tape recorder that has individual channel controls is available.

Finally, a device called a **mixer** can be used to blend different sound inputs together electronically. If such equipment is available, you will find it to be very useful in the production of high quality sound.

EDITING AND SPLICING

It is possible to edit a tape by re-recording it onto another tape. This is a difficult technique that requires practice, but it does have the virtue of eliminating the need for splicing. Hook two machines together as described in the section on dubbing. Start the recording machine first. As the tape feeds through, you will monitor the sound, stopping the recording machine whenever unwanted segments are encountered. It is helpful to have a dry run before trying this approach. One way that this can be done is to adjust the digital counter to "000" and then to note on a pad the position on the tape (as indicated by the counter) of any unwanted material.

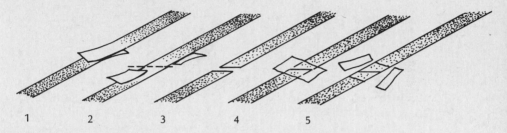

1   2   3   4   5

1. Overlap the tape ends; shiny side should face up.
2. Cut tapes on 45° angle.
3. Butt the ends together.
4. Press splicing tape over cut.
5. Trim excess tape; rub firmly with fingernail.

FIGURE 12-7

The scratching, popping sounds that result from the stopping and starting of the recorder are familiar to everyone and should be avoided if possible. You might turn the volume down before stopping the recording unit and then turn it up after starting it. This must be a well-coordinated process, otherwise obvious gaps in which the sound is missing will appear in the finished tape.

If you prefer to cut and splice, you should identify the portions to be removed by marking on the base (shiny) side of the tape with a grease pencil. De-magnetized scissors can be used to cut out any unwanted segments if a splicer is not available. After the predetermined length of tape has been removed, overlap the ends of the two pieces a sufficient amount so that a cut of 45° can be made through both sections. Fit the two ends together snugly and adhere a small piece of splicing tape over the joint on the base side. Rub the tape securely into place, then trim the excess that extends beyond the edges of the tape.

A splicer makes this process a bit more simple and the splice most generally will be a superior one. A splicer is so constructed that the tape segments are held in perfect alignment. The cut is made by following a recessed, angled groove which gives a perfect match to the two segments. Further, the butting process is much simpler because the tape is held in position after the cut has been made.

PROGRAMMING WITH THE TAPE RECORDER

A stereo recorder can be used to operate automatically one or several pieces of equipment. The two tracks are needed because one must be available for the inaudible signals that will trigger the projectors and change the images on the screen(s).

The typical approach involves recording the narration, music, and so forth on one of the two tracks. After this has been edited and perfected, the tape is placed on a machine that is connected to a programmer. The person operating the machine refers to a script which includes a key that coincides with the buttons on the programmer. As the operator listens to the tape, he or she presses the buttons at the appropriate times thus recording an inaudible electronic signal on the blank tape track. When the process is reversed and the signal track plays back through the programmer, the projectors are activated by the impulses that are fed to them. If the person in charge of programming did the job well, everything will be synchronized and the result will be an exciting combination of sights and sounds.

OTHER AUDIO TECHNIQUES

The 3M Company has introduced an innovative way in which to individualize instruction which is called **The Sound Page System.** A Sound Page consists of a sheet of paper which is plain on one side but coated with a magnetic film on the other. The plain side can be imaged by typing, writing or drawing on it. Or, a duplicator might be used to place pictorial or printed material on the surface. Up to four minutes of recorded sound can be placed on the treated side of the sheet.

An audio printer can be used to reproduce duplicates from the master at a rate of about twelve each minute. The sheet is placed on the playback unit with the magnetic side facing down. With the printed or plain side facing the operator, a number of techniques can be utilized which call for some kind of interaction with the printed materials. For example, the narrator might direct the students to write certain responses, or they might be asked to examine certain aspects of a diagram, map, or chart.

Bell and Howell's Language-Master® audiocard system consists of a machine that translates information encoded on a card into an audible message. The card contains large-format lettered material as well as a recorded version of the word. When the card is fed into the machine, young children have the experience of matching the sound with the lettered image. Blank cards with a recording strip are available for creating your own tailor-made units.

The 3M Company has a "Live Slide" system that includes a magnetic-striped slide and a projector that serves as both the recorder and player for the sound. A maximum of five seconds of sound is possible with this system.

Another 3M innovation is the "Sound on Slide" projector with its attendant software. The slide is positioned in the center of a disc upon which the audio portion of the presentation is recorded. Rather than passing across the recording as with the Live Slide, the head moves around the disc thus permitting an audio message of up to thirty seconds to be recorded and played back.

Record players, though not as popular as they once were due to the impact of the tape recorder, are frequently encountered in the classroom. Disc recordings of various kinds are available from any number of sources, including the corner super-market, and the selection and variety seem to be growing all the time. Frequently, discs and tapes are available of the same recording, thus giving the buyer a choice in the type of format that he selects. The record player is a relatively simple device to operate and can be mastered readily by anyone in just a few minutes. However, the proper care of disc recordings is one thing that many people overlook. Here are a few suggestions that should extend the life of your recordings:

1. Never turn the player off while the stylus is in contact with the rotating disc.
2. Avoid touching the disc except around the edges where there are no grooves.
3. When not in use, store the discs vertically in their covers. Inexpensive storage units can be purchased from a number of different sources.
4. Make certain that the record player is compatible with the type of disc to be played.
5. Use the proper stylus and replace it when necessary.

BIBLIOGRAPHY

Armsey, James W., and Dahl, Norman C. **An Inquiry into the Uses of Instructional Technology.** New York: The Ford Foundation, 1973.

Brown, Robert M. **Educational Media: A Competency-Based Approach.** Columbus, Ohio: Charles E. Merrill Publishing Co., 1973.

Bullough, R. Vern, and Duane, James E. **Utilizing the Tape Recorder in Teaching.** (Slide-Tape Program). Salt Lake City: Media Systems, Inc., 1975.

Creative Teaching with Tape. St. Paul, Minn.: The 3M Company, n.d.

Erickson, Carlton W. H., and Curl, David H. **Fundamentals of Teaching with Audiovisual Technology.** New York: Macmillan Co., 1972.

Giansante, Louis, "Learning to Listen." **Media and Methods** 12 (1976): 24-25.

Haney, John B., and Ullmer, Eldon J. Educational Media and the Teacher. Dubuque, Iowa: Wm. C. Brown Co., 1970.

Kinder, James S. **Using Instructional Media.** New York: D. Van Nostrand Co., 1973.

13

TELEVISION

INTRODUCTION

The electronic medium of television has two major characteristics that make it particularly useful for educational applications. First, television has the capability of distributing a given program simultaneously to any number of television sets at any number of different locations—this characteristic is referred to as the multiplication capability. Second, through the use of videotape, television has the ability to store information for immediate or delayed replay on a one-time, or repeated, basis.

In addition to those mechanical characteristics mentioned above television also exhibits a number of other features that enhance its effectiveness as a communication medium. Its universal presence, its potential for intimate and immediate reporting, and its visual impact are but a few of these virtues.

Among other things, television is very effective in the teaching of concepts. The teaching of concrete concepts is typically handled by such programs as Sesame Street, although abstract concepts are also stressed. The affective area, which is so rich in abstract concepts, is typically represented on commercial television by programs that might be labelled "entertaining" for want of a better term. The learning of abstract concepts is also stimulated by much of the programming on public television although in many cases neither the commercial nor the public television program developers would consider this to be their primary objective.

The term **educational television** (ETV) is generally used to identify programs of a cultural and general educational nature which are broadcast by public television stations. Commercial stations frequently present programs that would fit this category. **Instructional television** (ITV) is the term assigned to those programs that are more narrowly instructional or lesson-oriented in nature—the televised course is an example of ITV.

As would be expected, this chapter is devoted to production techniques that are most applicable to the realm of ITV. Much of what is covered relates to the creation of materials to be used in the development of instructional segments; however, some attention is given to the use of equipment such as the videocassette recorder. This device permits programs to be recorded and stored on tape (a process referred to as **canning).** A creative teacher will undoubtedly find uses for television that extend beyond the simple playback of canned material. The television lesson can become much more than a passive viewing experience through the use of such things as orientation activities that precede the program and follow-up activities that are conducted after it has been played.

TELEVISION GRAPHICS

Proportions

Materials that are prepared for television use should have an aspect ratio of three units high to four units wide. The size of the visual is not critical, it is the proportion of the height to the width that is important. For example, a visual might be six inches high and eight inches wide, or it might be nine inches by twelve inches (a good, average size) or any other size as long as the ratio is adhered to.

The visual should be of sufficient size that ample bleed area can be left around the edges. Within the bleed area is the scan area, that is, the total space which is seen by the camera. Finally, within the scan area is the critical or essential area which constitutes that part of the total card which is transmitted in sharpest detail by the camera.

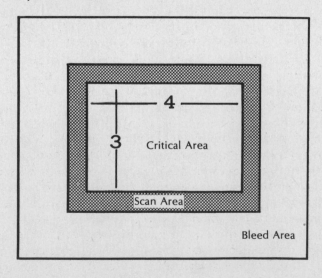

FIGURE 13-1 Proportions and Areas of a Television Card

You might wish to create a standard guide or mask that will serve as a pattern for all of your television cards. Such a mask can be made from scrap illustration board as shown in Figure 13-2. When using the mask, be certain that the critical area does not extend to the edges of the opening. Keep in mind that the total opening represents the scan area. You will, however, find it necessary to extend beyond the scan area and into the bleed area if detailed backgrounds are incorporated into your visual. If the colored or textured surface of the board constitutes the background, then the problem resolves itself.

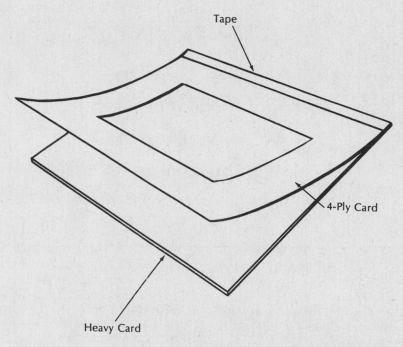

FIGURE 13-2   A Mask for Use in Television Card Production

Lettering

You may wish to refer to the chapter which is devoted to this subject for specific information on various ways in which letters can be formed. In addition to the techniques that are described in the lettering section, there are several specialized approaches that are often used by the television graphic artist. For example, the hot press is a machine that uses heated type to form sharp, clean letters on a variety of surfaces. The Reynolds Leteron and the Embosograph use type with raised edges to form cut-out letters in many sizes and colors.

Regardless of the specific kind of lettering that is used, you should observe a few basic rules as follows:

- Use simple letters, such as Gothic (sans serif) or an uncomplicated Roman style.
- Letters should be at least 1/25 the height of the critical area.

- A rule of thumb is to leave a space between lines of letters that is approximately the same height as the letters.
- Letters should be medium or bold face rather than light face.
- Words should be aligned in a horizontal format; avoid lettering that runs vertically or diagonally.
- Restrict the number of lettered lines to about six per card.

EXTINCT BIRDS

1. LABRADOR DUCK

2. PASSENGER PIGEON

3. CAROLINA PARAKEET

4. GREAT AUK

FIGURE 13-3   A Properly Lettered Television Card

Lettering and pictorial materials are frequently combined through the process of superimposition. **Supers** are typically black cards upon which captions, titles, credits, or other information has been printed in white letters. When one camera is used for the background picture, and a second for the lettering, the combined result appears on the receiver as a picture with a "dropout" of verbal information. Obviously, a similar effect could be obtained by applying white letters over a photographic print, but this approach would greatly diminish the flexibility that is a characteristic of the "super" approach.

The Gray Scale

If you were totally color blind and could see no hues you would move about in a world of varying degrees of gray, that is, in an achromatic world. Hues such as red and green would appear as a darkish gray while yellows, pinks, and other pastel hues would appear as a light gray. Because of the tendency for several hues to appear as the same shade of gray when a black-and-white television receiver is used it is a good idea to create colored visuals with this constraint in mind. If you will refer to the color wheel on page 000 you will be able to form a better idea as to what this discussion is all about. The original chart was made in full color, but it was photographed on black-and-white film, so what you see is essentially what a black-and-white television receiver would pick up if it were transmitting a visual that was rendered in color.

Note that only about six different values, including black and white, can be reproduced by black-and-white television equipment. Therefore, your visuals should be limited to this range of values. Use lights on darks and darks on lights where practical, but avoid combinations that are extremely contrasty because they do not pick up well and tend to appear overly stark.

The Television Card

Television cards consist of lettering or pictorial renderings, or a combination of both, that are created with the specific constraints of the television medium in mind.

When creating a card you should begin with a rough sketch that conforms to the dimensions that were previously mentioned. Any lettering is indicated with lines at this point, and objects are delineated in a generalized manner. The sketch is then transferred to the card (see the chapter on illustration for specific transfer techniques). Most visuals for black-and-white reproduction are rendered on a standard gray television board with ink, tempera, markers, gray pencil, or other suitable mediums.

Various media can be used in the production of visuals which will be reproduced in color. For a discussion of a wide range of such materials refer to the chapter on illustration. An excellent medium for colored cards that was not specifically described in the chapter mentioned is a paper called Color-Aid. This material is available in 18 X 24 inch sheets that are intensely pigmented with a wide selection of permanent hues. Shapes are cut from the paper and are glued to the background board; details are then added with ink, acrylics, markers, or other suitable mediums.

Remember to keep your illustrations simple and bold; available visuals that are overly detailed or complex may have to be redrawn and simplified for the best results.

Available Graphics

When available materials such as posters, charts, and flip charts are employed, the problem of incorrect aspect ratios is often encountered.

You can use such out-of-proportion materials without any problem if the scene to be photographed includes live talent. In this instance, the visual is placed on a tripod and the talent then refers to it. But if the aspect ratio does not approach the 3 : 4 unit standard it will be difficult to use a visual by itself unless some compromise is made. For example, most posters have a vertical format rather than one that conforms to the horizontal format of the television screen. If you must use such a poster, you will find it necessary to include some of the background in the image area—in this case, keep the background as plain and unobtrusive as possible.

In addition to aspect ratio, you should keep in mind such considerations as contrast, color, letter size and style, and simplicity as mentioned elsewhere in this chapter. If a particular visual meets these requirements, you may safely proceed to incorporate it into your program thus saving you the time and effort that would be required to produce a completely new visual. If, however, you find that it is necessary to start from scratch, the information given under the heading Television Graphics will be of assistance to you.

Photographic Prints

When creating photographs with television utilization in mind, you should leave ample bleed space around the subject that is to be emphasized. Remember that the specifications that apply to graphic materials such as cards are also important when photographs are involved.

Avoid photographs that are overly contrasty; work for a wide range of grays, rather than for deep blacks and clear whites. Glossy prints tend to reflect light sources thus causing "hot spots" that pick up as glare on the receiver. Use matte surfaced papers for your prints whenever possible or process the paper in such a way that a dull surface results. You might also use a dulling spray.

Slides

Slides, as well as other projected visuals should be created so that they conform to the horizontal format because this is the format of the TV screen; vertical slides are not suitable for television use under normal conditions.

Because image cropping takes place at a number of different stages during TV production, it is important that slides, as well as other visual materials, be produced with this problem in mind. For example, up to one fourth of the image area of a 35 mm slide can be lost by the time that the image appears on the receiver. If important detail is located in the lost area, the final image is likely to be unsatisfactory. The problem is compounded by the fact that television receivers tend to vary from one to another in the area of a given visual that is reproduced with some picking up a considerably greater proportion of the total visual than others.

Therefore, the rules that apply to cards and other graphic forms of art must also apply when projected materials are being prepared. Although many available slides will be suitable for TV use, a large percentage typically will prove to be unsatisfactory thus making it necessary for you to do some reshooting. An excellent way in which to make certain that sufficient bleed will be provided around the critical area is to make a mask which fits in the viewing system of the camera.

To create a mask, you should first draw it on a piece of paper or card so that the outside dimensions are two units high and three units wide (the dimensions of a 35 mm slide). The inside dimensions should be three units to four (TV proportions), and the bleed area should be about one-sixth of the total area on all four sides.

The mask is now photographed on colored film to create a positive image. If you elect to use black-and-white film, it will be necessary to contact print the negative to a second sheet of film in order to achieve the desired positive effect.

The image area of the slide is carefully trimmed around the margins; this will give you a finished mask that should exactly fit over the viewing screen of your camera. Next, remove the lens (most single-lens reflex cameras have removable lenses) thus exposing the ground-glass screen. Place the mask over

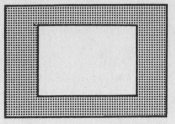

1. Draw The Mask

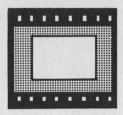

2. Make A Slide

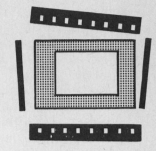

3. Trim Around Image Area

4. Install In Camera

SLR Camera With Lens Removed

FIGURE 13-4   Making a Viewfinder Mask

the screen, and carefully press it into position. The natural springiness of the film should hold it in position over the glass. The bleed area on the mask should be sufficiently transluscent to permit you to read the light meter if it is the type that has the scale printed on the side of the glass screen. Simply flick the mask with your fingernail to release it from its position when you no longer need to use it.

Of course, all of the trouble of making and installing a mask can be circumvented if you simply develop an eye for the critical area, and then remember to exercise this skill as you create your slides.

The importance of working within the brightness tolerances of the medium has already been mentioned. You should try to avoid such things as white backgrounds, sun on snow, etc., whenever possible. A slightly overcast day is preferable to a clear one when working out-of-doors. Indoor control is simpler to achieve and can be handled with appropriate backgrounds, fill lights, and so on.

Both the color and the density of the slide should be consistent for best results. Slides that are overly dark do not show up well, and those that deviate from accurate color representation will appear out of place, particularly if other slides in the series portray color accurately.

It is a good idea to test colored slides that are to be used with a black-and-white system by projecting a few of them to see if adequate value separation occurs when they are viewed on the receiver.

Slides as well as other projected materials can be transferred to the television screen through the use of a number of different techniques which include the following:

Croma Key. Professional television studios use a combination of cameras to accomplish an electronic mixing effect which most often includes live talent in the mix. A blue background provides the neutral base for the build-up of various visual combinations.

Rear Projection. Slides, transparencies, and motion pictures can be projected onto the rear-projection screen with excellent results. The brilliant image is then transmitted to tape or the TV set via the camera. If the croma key capability is not present, and talent is to be included, the rear projection technique is commonly used; however, with the newer front-projection screens (such as the 3M type 7510) it is possible to position both the talent and the projector in front of the screen.

Front Projection. If a suitable front-projection screen is available, it is possible to achieve satisfactory results by using a setup that includes a slide

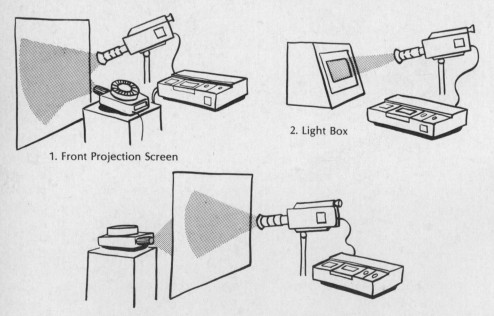

1. Front Projection Screen

2. Light Box

3. Rear Projection Screen

FIGURE 13-5 Three Projection Methods for Local Television Production

projector which is positioned in front of the screen and a camera that is situated in close proximity to the projector.

Light Box. Larger visuals, such as overhead transparencies, are frequently placed over a light source such as a light box in order to make them suitable for transmission.

Film Chain. A description of this approach is given in the discussion on motion pictures.

Overhead Transparencies

Most of the various kinds of transparencies that are described in the chapter on this subject can be adapted to the TV medium through one of several approaches. You might project them onto the screen in the normal fashion and then pick up this projected image with the television camera. A better approach involves projecting the image onto a rear-view screen. The concentration of color and the clarity of detail is considerably enhanced when this technique is used.

Or, better still, you might place the transparency over a light box of some kind. A typical light box contains one or two flourescent tubes which direct the light onto a diffusion screen such as opal or frosted glass. The box might be

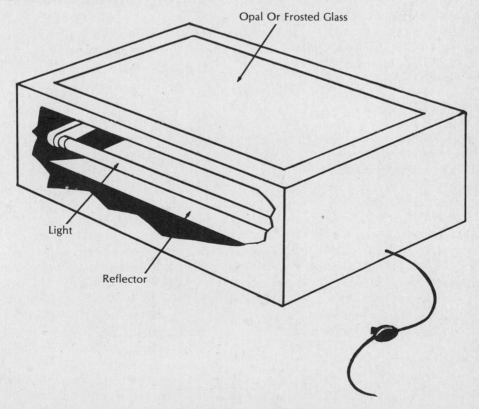

FIGURE 13-6 A Light Box

vertical, in which case the horizontally-mounted camera would be used; or, it might be a horizontal arrangement which would require the use of an overhead camera.

Motion Pictures

The suggestions which were given for the production of 35 mm slides apply in large part to the motion picture. As a general rule, however, available motion pictures are used and it is necessary to adapt them as best you can to TV use—remember that there will be some loss of image area, but there isn't a great deal that you can do about this problem.

The television camera can be stationed in front of a rear-view screen upon which the images from slides or a motion picture are projected. In this way, such images can be transmitted to receivers where they are viewed by an audience. This approach is not the typical one but is sometimes used when special equipment such as a film chain is not available. The film chain consists of a system that integrates slide and motion picture projectors with a special television camera. This system provides the operator with considerable flexibility while at the same time producing high-quality images.

Another type of film chain is the film videoplayer which is manufactured by Eastman Kodak. It utilizes super 8 film as the source for televised images. With this machine, it is possible to make video insertions rather simply; that is, you can transfer images from film to a videotape, and mix them with other materials that have been derived from other sources.

THE SCRIPT

A television script can assume a number of different forms but the basic information is essentially the same on all of them in spite of superficial differences. The script has two major columnar divisions, the right-hand one, which is the larger of the two, is devoted to the audio portion of the presentation, while the left-hand one is used for the video portion. The text should be organized into natural blocks of audio and video materials. The video description or illustration should conform to the placement of the accompanying audio quite precisely; an obvious spatial break should occur between the frames or segments.

A basic script that relies on verbal descriptions of the video portion of the program might look like the one illustrated below. It is common for producers to write in any information that will assist them and their crew to understand and follow the script more adequately.

A modified version that utilizes illustrations to portray the video is shown on next page. The visuals need not be polished, a quick pencil sketch is generally adequate.

One disadvantage of the second version is that the blank script form is generally printed from a standard master and therefore the boxes are a standard, fixed distance from each other. If additional space is needed for a partic-

Video	Audio

ECU: title card

ANNC: Single-lens reflex cameras are popular and versatile. This program will cover several innovative ways in which they can be used.

Pan from one camera to another in the display

ANNC: When you look at the many different models of SLR cameras on the dealer's shelf you are likely to conclude that there is little standardization amongst them.

CU: SLR camera

ANNC: Fortunately, all of these diverse models work on the same basic principles.

FIGURE 13-7 One Type of Script

ularly lengthy frame, the information might run into the next frame-space. The fixed position of the boxes sometimes makes it difficult to follow the suggestion that the script be double spaced with four spaces between each segment. However, the visual feature of such a script makes it particularly easy to follow.

Note that directions relating to camera movements and types of shots are included along with other information that is meant to supplement the audio and video portions of the script. Camera movements are discussed in the section on using TV equipment; types of shots will be discussed briefly at this point.

Several terms are used to designate specific kinds of shots that are based on the amount of the visual field that is included within a frame. When the various

Video	Audio

ECU: card

Introductory music

MCU: talent

HOST: Tonight, folks, we plan to take you on
a trip into the world of that aristocrat
of the game fish clan--the trout. But
first, let's meet the members of the clan.

ECU: card

HOST: The colorful brookie is native to the
eastern portion of the United States,
but has been planted in many of the
high, clear lakes and streams of the west.

FIGURE 13-8 A Script With Illustrations

shots are intermixed within a presentation a certain amount of clarification along with considerable aesthetic improvement can result.

Long shots include the environment around the subject. Extreme long shots show even more of the environment and may actually consist of a panoramic view. The designations are LS for long shot, and ELS for extreme long shot.

Medium shots include a much closer view of the subject, perhaps the torso and head of an actor. MS is the designation used.

Close-up shots exclude everything except for that item being emphasized or discussed. An example might be a shot of the actor's face. An extreme close-up could include a zoom to the lips, or an eye. CU for close-up and ECU for extreme close-up are the designations used.

USING TELEVISION EQUIPMENT

Portable Units

Such battery operated recording units that can be carried out to "where the action is" are often referred to as **back packs** (a term which has been popularized by Sony Corporation).

Portable Unit

The procedures that apply to cameras in general also apply to the cameras in this system (refer to the section on TV cameras). The same can be said for the recorder also. But there are some characteristics that are unique to this system due to its portable nature. For one thing, the unit is battery powered which means that periodic recharging sessions will be necessary. The batteries are good for approximately thirty minutes to two hours use without a recharge. You should make it a habit to check the meter periodically when the unit is in use in order to prevent complete draw-down which can result in permanent damage to the batteries.

Because your camera is transportable, it will be exposed to a number of environmental factors, including direct sunlight, that can cause damage. As with any camera, the lens should be closed and the cap placed over it when the unit is not in use. This is a standard procedure that becomes particularly critical with cameras that are being used out of doors.

Another light-related problem has to do with the manner in which scenes are photographed. You should avoid photographing such things as sunrises or other situations, such as the sun's rays coming through the trees, in which the camera is pointed directly into the light source.

Finally, with some back pack units, it is possible to plug in the battery incorrectly. Make certain that the pins match correctly in order to prevent severe damage from occurring.

Cameras

Color cameras with their attendant recorders are considerably more expensive than are comparable black-and-white models, but for some purposes they are definitely worth the extra cost. A dissection, for example, not only has more impact on the students when transmitted in color, it might also be more readily comprehended by them due to the color differentiation among the various features.

Cameras consist of three main elements; these are the camera body, the viewfinder, and the lens system.

The **camera body** contains the electronic components that translate the incoming light energy into an electrical output.

The **viewfinder** is a small monitor that has a screen and controls that are similar to those on a standard TV set (but without the tuning feature). The controls permit the person who is using the camera to adjust the monitor so that an image of optimal quality is obtained.

The **lens system** has an aperture adjustement which controls the amount of light entering the camera. It also has a focus arrangement.

Although standard lenses can be used effectively for some kinds of production, greater variety can be achieved in less time with a zoom lens. Zoom lenses move smoothly from a telephoto to a wideangle position thus making it possible to modify the image without moving the camera. Zoom lenses have either a manual or a remote zoom control.

Although the specifics might vary somewhat from one brand of camera to another, the following standard procedures tend to apply to all of them:

- Keep the lens closed and the cap in place when the camera is not in use.
- As a general rule, a wide lens opening rather than a small one should be used when working indoors. Although images will be obtained with the smaller opening, those that involve action are likely to appear blurred or streaked when they are played back due to insufficient light.
- The problem of excessive light has been mentioned in conjunction with slides and motion pictures and applies also when the camera is being used to shoot live action. Do not shoot against a white wall or a light source such as a window or open door—your subject will invariably appear overly dark in value under these conditions.
- It is a good idea to keep the camera contrast and brightness controls somewhere in the middle range while using the aperture adjustment to achieve a quality image in the viewfinder.

Camera Techniques. Smaller cameras exhibit a number of positive traits, some of which have already been mentioned, but they also are heir to some deficiencies. Small, light cameras do not as readily lend themselves to the smooth, professional effects that are characteristic of productions that are made with the larger, heavier studio camera. Such movements as pans, tilts, and zooms can take on the characteristics of a roller-coaster ride if the operator of the small camera fails to exercise a considerable amount of care as he manipulates the equipment.

Incidentally, the term **pan** refers to the horizontal following movement of the camera while the term **tilt** is used to identify the vertical movement. Tilts are commonly used in conjunction with lists of credits and other information that are arranged on a long card with a vertical format.

A sure way in which to upgrade the quality of a taped segment is to replace light-weight tripods with heavier ones. The simple expedient of using a tripod that permits smooth pan and tilt movements should lead to instant improvements where these techniques are concerned. Of course, this doesn't solve the difficulties that are common to hand-held cameras.

With either hand or tripod support it should be possible to greatly improve zooming techniques with a bit of practice. Before you begin the shooting sequence, zoom out to telephoto and focus on the subject. When you then move back to the wide angle position, the subject should remain in focus. This simple strategy permits you to move through the necessary zoom and wide angle shots without the need to worry about refocusing.

Pans should normally be executed with the lens at the wide angle setting. Any irregular camera movements will then appear less conspicuous than they would if a telephoto setting were used. Pans are much smoother if a tripod is used, but can be accomplished without one if the camera is supported securely with some kind of body harness.

A selection of special harnesses or "shoulder pods" are available for use with hand-held cameras that afford a large measure of both mobility and stability. Generally, both a shoulder brace and a strut that runs to a waist support are incorporated to give maximum strength. A number of adjustments are provided that permit modifications to be made so that virtually any operator can be comfortably fitted. Although this arrangement cannot provide the support of a heavy tripod, it nevertheless provides a means for achieving improved results where hand-held cameras must be used.

When panning, have the talent move toward the center of the viewfinder; pick up the action before she passes through the center, and then follow as necessary to achieve the desired effect. Unfortunately, there is no secret to making a nice, smooth tilt. Only through continued practice can mastery be achieved. This is one movement that is definitely made easier if a well-mounted camera is being used.

Video Recorders

Open-reel videotape recorders (VTR) are similar to reel-to-reel audio recorders in that they require hand threading of the tape. Videocassette recorders (VCR) resemble their audio counterparts to the extent that the tape is housed in a cassette and does not require manual threading.

There are advantages and disadvantages to each of the systems, but the ease with which the videocassette can be used has made it a favorite with many teachers and students. Videocassettes are handy also from the standpoint of storage and retrieval. The compact cassettes fit snugly on the shelf right along with the books and can be put into service at a moment's notice.

A number of school districts have moved to what amounts to a virtually total videocassette system for program storage. Some have converted their open-reel programs to cassette formats while others have gone so far as to tape selected 16mm films onto cassettes which are used in place of the traditional motion pictures. This has been done through contractual agreements with the film producers of course; copyright regulations apply to television as they do to all other forms of media.

Placing a number of videocassette copies of a given motion picture in a central repository in the school is one very effective way in which the well-known problems of obtaining a film are resolved. No longer must the teacher wait her turn to use a particular film; no longer must she wait at the loading dock to see if the delivery truck will arrive on time with the precious film.

VIDEOCASSETTE RECORDER-PLAYER
Courtesy Sanyo Electric Inc.

Additionally, programs that are shown on commercial or public stations inflict a scheduling constraint which causes the teacher to structure her class around the TV time slot. A cassette library of appropriate titles gives her the latitude to introduce the material at the precise moment when it will have the greatest impact.

All of this is not meant to deprecate the value of the open reel system for it has many positive values. The open reel VTR is generally less expensive than a comparable cassette model. It has fewer moving parts, so the wear and maintenance are reduced. Also, editing is much less complicated with this type of equipment due to the accessible nature of the tape. Additionally, the open reel system is the preferred one when a camera is being used in production.

Operating the Recorder. The instructions for operating a particular model of video recorder can be found in the manual that is furnished by the manufacturer. Most media centers, both at the district and school levels, and other facilities that have television equipment will have a media specialist or technician that will either set up and operate the equipment for you, or show you how this can be done. Sometimes, self-instructional packages are provided that permit you to gain proficiency in the desired area while working at your own pace.

For the sake of familiarizing you with the operation of a typical recorder let us proceed through the steps of recording and playing back using a generalized videocassette recorder.

Some viceocassette machines lack the "record" feature, and are used for playback purposes only. In order to record a new program onto tape, it is necessary that a machine with this capability be available to you. A "play-and-record" machine might also have a "TV tuner" feature which makes it possible to tape television programs that are broadcast by commercial and public networks.

First, let us examine the procedure for playing (not recording) a cassette tape.

1. Connect the video machine to the television set using a special matching device that is usually included with the cassette connecting cord. Some sets, called **monitor recorders,** are also made to accommodate a closed-circuit feed which runs directly from a camera or other video source to the set. Ordinary TV sets cannot use this feed unless they are modified for this purpose. Such sets require an rf modulator which is connected to the VHF terminals on the back of the set.
2. Plug both power cords into a wall socket.
3. Adjust the channel selector on the back of the video machine to a channel that is not used in your local area. Adjust the selector on the set to the same channel.
4. Turn both the TV set and the video machine to "on."
5. Depress the "eject" lever (On some machines you must pull out on the lever). This will open the machine so that the cassette can be inserted. Close the machine after the cassette has been properly seated.
6. Press the "play" button; adjust the sound source for volume. You will have to wait for about five seconds for the machine to move from the "standby" mode, then the program will begin. You may have to readjust the sound for the best listening level.
7. Press the "stop" button when you wish to terminate the presentation. At this point, the "standby" light will turn on. Do not attempt to operate the machine as long as the light is on.
8. After the "standby" light has turned off, you may proceed to rewind the tape. Merely press "rewind"—the machine will stop automatically when all the tape has been returned to the delivery reel.

Now, let us consider the process of recording a cassette tape. There are a number of ways in which this can be done including recording off-the-air, from another tape, and from a TV camera. As a word of caution, you should be aware of the potential for copyright infringement whenever the works of others are being copied or reproduced in any manner. Once this problem has been resolved to everyone's satisfaction, you can proceed to record off-the-air as follows:

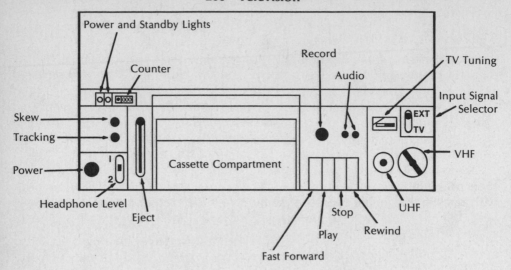

FIGURE 13-9 Videocassette Recorder

1. You must have the "play-record" type of machine with a "TV tuner" feature for this operation. Your cassette must have the "record tab" intact. As with an audiocassette, removal of this tab prevents accidental erasure of the program.
2. Connect the lead from the TV antenna to the "VHF antenna inputs" on the back of the recorder.
3. Turn the channel selector to the channel upon which the program is to be broadcast.
4. Press the "record" button.
5. Adjust the "fine tuning" control until the needle is in the specified position (generally centered).
6. When the program comes on the air, depress the "record" and "play" buttons simultaneously.
7. When the program is over, press the "stop" button. Wait for the "standby" light to turn off, then press the "rewind" button.

To record directly from the camera a slightly different sequence is involved as follows:

1. Connect the camera to the "video input" and the microphone to the "microphone #1" input on the back of the recorder.
2. If your recorder has a built-in tuner, move the "record selector" from "TV" to "external".
3. Press the "record" button. You should now see the picture on the screen.
4. Depress the "record" and the "play" buttons simultaneously.
5. After you have finished recording, press the "stop" button, wait for the "standby" light to go out, then press the "rewind" control.
6. Press the "play" button to play back the program that you have just recorded.

Videodiscs

A development that holds great promise for audiovisual communication is the videodisc. Although this device can be used in the traditional manner to encode from live and canned programs, its real potential lies in the fact that it will give to the viewer a true interactive experience with the television medium. Up until now, television has been for the most part a one-way affair—indeed this is perhaps the greatest criticism that is leveled against it by detractors. But, if the videodisc lives up to its promise, this will be a thing of the past.

Videodiscs are small, flexible, easily stored items whose appearance belies their potential. Information on the disc is encoded on a frame-by-frame basis with each frame being represented by a full 360° rotation of the disc. Over 50,000 single frames can be represented on one side of a given disc, and these can be retrieved either sequentially or one at a time. In other words, a program can be stopped at any time and a single frame can be frozen on the screen. Additionally, a manual or automatic search capability makes it possible to find in a very short time-span any specific frame for which you have a need.

By incorporating a keyboard (similar to a computer terminal in function) with a videodisc system, it will be possible to interact with a limitless array of simulated situations. The potential for education, particularly of the correspondence or home-study variety, is exciting to say the least.

Videogames

Although the initial application of the videogame was in the entertainment area, the educational potential of this popular toy is now being recognized and developed by an ever-increasing number of manufacturers.

The system includes a miniature computer-type device that attaches to the television set and some kind of a control that permits the individual to interact with the program. To prepare the unit for use, a videocartridge which contains the information and instructions (that is, the program) is plugged into the microprocessor or minicomputer. When a new game is desired, a cartridge containing a different program is substituted for the one in use.

Learning games based on mathematics and social studies are currently being developed and perfected. Subject areas that will be treated in the future are impossible to anticipate but might well include everything from the baking of a cake to the study of astronomy. Videogames lend themselves to traditional as well as innovative kinds of programed instruction. Retrieval from such a system is incredibly rapid since it is based on computer technology.

As the technologies of the videodisc and the videocartridge evolve and develop, it will become increasingly more feasible for individuals who are involved in the design and production of instructional materials to develop tailor-made programs for use in various educational settings.

FINAL COMMENT

As with certain other chapters in this text, notably photography, the coverage of television must of necessity be of a general nature. Entire books have been written that deal with but one single aspect of this fascinating and everchanging technology. Such books are available from a number of sources and make up a formidable section in many libraries. It is suggested that those who would like to delve into television in greater depth refer to the bibliography that accompanies this chapter for a cross-section of various books, periodicals, and programs that address themselves to television production and utilization.

BIBLIOGRAPHY

Ackerman, Jerrold, and Lipsitz, Lawrence. **Instructional Television: Status and Directions.** Englewood Cliffs, N.J.: Educational Technology Publications, 1977.

Adler, Richard, and Cater, Douglass, eds. **Television as a Cultural Force.** New York: Holt, Rinehart and Winston, 1976.

Arnove, Robert F. **Educational Television, A Policy Critique and Guide for Developing Countries.** New York: Holt, Rinehart and Winston, 1976.

Barcus, F. Earle, and Wolkin, Rachel. **Children's Television.** New York: Holt, Rinehart and Winston, 1977.

Brown, James W., Lewis, Richard B. and Harcleroad, Fred F. **A-V Instruction: Technology, Media and Methods.** 5th ed. New York: McGraw-Hill, 1977.

Brown, Robert M. **Educational Media: A Competency-Based Approach.** Columbus, Ohio: Charles E. Merrill, 1973.

Bullough, R. Vern, and Duane, James E. **Utilizing Instructional Television.** Salt Lake City: Media Systems Inc., 1975. (sound-filmstrip program).

Cater, Douglass, and Adler, Richard. **Television as a Social Force.** New York: Holt, Rinehart and Winston, 1975.

Educational and Industrial Television. Danbury, Conn.: C. S. Tepfer Publishing Co., Inc. (Periodical)

Gordon, George N. **Videocassette Technology in American Education.** Englewood Cliffs, New Jersey: Educational Technology Publications, 1972.

Haney, John B., and Ullmer, Elden J. **Educational Communications and Technology.** Dubuque, Iowa: Wm. C. Brown, 1975.

Harwood, Don. **Everything You Always Wanted To Know About Tape Recording.** Bayside, New York: VTR Publishing Co., 1975.

Murray, Michael. **The Videotape Book.** New York: Bantam Books, 1975.

Potter, Rosemary Lee. **New Season: The Positive Use of Commercial Television With Children.** Columbus, Ohio: Charles E. Merrill Publishing Company, 1976.

Vasche, Gertrude A. **Utilizing Television in the Classroom.** Menlo Park, Calif.: Pacific Coast, 1974.

Witherspoon, John P. **State of the Art (A Study of Current Practices and Trends in Educational Uses of Public Radio and Television).** Washington, D.C.: Advisory Council of National Organizations, 1974.

Wittich, Walter A., Schuller, Charles F., Hessler, David W., and Smith, Jay C. **Student Production Guide to Accompany Instructional Technology, Fifth Edition.** New York: Harper and Row, Publishers, 1975.

MATERIALS AND EQUIPMENT SOURCES

Most of the materials that are required to produce the projects that are described in this book can be acquired from the typical school or district media center. However, if certain items are not available, the following sources will be useful in providing them:

A. B. Dick, Co., 5700 West Touhy Ave., Chicago, Ill. 60648 (duplicating materials for offset, photocopy, and spirit duplicator processes)

Addressograph-Multigraph Corp., 1200 Babbit Road, Cleveland, Ohio 44117 (multi-color diazo transparencies; duplicating materials)

Agfa-Gevaert, Inc., 275 North St., Teterboro, N.J., 07608 (photocopy supplies; Transparex transparency materials)

The American Crayon Co., 1706 Hayes Ave., Sandusky, Ohio 44871 (drawing and coloring materials; display materials)

Ampex, 401 Broadway, Redwood City, California 94063 (audio tapes)

Arkwright Incorporated, Fiskville, R.I. 02823 (thermal transparency films, electrostatic transparency films and supplies)

Artype, Inc., 345 E. Terra Cotta Ave., (Rt. 176), Crystal Lake, Ill. 60014 (pre-made lettering)

Avcom, Inc., 159 Verdi St., Farmingdale, N.Y. 11735 (frosted acetate and carbon film for overhead transparencies)

Beckley-Cardy Co., 1113 South Ninth St., Springville, Ill. 62705 (art and AV supplies)

Bell and Howell Co., 7100 McCormick Rd., Chicago, Ill. 60645 (duplicating materials; tape recording equipment, cameras, projectors)

Charles Beseler Company, 8 Fernwood Road, Florham Park, New Jersey 07932 (slide, overhead, and opaque projectors)

Dick Blick, P.O. Box 1267, Galesburg, Ill. 61401 (drawing and coloring materials; lettering, etc.)

Bogen Photo Corp., P. O. Box 448, Englewood, N.J. 07631 (dry mount presses, materials)

Bourges Color Corp., 80 Fifth Ave., New York, N.Y. 10017 (colored adhesive film for non-projected visuals and transparencies)

Milton Bradley Co., 74 Park St., Springfield, Mass. 01101 (rubber magnets and other art supplies)

Arthur Brown and Bro., Inc., 2 West 46th St., New York, N.Y. 10036 (artists' materials, drawing and drafting supplies)

Charles Bruning Co., 1800 W. Central Rd., Mount Prospect, Ill. 60058 (overhead transparency materials)

Calumet Scientific, Inc., 1590 Touhy, Elk Grove Village, Ill., 60007 (view cameras)

Carter's Ink Co., Cambridge, Mass. 02142 (materials for lettering and coloring)

Chartpak Rotex, One River Road, Leeds, Mass. 01053 (adhesive tapes for charts and transparencies)

Color-Stik Company, 8 Fernwood Road, Florham Park, New Jersey 07932 (transparency materials)

Columbia Ribbon-Carbon Mfg. Co., Inc., Herbhill Rd., Glen Cove, N.Y. 11542 (duplicating materials; transparency materials)

The Craftint Mfg. Co., 18501 Euclid Ave., Cleveland, Ohio 44112 (inks; materials for drawing and coloring)

Ditto, Inc., 6800 McCormick Rd., Chicago, Ill. 60645 (materials for spirit duplicator processes)

Eastman Kodak Co., 343 State Street, Rochester, N.Y. 14608 (audio tapes, films, cameras, projectors)

Embosograf Corporation of America, 38 W. 21st St., New York, N.Y. 10010 (lettering presses and supplies)

Geller Artist Materials Inc., 116-120 East 27th St., New York, N.Y. 10016 (Color-Aid art paper)

General Binding Corp., 1101 Skokie Blvd., Northbrook, Ill. 60062 (mounting and laminating materials)

Gestetner Corp., 216 Lake Ave., Yonkers, N.Y. 10702 (duplicating materials)

Graphica International, 1936 Euclid Ave., Cleveland, Ohio 44115 ("Permatype" vinyl letters)

Higgins Ink Co., Inc., 271 Ninth St., Brooklyn, N.Y. 11215 (inks; pens, drawing and coloring materials)

Honeywell, P. O. Box 1010, Littleton, Colorado 80120 (Pentax cameras)

Hunt Mfg. Co., 1405 Locust St., Philadelphia, Pa. 19102 (lettering pens, inks)

Instantype, Inc., 7005 Tujunga Ave., No. Hollywood, Calif. 91605 (pre-made lettering)

Instructo Products Co., 1635 No. 55th St., Philadelphia, Pa., 19131 (materials for transparencies)

Keuffel and Esser Co., P. O. Box 2947, South San Francisco, Calif., 94080 (lettering equipment, transparency materials)

Koh-I-Noor, Inc., 100 North St., Bloomsbury, N.J. 08804 (lettering and drawing materials)

Labelon Corp., 10 Chapin St., Canandaigua, N.Y. 14424 (thermal and xerographic transparency materials)

Lea A-V Service, 182 Audley Dr., Sun Prairie, Wisc. 53590 (bulletin board adhesive)

Letraset, Inc., 2379 Charles Rd., Mountain View, Calif. 94040 (pre-made lettering)

Letterguide Co., Inc., P.O. Box 30203, Lincoln, Nebr. 68503 (lettering equipment)

Charles Mayer Studios, Inc., 140 E. Market St., Akron, Ohio 14308 (Hook-n-Loop materials)

Minnesota Mining and Manufacturing Company, Visual Products Div., Box 3100, St. Paul, Minn. 55101 (thermal transparency materials, adhesive-back color film, duplicating materials, audio tapes)

National Adhesive Products, Inc., The Penthouse, Cleveland Plaza Towers, Euclid Ave. at E. 12th St., Cleveland, Ohio 44115 (lamination supplies and equipment)

Ozalid Div., General Analine and Film Corp., 140 W. 51st St., New York, N.Y. 10020 (diazo transparency materials)

Polaroid Corporation, Cambridge, Mass. 02139 (instant cameras, film)

Frederick Post Co., Box 803, Chicago, Ill. 60690 (lettering equipment, transparency materials)

Pressure Graphics, Inc., 1725 Armitage Court, Addison, Illinois 60101 (graphic materials such as lettering and tone sheets, tapes, etc.)

Prestype, Inc., 194 Veterans Blvd., Carlstadt, N.J. 07072 (pre-made lettering)

Radmar, Inc., P.O. Box 425, Northbrook, Ill. 60062 ("Filmaker" filmstrip production system)

Reynolds Leteron Co., 13425 Wyandotte Street, North Hollywood, Calif. 91605 (Leteron tapesign system)

Rheem Califone, 5922 Bowcroft Ave., Los Angeles, Calif. 90016 (tape recorders)

Sanford Ink Co., 2740 Washington Blvd., Bellwood, Ill. 60104 (ink, pens, drawing and coloring materials)

School Pen Co., P.O. Box 407, Chatham, N.J. 07928 (transparency pens and markers, coloring and drawing supplies)

Scott Graphics, Inc., 104 Lower Westfield Road, Holyoke, Mass. 01040 (Tecnifax transparency materials and equipment)

Seal Incorporated, Derby, Conn. 06418 (dry mounting and laminating supplies and equipment)

Spiratone, Inc., 135-06 Northern Blvd., Flushing, N.Y. 11354 (photographic supplies)

Standard Projector and Equipment Co., Inc., 1911 Pickwick Dr., Glenview, Ill. 60025 (Gatling filmstrip cameras and accessories)

Starex, Inc., P. O. Box 248, Kearny, N.J. 07032 (transparency materials, polarizing kits)

Stik-A-Letter Co., Rt. 2, Box 1400, Escondido, Calif. 92025 (pre-cut letters)

Technamation, Inc., 30 Sagamore Hill Dr., Port Washington, N.Y. 11050 (materials for overhead transparencies)

Varigraph, Inc., P. O. Box 690, Madison Wisc. 53701 (lettering equipment)

Volk Corporation, Box 72, Pleasantville, New Jersey 08232 (clip art)

Ward's Natural Science Establishment, Inc., 300 Ridge Road, E. Rochester, N.Y. 14622 (resins and catalysts for specimen preservation)

Winsor and Newton, Inc., 555 Winsor Dr., Secaucus, N.J. 07094 (drawing and coloring materials)

Wood-Regan Instrument Co., Inc., 184 Franklin Ave., Nutley, N.J. 07110 (Wrico lettering Equipment)

Xerox Corp., 1250 Midtown Tower, Rochester, N.Y. (duplicating materials)

INDEX

Acetate
  clear, 141
  frosted, 143
  in passe-partout production, 38-42
  in rubber cement lift, 145
  self-adhering, 146
  treated, 143
Affective behaviors
  development of, 3-4
  as learning domain, 16
  and media selection, 6
  and posters, 113
  and television, 249
Animation, 228
ASA, 210
Attention, 106-107
Audio recording
  advantages and disadvantages of, 13
  applications of, 235-36
  characteristics of, 13, 235-38
  dubbing techniques, 242-44
  editing, 245-46
  equipment, 239-42
    cassette recorder, 239-40, 241
    cassettes, 242, 243
    reel-to-reel recorder, 240-42
  miscellaneous audio techniques, 246-47
  mixing, 244
  principles of, 236-37
  selection in, 7, 13
  splicing, 245-46

Balance, 91-93
Bulletin boards
  characteristics of, 173
  construction of, 173, 175-76

Cameras
  copying techniques, 217-19
  filmstrip, 214-17
  instant, 222-23
  motion picture, 224-26
  simple, 206-207, 209
  single lens reflex, 203-204, 208
  television, 261-63
  35mm
    characteristics of, 208, 213
    operation of, 208, 210-14
    parts of, 211
    use in television production, 254-55
  twin lens reflex, 204-205
  view, 205-206
  viewfinder, 203
Cartooning, 55, 56-59
  expressions, 56
  figures, 58

Cartooning (continued)
  figures in action, 59
  heads, 57
  techniques of, 55
Cartoons
  characteristics of, 21
  as embellishments, 110
  uses of, 55
Cassettes
  audio, 239-40
  super-8 motion picture, 202
  35mm, 202, 213
  video, 263-64
Center of interest. See Composition.
Chalkboard
  care of, 169
  characteristics of, 166, 167
  construction of, 167
  magnetic, 169, 171-72
  marking on, 168
  tools for, 168-69
Chartex, 31-32
Charts, 118-19
  flipcharts, 119-21
  and television, 253
Clay coated paper, test for, 145
Color
  in attracting attention, 106
  characteristics of, 101
  complements, 103-104
  as cueing device, 109
  as element in design, 91
  as embellishment, 110
  in mounting of pictures, 103-105
  in photographic film, 218-19
  in posters, 103, 115
  primaries, 102
  psychological effects of, 104-105
  secondaries, 102
  shades, 103
  in spirit duplicator master, 130-31
  in television, 252-53, 256
  tertiaries, 102
  tints, 103
  tones, 103
  in transparencies, 140, 143, 158, 161
Color Key, 161
Color wheel, 101-104
Coloring techniques, 53-55
  colored papers, 54
  colored pencils, 54
  felt markets, 53
  pastels, 54
  poster paints, 53
  pressure-sensitive colored film, 54
  in transparencies, 140, 142

Coloring techniques (continued)
transparent watercolors, 53
wax crayons, 54
Communication
example of, 15-16
model of, 13-15
Composition. See also Design.
in bulletin boards, 173, 176
elements and principles of,
balance, 91
center of interest, 93
contrast, 96
emphasis, 94
form, 89
line, 88
rhythm, 97
shape, 89
space, 88
surface, 90-91
unity, 94-95
in photography, 98-99, 223
Concept development
abstracting skills in, 4
and age, 4
classes of, 2
definition of, 4
and discrimination, 107
with display and demonstration boards, 165-66
and graphs, 121
with handouts, 126
with overhead transparencies, 137-38
with photography, 201-202
and posters, 113-14
relationships in, 107
with still pictures, 19
with television, 249
with verbal materials, 2, 4, 19, 63-64, 126
Copy stand
home-made, 217
Kodak "Visualmaker", 207
use of, 217-18
Copying and duplicating processes, 125-36
definition of, 125
electrostatic process, 127-28, 150
mimeograph, 133-34
photocopy, 128-29
planographic, 135-36
spirit duplicator, 130-33
thermal transfer, 129-30, 131
uses for, 125
Copyright
and illustrations, 43-44
and television, 264
Cropping
in design and photography, 99, 208
in television production, 254
Cues
to direct attention, 109
varieties of, 109
verbal, 19

Decoding, in communication process, 14, 16
Depth of field, 213-14
Design. See also Composition.
eye movement in, 98
mergers in, 99
research in, 105-10
in transparencies, 138-40
Diazo process. See Overhead transparencies.
Diffusion-transfer process. See Overhead transparencies.
Dioramas
construction of, 183-84
uses and characteristics of, 182
Display and demonstration boards
bulletin boards, 173, 176
chalkboards, 167-71
description of and uses for, 165-66
flannel boards, 171, 173, 174
hook and loop, 176
miscellaneous types of boards, 176-77
Display stands, 177-78
Domains of learning. See Learning.
Drawing devices, 52-53
brushes, 52
crayons, pencils, 53
markers, 53
pens, 52
tapes, 53
Dry mounting, 28-32
on cloth, 31-32
on a hard surface, 28-31
Dry-transfer letters, 81-82
in transparency production, 143
Duplicating masters
mimeograph, 133-34
planographic, 135-36
spirit duplicator, 130-32
Duplicating processes. See Copying and duplicating processes.

Editing
of audio tape recordings, 245-246
of motion pictures, 229, 231, 232-33
of videotapes, 264
Electrostatic process (Xerox)
copying with, 127-28
in transparency production, 150, 161
Encoding, in communication process, 14, 15
Enlarging and reducing techniques. See also Photography.
graph method, 46, 48, 49
pantograph, 48, 50-51
in poster production, 115
projected, 51-52

f-stop, 208, 210, 211
Faxability, 129, 131
Feedback
in communication process, 14, 15
in instructional system, 18
Felt board. See Flannel boards.

Felt markers
  in illustration, 53
  in lettering, 74
  in transparency production, 142-43
Film
  black-and-white, 218, 219-22
  color, 218, 219
  for overhead transparencies. *See* Acetate.
  processing of,
    continuous tone, 220-21
    line (high-contrast), 220, 222
  speed of, 210
  35mm slide format, 208, 214
  tungsten, 218, 219
Film chain for television, 257, 258
Filmstrips
  characteristics of, 214-16
  production of, 215-16, 217-19
  projector, 217
  proportions of, 214, 215
Flannel boards
  characteristics of, 171
  construction of, 171, 173, 174
  figures for, 173
Flip charts, 119-21

Generalizing skills in concept development, 4,
  107
Graphs, 121-23

Handouts, advantages and disadvantages of,
  11-12. *See also* Copying and duplicating
  processes.
Heat transfer process. *See* Copying and duplicating processes; Overhead transparencies.
High contrast film. *See* Film.
Hook and loop boards
  characteristics of, 176
  creation of, 176

Illustration
  coloring techniques, 53-55
  definition of, 43
  inking and outlining, 52-53
  steps in creating, 60
  in television production, 252-53
Individualized instruction. *See also* Self-instructional materials.
  with display devices, 166
  and filmstrips, 216
  with photography, 202
Ink and inking techniques
  in illustration, 52-53
  in transparencies, 141-43

Laminating, 32-36
  heat lamination, 32-33
  mechanical, 35
  picture-split, 35, 154
  self-adhering, 35-36
  for transparency lifts, 145, 146, 154, 156

Learning, domains of, 16
Legibility standards
  for nonprojected materials, 65, 168
  for projected materials, 64-65
LeRoy lettering system. *See* Lettering.
Lettering
  for bulletin boards, 173, 175
  on chalk boards, 168
  families of, 65-67
  groups of, 64
  handmade, 67-74
    advantages and disadvantages, 67
    cut-paper display, 68, 70, 71
    felt marker, 74
    hand-drawn, 67-68, 69
    pen letters, 70, 72-73
  legibility standards,
    for nonprojected materials, 65
    for projected materials, 64-65
  mechanical, 74-80
    advantages and disadvantages of, 74-75
    pens and guides (Wrico), 76-77
    rubber stamps, 79-80
    scriber and template (LeRoy), 78, 79
    stencil, 75-77
  in poster making, 115
  premade, 80-83
    advantages and disadvantages, 80
    die-cut, 80-81
    dry-transfer, 81-82
    paste-up, 82-83
    three-dimensional, 81
  spacing, 83-84
  in television production, 251-52
  uses for, 63-64
Lift transparencies. *See* Overhead transparencies.
Light meter, 35mm camera, 210
Lighting
  for photography, 218
  for television production, 261, 262
Line film, 220, 222

Marionettes, 185-87
Masks
  uses of, 190
  varieties of, 192
    balloon, 191
    construction paper, 191
    paper bag, 190-91
    papier mâché, 191
Media, selection of, 5-8
Mergers, in display and photography, 99
Models
  construction of, 193
  uses and characteristics of, 193
Motion pictures
  advantages and disadvantages of, 10-11
  camera, super-8, 224-27
    operation of, 226-27
    parts of, 224-26

Motion pictures (continued)
  special techniques with, 227-29
  characteristics of, 10
  production of, 224, 226-33
    editing, 229, 231, 232-33
    script writing, 231, 232
    sound, 229
    special effects, 227-29
    steps in, 226-27
    story board, 229-31
    suggestions, 224
  uses of, 201, 202
Mounting
  color, selection in, 104
  of pictures to be photographed, 208
  processes for pictures, 23-42
    dry mounting on cloth, 31-32
    dry mounting on hard surface, 28-31
    lamination, heat, 32-35
    lamination, mechanical, 35
    lamination, self-adhering, 35-36
    passe-partout, 38-42, 197
    picture-split, 35, 154, 156
    positionable mount, 27-28
    rationale, 23-24
    rubber cement, double coat, 24-26
    rubber cement, one coat, 27
    spray adhesive, 27
    wet mounting, 36-38
  of specimens in plastic, 197-99
  of transparencies. *See* Overhead transparencies.
Movement
  animation, 228
  in motion pictures, 10
  in pictures, 110
  with polarization, 106, 161-62
  simulated, 100
  television, 262-63

Noise, in communication process, 14, 15

Objectives, behavioral, 17
Opaque projector, for enlarging. *See* Enlarging and reducing techniques.
Originals for reproduction, 55, 60-61
  continuous tone, 61
  halftone, 60-61
  line, 60
  in transparencies, 150
  uses of, 61
Overhead projector
  characteristics of, 141
  for enlarging. *See* Enlarging and reducing techniques.
  with shadow puppets, 187
Overhead transparencies
  advantages and disadvantages of, 9-10, 149, 162
  characteristics of, 10, 137-38, 140-41
  design of, 138-40
  groups of, 141

Overhead transparencies (cont.)
  handmade, 141-49
    clear acetate, 141-43
    frosted acetate, 143
    lifts, 143-49
    treated acetate, 143
  machine-made, 149-61
    Color Key, 161
    diazo, 158-61
    electrostatic, 161
    lifts, 154, 156
    photocopy, dry, 158
    photocopy, wet, 156-58
    spirit duplicator, 149-51
    thermal transfer, 150, 152-54
    Transparex, 154-56
  masters, 159
  mounting, 163
  overlays, 140
  polarizing materials, 161-62
  techniques of utilization, 162, 164
  in television, 257-58

Papier mâché
  masks, 191
  objects, 191, 193, 194
  puppet heads, 187
Parallax, 203
Passe-partout mounting. *See* Mounting.
Paste-up, in illustration, 44-45
Paste-up letters. *See* Lettering.
Pen and guide lettering. *See* Lettering.
Pens
  for drawing, 52
  for lettering, 70
Perception
  and attention, 106-07
  in children, 108
  and concept development, 1-2
Photocopy
  copying with, 128-29
  transparency production with, 156-58
Photographs
  characteristics of, 20
  and depth cues, 19
  in television, 254
  uses of, 201-02
Photography
  characteristics of and uses for, 201-02
  enlarging process, 221
  in silk screen production, 117
Picture split. *See* Laminating.
Pictures
  advantages and disadvantages of, 9, 22-23
  color in, 21-22
  criteria for selection, 21-22
  description of, 19
  distortion of, 21-23
  enlarging and reducing of. *See* enlarging and reducing techniques.
  function of, 19, 21
  kinds of 20-21

Pictures (continued)
motion. *See* motion pictures.
mounting. *See* mounting, processes for pictures.
photographic copying of. *See* cameras, copying with.
placement on mounting board, 24-25
Plastic. *See also* Acetate.
spray, for pastels, 54
spray, for transparencies, 143, 146, 154
Polarization
in overhead transparency production, 161-62
in photography, 219
Posters, 113-18
creating, 114-16
Pressure sensitive film
in illustration, 54
in transparency production, 143
Principles, development of, 4-5
Problem solving, 5
Projectors. *See* Opaque projector, Overhead projector.
Psychomotor skills
as domain of learning, 16
and media selection, 6
and motion pictures, 10, 201, 202
Puppets, 184-190
hand, 189
marionettes, 185-87
rod, 187, 188
shadow, 187, 190
uses and characteristics of, 184-85
varieties of, 185

Realia, in teaching, 1, 5
Research applied to design, 105-10
Rubber cement
for lift transparencies, 145-47. *See also* Mounting.

Scripts
for photographic productions, 231, 232
for television, 258-60
Sculpture, paper, 195-97
Seal-lamin film. *See also* Laminating.
for mounting specimens, 32, 197
Self-instructional materials, 6. *See also* Individualized instruction.
Shutter speed, 210, 212
Silk screen process, 117-18
Slides
advantages and disadvantages, 8-9, 215
characteristics of, 8-9, 215
creating, 217-19
proportions of, 214-15
in television production, 254
uses of, 201
Slow motion, 228
Sound. *See also* Audio recording.
in super-8 motion picture production, 229

Space
as design element, 88
division of, 100-101
Speedball pens. *See* Pens.
Spirit duplicator
for handouts, 130-33
operation of, 132-33
and thermal-transfer master unit, 131
in transparency production, 149-51
Stencil. *See also* Lettering, stencils.
and mimeograph process, 133-34
in poster production, 115
in silk screen process, 117
Still pictures. *See* Pictures.
Story board, 229-31
System
in instruction, 16-18
model of, 18

Tape recording. *See* Audio recording.
Television
advantages and disadvantages of, 12-13
characteristics of, 12, 249-50
equipment, 261-66
graphics, 250-58
available graphics, 253-54
gray scale, 252-53
lettering, 251-52
projected materials, 254-58
proportions, 250-51
script, 258-60
videodiscs, 267
videogames, 267
Tests
as feedback, 15, 18
posttests, 17-18
pretests, 17-18
Thermal transfer process
for duplicating masters, 131-32, 134
in overhead transparency production, 150, 152-54
for paper copies, 129-30
Three-dimensional teaching materials
dioramas, 182-84
masks, 190-92
models, 193
mounted specimens, 197-98
papier mâché, 191, 193-94
paper sculpture, 195-97
puppets, 184-90
uses of, 181-82
Time-lapse, 228
Titling
in motion picture production, 228
for television, 251-52
Tracing techniques, 45-46, 47
Transmission, in communication process, 14, 15
Transparencies. *See* Overhead transparencies.

Value
in color, 101
definition of, 91

Verbal materials
  in concept development, 2, 63
  as handouts, 11-12
  as recordings, 13, 235-36
Video recorder, 263-66
Videodisc, 267
Videogame, 267
Videotapes and videocassettes
  advantages of, 12
  characteristics of, 263-64
  selection, 6

Wet mounting, 36, 38
Wheat paste, 36
  in papier mâché, 185, 191-93
Words. See Verbal materials.
Wrico lettering system. See Lettering.

Xerox process. See Electrostatic process.

Zoom effects
  in photography, 227
  in television, 260, 262